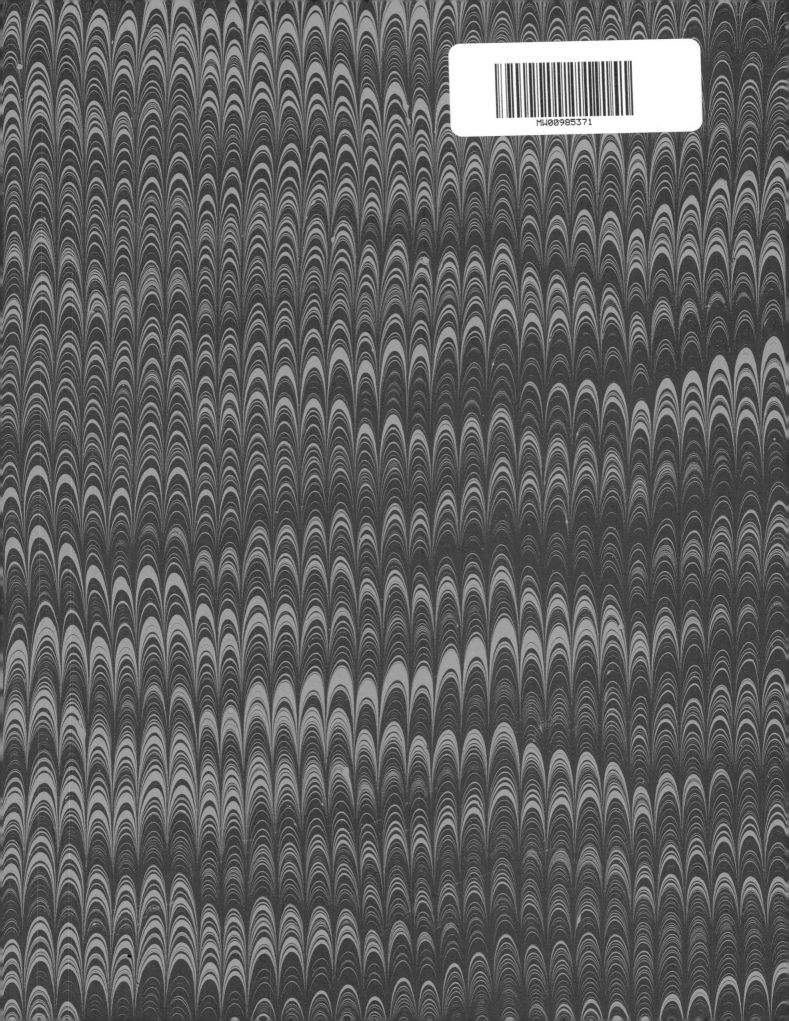

THE FIRST 300:

The Amazing and Rich History of Lower Merion

The Amazing and Rich History of Lower Merion

THE FIRST 300

The Lower Merion Historical Society

Limited Edition, Published in the Year 2000
by The Lower Merion Historical Society.

Distributed by Diane Publishing Co.

Library of Congress Cataloging-in-Publication Data

The first 300 : the amazing and rich history of Lower Merion / The Lower Merion
Historical Society. - - Limited ed.
      p. cm.
   Includes index.
   ISBN 0-7881-8500-4
   1. Lower Merion (Pa. : Township)- -History. 2. Lower Merion (Pa. :
Township)- -History- -Pictorial works. I. Title: First three hundred. II. Lower Merion
Historical Society.
F159.L9 F57 2000

                                                              99-057322

Published by:
The Lower Merion Historical Society,
Box 51, Ardmore, Pennsylvania 19003

Distributed by:
Diane Publishing Co.,
330 Pusey Avenue, Unit #3,
Collingdale, Pennsylvania 19023

Printed by:
Stauffer Printing,
505 Willow Lane,
Lancaster, Pennsylvania 17601

Inquiries should be directed to:
The Lower Merion Historical Society,
Box 51, Ardmore, Pennsylvania 19003

INTRODUCTION

The First 300 is an ambitious three-year community project. Initiated by The Lower Merion Historical Society, the book has involved not only its members, but a cast of over 75 historians, educators, archivists, artists, photographers and just-plain-folks. *The First 300* presents a panoramic view of the human history of a special Pennsylvania territory. I thank all of those who worked with me to devote their skills, their time and their energies to further the Society's mission: *Preserving our past for the future.*

— DICK JONES, Editor-in-Chief/Designer

DEDICATION

To W. Robert Swartz: A former President of The Lower Merion Historical Society, Bob operated a popular photo shop on Lancaster Avenue in Ardmore for 49 years. He soon began adding pictures to the Society's archives. Customers knew of his interest in visions of yesteryears and would loan photographs for Bob to copy. The collection grew to thousands of pictures. Those images, and others, formed the basis of our local history as seen through the lens of a camera.

FINANCIAL SUPPORT

The Lower Merion Historical Society acknowledges its gratitude for the generous financial backing from these organizations. They helped to make the publication of *The First 300* a reality. Patrons, Sponsors, Contributors and Subscribers are listed on pages 276 and 277.

GRANTS

Thanks to the enthusiastic support of State Senator Richard A. Tilghman, this project was financed in part by grants from **The Commonwealth of Pennsylvania, Department of Community and Economic Development** and **The Pennsylvania Historical and Museum Commission**

The project was also supported by grants from **The McLean Contributionship** Bryn Mawr, Pennsylvania

and

The Merion Community Association Foundation serving the community through the Tribute House for 75 years

CONTENTS

OBSERVATIONS. Far away people heard with awe of the privileged Main Line of Philadelphia. (That it actually was not in Philadelphia didn't matter.) The likes of Christopher Morley and James Michener described its ambiance, extolled its wealth and civility which, of course, depended on the urbane money-making apparatus of Philadelphia, immediately at hand.

The string of suburban communities that constitute the Main Line are braided together along the tracks of the once-powerful Pennsylvania Railroad, linking East with West through this part of the U.S.A. The railroad, early named the Main Line of Public Works, gave it birth in its modern form. Quaker elements of its colonial roots were long ago forgotten.

First of all...now speaking in the beginning of the 21st century...the schools (both public and private) attract families. This generous helping of educational opportunities not only brings ambitious parents to the area, but also brings their academic faculties to nest nearby.

Medical resources are first rate. Doctors, lawyers, manufacturers and scholars live here, even if they work elsewhere; they add some altitude to the level of conversation at cocktail parties.

Here and there, retirement enclaves of grand scale spread over landscaped acres, often set in recyled mansions of yesteryear. Now and then, a rich man's magnificent stone castle, sometimes disguised as a school or enveloped in a forest, may be glimpsed from a formal gateway. Alas, some have disappeared entirely. A few old, old colonial houses, still inhabited, have influenced local domestic architectural styles since World War I.

Once upon a time, the population of the Main Line (between roughly the 1870s and 1930s) was clearly layered and labeled, and money had everything to do with it. Gradually, second and third generations ascended the social scale, rising from immigrant serving class folk to float to the top, propelled by excellent free education and their hard work that forced open the barriers.

In these next hundred years, new people will continue to arrive, many from places even the professors have to be shown on the world map, and they will be inspired and educated by, and absorbed into the Main Line atmosphere...elevated slightly above the city as it is: cool, charitable and civilized.

1 *(left page)* 1851 map of Lower Merion by John Howell Levering (1830-1885). His survey showed all of its buildings, names of property holders and the boundaries of lots and farms. Levering, a Trustee of the Lower Merion Academy, was employed in the surveying and civil engineering departments of the City of Philadelphia. His family had owned grist and saw mills in the Township since the 1700s.

THE NATURE OF LOWER MERION. Lower Merion is twice blessed: not only do we possess a rich and wonderful history...as you will soon discover...but that history occurred on a rich and wonderful stage, the land itself. Even today, 300 years after European settlement, Lower Merion is one of the most physically stunning townships in the Philadelphia region. Our roads wind around rolling hills lined with magnificent street trees, we boast expansive forests of oak, beech and tulip poplar, and our clear, clean creeks slice through sparkling mica-flecked stone studded with innumerable garnets.

Our land is still rich in wildlife. Here, red fox stalk white-footed mice; there, great horned owls drop silently out of the night sky on unsuspecting skunks. Raccoons hunt crayfish in our creeks, migrating songbirds rain out of the sky to rest in our backyards and preserved open spaces, butterflies gambol in our gardens, and white-tailed deer...No, please, don't get us started about white-tailed deer.

But while nature seemingly abounds, it may come as a surprise to you that nature has only recently returned to Lower Merion. As nature plays out on our landscape's stage, we are already deep into Act Three.

Act One, of course, is the pre-Columbian era, when it has been said a squirrel could cross North America from treetop to treetop without ever touching ground. Certainly, any squirrel could easily cross our densely timbered land, with its ancient trees the size of which we don't see anymore—immense trees in an unlogged landscape. And in that forest lived animals long gone: bear, cougar, wolf, rattlesnake, otter, beaver, weasel, turkey, grouse, even woodland bison. Trout swam in our streams; bald eagles soared over the Schuylkill snaring fish in their claws.

European settlement ushered in chapter two. Immediately, the land was logged, the timber an invaluable resource for building homes, fueling hearths, and establishing safe borders, pushing those bears and wolves away from family. Within moments of the establishment of the Welsh Barony, saw mills were logging Lower Merion. By 1900, Lower Merion was a wholly altered landscape: little virgin timber anywhere, and one could see for miles in some places.

As farms gave way to genteel estates, fields became lawns and the forests stayed away. As more houses were built, the forest retreated. An 1895 list of local birds carefully kept by a Narberth physician showed that deep-forest birds like thrushes, vireos and warblers were disappearing or gone, and in their stead were new strangers, a profusion of farm and grassland birds like bobolinks, meadowlarks and sparrows.

But times changed. After the world wars, farming quickly vanished and large estates became as rare and endangered as barns and silos. The land was subdivided, and we enter the next 300 years in our third chapter of land use as a suburban landscape.

And in that landscape, street trees have grown large and shade-rich, and once farmed places like Saunders Woods, Rolling Hill Park, and the Riverbend Environmental Education Center have reverted back to forest. The deep green woodland is slowly returning. Farm birds like meadowlarks and bobolinks are gone, and thrushes and vireos, woodpeckers and warblers are perhaps more common today than they were in the 1890s.

But it's not entirely the same. No squirrel can travel the township from tree to tree, nor ever will again. Many of our natural neighbors—that list above—are gone, and will never return. The only trout in Lower Merion are state-stocked and ephemeral; streams like Mill Creek are too hot in the summer (from warm stormwater and lack of streamside forests) to support natives like brook trout.

Our forests are overgrown by non-native species like mile-a-minute vine, *Wisteria,* Norway maple, and garlic mustard. American chestnut trees were killed by a blight, and wildflower species are declining. Deer proliferate, grazing young trees and shrubs out of the landscape, collaborating with white-footed mice to spread deer ticks and Lyme disease.

The forest has returned, but it is a shadow of its once-proud self. *That* would be a great gift to Lower Merion in the next 300 years: preserving and restoring the nature that remains with us on our beautiful land.

1 Tish-Co-Han, an elder of the Toms River, New Jersey band (Lenópeh). His name may mean "He who never blackens himself." This 1735 portrait, by Swedish artist Gustavus Hesselius, shows him as a man of stout muscular frame, about 45 to 50 years old. In 1737, he signed the treaty known as the "Walking Purchase." The Penn family considered him "an honest, upright Indian."

2 "Delaware" Indian family (detail from a 1653 Swedish map). This drawing was produced in response to the curiosity that Europeans had about what American Indians looked like. The artist drew what he wanted to see, with the intent to advertise the New World, which resulted in this inaccurate picture of Lenape appearance.

THE LENAPE. The ancestors of the Lenape had hunted in eastern regions of North America for thousands of years, adapting through time to the changes in climate and landscape. By 1200 A.D. these small and highly mobile bands had developed new strategies that gave them more efficient use of the land and its resources. Within a few hundred years they had formed into the several nations who met the Europeans after 1500. One of these bands called themselves *Lenape* (len-AH-puh).

What today we know as the Delaware River takes its English name from Sir Thomas West, Lord de la Warr, the first governor of the Virginia colony. To the Lenape, this river and the land around it was called *Makeriskhickon* and, in many ways, this always flowing river was the lifeblood of these people. In their own terms these people called themselves *Lenape*, meaning "the people."

The Europeans first referred to all of the Lenape bands along the western side of *Makeriskhickon*, as well as to two other nations whose territories touched the "Delaware" River, by the collective designation of "River Indians." All of these groups were later called "Delaware." They spoke a variety of Algonkian tongues, now collectively called the "Delawarean" languages.

THE LENAPE BANDS

At the time of the arrival of Europeans in the Middle Atlantic region, the Lenape people were organized into more than a dozen different bands, each with its own area for winter hunting, and its own summer station along the Delaware River. Most of the year was spent at these summer fishing stations. The individual band would "aggregate" into a social and economic unit for the warm months. Each individual family within the band would then "disperse" for winter hunting.

While these bands were somewhat flexible in membership, each tended to have a core group composed of closely related members. The young men in each band stayed within their birth band until they married, then would join the band of their wife.

The Lenape band living in the Lower Merion area was one of the largest of all. They traditionally summered in the rich swamps at the mouth of the Schuylkill, but hunted over the entire southwestern side of the Schuylkill River drainage which was their foraging territory.

LENAPE LIFE

The Lenape living in the resource-rich area of southeastern Pennsylvania developed a sophisticated foraging life-style during the Late Woodland period (c.1100-1600 A.D.). They hunted and fished and gathered many different kinds of plants, such as goose-foot and wild millet, in order to feed themselves. In the fall, hickory nuts and acorns were gathered and processed for food. Among the animals collected by Lenape women for food were bird eggs, nestlings, frogs, turtles and shellfish.

During the summer, everyone helped fish for shad, sturgeon, striped bass, eel and many other water-dwelling creatures, using complex woven traps, large nets and harpoons. Lenape men also hunted in the surrounding forests for deer, elk, bear and birds, using the bow with arrows tipped with flat, triangular stone heads...finely chipped and very sharp. Other foods that now sound less inviting, such as caterpillars, also were important to the Lenape.

The Lenape lived simply; each

band was made up of several related families who worked and ate together. The members of any band could marry into any other band within the Lenape area, and rarely did they marry someone who was not a Lenape.

In 1985, excavations undertaken for the University Museum in Philadelphia located evidence of some small structures of the kind described by William Penn, who provided most of the direct descriptions of Lenape constructions:

> "Their Houses are Mats, or Bark of Trees set on Poles, in the fashion of an English Barn, but out of the power of the Winds, for they are hardly higher than a man..."

NEW PROSPECTS

The arrival of Europeans provided the Lenape with a new set of opportunities. Dutch traders from Fort Amsterdam, located on the North (Hudson) River, came down to what they called the South River in 1623 specifically to trade with the **Susquehannock.** Those people, the most powerful native nation in Pennsylvania, brought furs overland to the Delaware River to avoid the renewed conflicts between the **Powhatan Confederacy** and the English colonists on the Chesapeake River.

The Dutch put up a tiny trading post, Fort Nassau, on the Jersey

2 Aerial view of the Schuylkill River in Gladwyne where there is a bend in the river. At this location, due to the water's change in direction, there is a natural pool of warm water where fish congregate. This is where the Lenape set up their "summer station" to trap fish, which was a staple in their diet.

side of the river opposite the mouth of a river they called the "Hidden Stream" (*"schuylkil"* in Dutch). The swamps and islands at the mouth of the Schuylkill made it difficult for early sailors to identify the true course of this river, so well-known and easily traveled by the Lenape.

The people of the **South Schuylkill** band became important figures in the quests of these various European traders for "legitimacy" as regards trading rights and land claims. Until the Swedes arrived in 1638 and bought land at *Hopokehocking* (now Wilmington) from the **Brandywine** band, the **Schuylkill River** people were the best known of the Lenape bands.

The Dutch came to "their" South River primarily to trade with the Susquehannock, but did not set up a permanent fort or individual homesteads. Before their Swedish competition arrived, there was little concern with land claims and territorial rights.

The Swedish colony was established principally to trade for furs, but failed to make a serious dent in the Dutch fur market. Taking a lesson from the Virginia Company, the Swedes went into the production of tobacco. The expansion of Swedish farmsteads and their continuing efforts to crack the Dutch fur monopoly, led to an interesting contention be-

1 Contemporary artwork depicts Lenape contact with new European arrivals and their neighbors to the west, the Susquehannock.

tween the Swedes and the Dutch over land rights.

To counter the Swedish expansion into the Schuylkill Valley, the Dutch bought a few acres from the Lenape and built a small fort called *"Bevers Rede"* on the west banks of the Delaware. These deeds provide us with clues to the membership and territory controlled by the dominant Schuylkill River bands of Lenape.

FUR TRADE

During the period following the Swedish entry into the South River (c.1638-1660), the local Lenape had slight profits from the European competition for furs. The Lenape and their immediate neighbors had only the furs that they hunted from their own territories to trade; the Susquehannock were middlemen in the fur trade that extended out into the Mississippi Valley! Thus the Lenape were, as Swedish Governor Printz put it, "poor in furs." These sales provided the Lenape with one means of access to highly valued trade items such as metal goods and blankets.

A second source of European goods derived from the sale of maize to the Swedes. The Lenape had always grown a bit of maize in their summer gardens, but after 1640 they increased the amount planted to sell to the Swedish colonists. The Swedes were concentrating their planting on tobacco for export, and bought maize from these Lenape foragers at lower costs than the value of tobacco. In this way the Lenape gained trade goods while not having to deal with the problem of food storage.

In addition, the Swedish provided a new and useful means by which the Lenape could make it through particularly bad winters. If the hunting were bad, Lenape families could rely on the Swedes for supplementary rations during the "starving time."

LAND SALES

Another Lenape technique for gaining access to European goods involved the sale of land. In general, the plots sold were small holdings and

1 The turtle was part of the Lenape story of creation. As the story goes, Kishelemukong, the Creator, brought a giant turtle from the depths of the great ocean. The turtle grew until it became the vast island now known as North America. The first woman and man sprouted from a tree that grew upon the turtle's back. Kishelemukong then created the heaven, the sun, the moon, all animals and plants, and the four directions that governed the seasons.

the goods received were considerable. Lands sold to one group could often be promised or "sold" to another group at a later date.

At a major gathering in 1654, six members of the North Schuylkill band were joined by two Lenape from the South Schuylkill band and two other Lenape from a third band. This gathering led to a major land sale. The North Schuylkill band sold a huge portion of the lower part of their territory, excepting out *"Passaijungh,"* where they continued to spend the warm months doing their traditional fishing.

PENN'S GRANT

The lands that became Pennsylvania came as a Crown grant to William Penn. Penn believed that the wholesale purchase of land from its native owners, and the subsequent division and resale of small plots, would make him fabulously wealthy. By the time Penn

received his grant and developed his plans for what became "Pennsylvania," thousands of English colonists already had come into the area.

This increase in population, most of whom purchased small tracts of land along the Delaware River, began to influence native fishing and foraging strategies by the 1660s. Rather than sustaining their summer fishing stations directly on the Delaware, individual Lenape bands began to shift their summer stations further up their respective streams. From c.1660 to 1680 the Schuylkill River and other other bands were also relocating their summer stations further up river, with the South Schuylkill band shifting to a location in the Lower Merion area.

PENN'S PURCHASES

Between 1682 and 1701, Penn patiently negotiated the purchase of *all* of the holdings of every one of the Lenape bands, except those areas on

2 Black rocks, different from other rock formations in the area, cover some four to five acres near Mill Creek as it passes under Black Rock Road in Gladwyne. Geologists say the nature of the rock represents

gradations from serpentine to talc. Tradition holds that the Lenape camped in the area because it was the source of chert, a flint-like stone used in the manufacture of spearpoints and arrowheads.

which the individual bands "were seated" (had their summer stations). The first of these deeds were drawn up in July 1682 by William Markham, Penn's agent, shortly before Penn himself arrived in the New World. The deed that is of most interest concerns the sale to Penn of all of the lands claimed by the South Schuylkill band (what is now Montgomery County).

The following July, two different Lenape bands came to negotiate sales of their lands to Penn for an incredibly rich array of trade goods. The first of these sales was made by the band living west of the Schuylkill. They sold all the land lying between *"Manaiunk* alias *Schulkill"* and Macopanackhan (Upland or Chester) Creek. This sale included land *only* up as far as the hill called Conshohockan.

These sales did little to change Lenape lifeways, other than to provide them with a vast quantity of useful goods. From the list of goods that Penn used to "buy" this tract, we can estimate the band size: 30 adults and possibly an equal number of children, since the goods involve items in multiples of 15. For the men, there are 15 guns, knives, axes, coats and shirts plus 30 bars of lead. For women, there are 15 small kettles, scissors and combs, but 16 pairs of stockings and blankets.

WESTWARD MOVES

All of the Lenape bands continued to live in the Delaware Valley for another 50 years, but at locations further up the streams. They lived in much the same way that they had for centuries before ...and continued to reside in these areas for another 50 years.

Only in the 1730s was the density of the English settlement and the subtle influences it had on native lifeways considered a potential problem to the Lenape. Many were marrying or settling among the colonists and the traditional modes of living were becoming difficult to follow in the lower Delaware Valley.

Between 1733 and 1740, all of the conservative members of many Lenape bands had decided that eco-

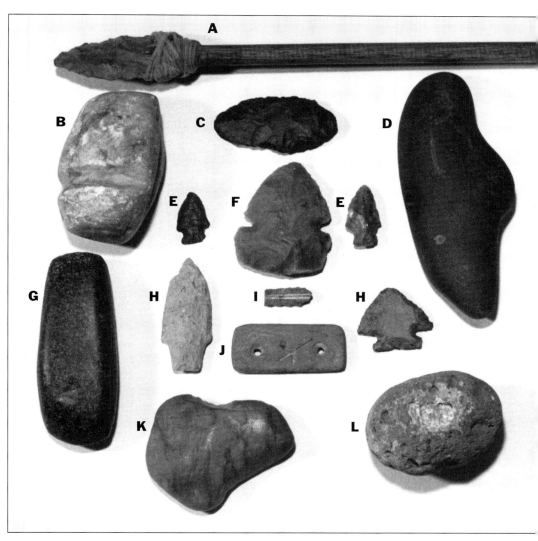

Lenape Artifacts
A. Archaic period spear head
B. Full-grooved, pecked, cobblestone axe head, c.8000 BC to 4000 BC
C. Sway-backed knife, c.10,000 BC to 8000 BC
D. Bannerstone/Atlatl weight, c.4000 BC to 1000 BC
E. Jasper (a variety of quartz) point and scraper
F. Knife point (handle added) c.1000 BC to 1550 AD
G. Pecked & polished chisel, c.8000 BC to 4000 BC
H. Dart heads or knives
I. Antler harpoon
J. Gorget (soapstone) pictograph, c.1000 BC to 700 AD
K. Chopper/hoe blade c.1000 BC to 700 AD
L. Pitted stone, 8000 BC to 4000 BC

nomic opportunities and the chance to maintain the old ways lay in moving west. In leaving the coastal plain, these Lenape set the pattern that would be followed by early colonists and other immigrant groups to follow...moving west for opportunities that lay beyond the Atlantic shore.

Lenape had been moving west since at least 1661. When William Penn arrived, many Lenape already had left the Delaware Valley and others were ready to sell their lands and move out to central Pennsylvania and beyond. Most of the con-

servative and traditional Lenape people had left the Delaware Valley by 1740.

The numbers of Lenape who simply merged into the colonial society explains some "disappearances" of many aboriginal groups. For the Lenape, the attraction of wealth to be gained from the fur trade pulled many people west more forcefully than they were being pushed west by colonial population expansion. These Lenape people have joined with many other peoples to become the foundation for modern American society.

THE EARLIEST SETTLERS. Far and away the best pioneers and precursors of Penn's Holy Experiment were the Swedes and their then-compatriots the Finns, who, as Penn observed, were settlers, not mere traders. The Dutch laid claim to the Delaware Bay region via Henry Hudson's explorations in 1609, but their desultory stabs into the wilderness to trade with the Indians for furs left little of permanence. Their early town Swanendael at the site of Lewes, Delaware, lasted about one year, was burned and the residents killed by Indians.

Peter Minuit lost his job running New Amsterdam up on the "North River" (the Hudson..."South River" was the Delaware) and was ordered home by the Dutch West India Company, whereupon the Swedish government hired him to lead an expedition to Delaware Bay. This venture resulted in founding, in 1638, New Sweden based at Fort Christina near present-day Wilmington.

The farmers of New Sweden, some fleeing the uproar of the Thirty Years' War, and unlike the volatile Dutch of New Netherland (where shouting matches were the norm), built their log cabins, were friendly toward Indians and prepared a solid foundation for the sort of society William Penn had in mind.

Swedish governor John Printz negotiated with local natives to claim all the western shore of the Delaware from Cape Henlopen to the Falls of Sanhickan (Trenton), and Scandinavians spread north into small farms and settlements at Upland (Chester), Wicaco (now part of Philadelphia) and Kingsessing ("a place where there is a meadow") between Cobbs Creek and the Schuylkill.

But all this bucolic peace was terminated by two major events: Peter Stuyvesant (whose name translated means "stir up sand") stormed down from Man-a-hatta to chase out the interlopers of New Sweden in 1655, thus igniting skirmishes between Dutch and Swedes for the next nine years,

Then, in 1664, a second military adventure had an impact that ended all arguments once and for all: the British navy arrived. John and Sebastian Cabots' exploration of 1497 planted in the British mind the notion that North America belonged to them and, by St. George, they intended to keep it, though lenience had prevailed almost 200 years.

Far from flinging out the foreign residents, the British encouraged existing settlers to stay, indeed gave them extra land in some cases.

Of the 2000 Europeans living in the area (fifty families within the modern limits of Philadelphia), almost half were Swedish/Finnish folk.

So it was that, to begin the Holy Experiment and build a city on the Delaware River, Penn's commissioners had to purchase about a mile of waterfront, high firm ground (between today's South and Vine Streets) from owners Sven, Olaf and Andrew, sons of Sven Gunnasson.

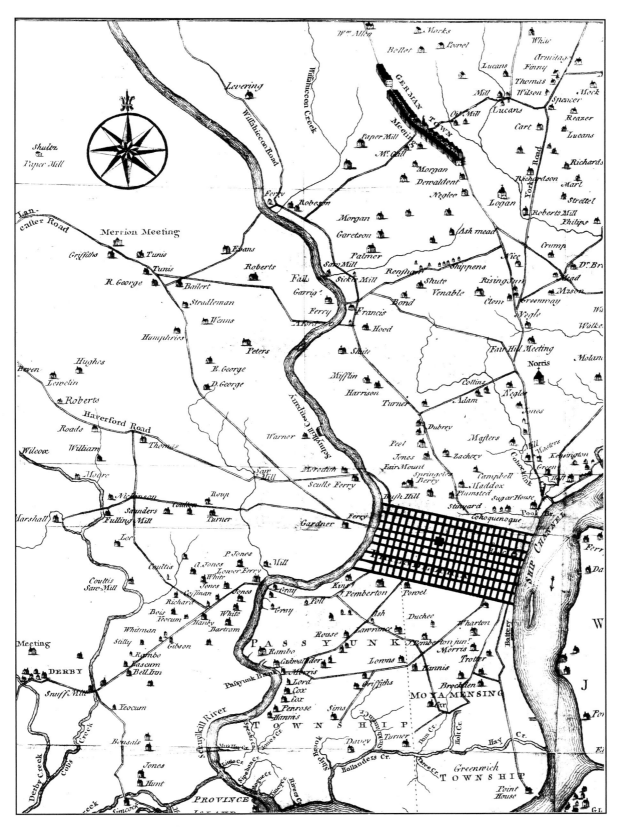

1 Scull & Heap map of Philadelphia and environs by George Heap (c.1715-1752), He drew "An East Prospect of the City of Philadelphia," engraved by George Vandergucht. Nicholas Scull (1687-1761) was Surveyor General of the Province of Pennsylvania.

PENN'S CHARTER. Just about everybody knows that Quaker William Penn was given Pennsylvania in 1681 by the King of England to pay a debt owed to his late father, Sir William Penn (Admiral of the British Navy) who fought for the crown and was a particular friend of the royal Stuarts. Curiously, young William (though considered a religious renegade and often in jail) remained on good terms with his king and the Duke of York (the king's brother, who owned, but relinquished, the land to pay the debt). But not many know that in 1675, six years earlier, the younger Penn, without leaving England, had helped to settle an argument between two Quaker landowners in West New Jersey. This provided him the opportunity to foreshadow things to come when he wrote a liberal frame of government, "Concessions and Agreements of the Proprietors, Freeholders and Inhabitants of West Jersey in America," emphasizing freedom of conscience and planting seeds of a new order...the *Novus ordo seclorum*...from which we benefit and acknowledge every time we salute the flag and the republic with "liberty and justice for all."

As he received reports from New Jersey so Penn learned about the Delaware Valley, how rich the soil, how well wooded the countryside, how plentiful the game and fish. George Fox, founder of the Society of Friends (Quakers) had traveled from Maryland to Long Island in 1672, dreaming all the while of a refuge for his beleaguered followers. As early as 1661, Parliament passed an act labeling Quakers with their uncomfortable penchant for speaking truth to power, as "dangerous and mischievous," and real persecution of Friends began.

Consequently, when William Penn petitioned the king for the grant of land that turned out to be almost as big as England, it was at least partly to be a refuge for the persecuted. In 1681 the Great Charter, boldly inscribed on pages of large parchment today in Pennsylvania's state archives and displayed on Charter Day (March 4), gave into Penn's hands what he intended to name "New Wales," but the king's secretary called "Pennsylvania" to honor his father.

Penn also advertised his American lands widely on the Continent and throughout Britain and caught the attention of merchants, farmers, artisans, educated gentlemen intrigued by "liberty of conscience," as well as those simply seeking wealth, who together created a colony that became a seedbed for a new nation one hundred years in the future.

1 Thomas Hicks, *Portrait of Edward Hicks*, (c.1850) James A. Michener Art Museum. Doylestown, Pennsylvania.

2 Edward Hicks, *The Peaceable Kingdom*, (c.1828-30), The Friends Historical Library, Swarthmore College, Swarthmore, Pennsylvania.

THE PEACEABLE KINGDOM

Edward Hicks, whose painting (c.1828-30) appears on the jacket, is known today as one of America's most recognized folk painters. A devout Quaker, Hicks admired William Penn's "holy experiment" that resulted in the the establishment of religious freedom and self-government in the colony of Pennsylvania. It seemed to be a fulfillment of Isaiah's Old Testament prophecy: "The wolf shall also dwell with the lamb, and the leopard shall lie down with the kid; and the calf and the young lion and the fatling together; and a little child shall lead them." • Hicks became fascinated with the *Peaceable Kingdom* theme and painted over sixty with that subject matter (many given as gifts to friends). Like other folk artists, he used popular prints and engravings as source material (like Benjamin West's great historical canvas *Penn's Treaty with the Indians*). And furthermore, William Penn and George Washington were Hicks' great heroes. Hicks combined the Biblical menagerie from Isaiah with a scene of Penn purchasing Pennsylvania from the Lenape Indians. Penn's dealings with the Indians were unique in the sorry history of relations between the white man and native Americans. As a Quaker, he admired Penn's treaty; the only one between Christians and Indians that was never broken. • Born in 1780 (in Bucks County) into an affluent family, his grandfather's wealth was wiped out by the American Revolution. Following his mother's early death, Hicks was raised by an upright and dignified Quaker family named Twining. At age 13, Edward was apprenticed to coachmakers where he was trained to paint both coaches and houses. His expertise at lettering trade and tavern signs can be seen on the four rhymed borders. Hicks combined the Biblical menagerie with a scene of Penn purchasing Pennsylvania from the Lenape Indians. The landscape is probably inspired by the Neshaminy Creek near his home in Newtown (though the actual treaty site was on the banks of the Delaware). • A respected minister in the Society of Friends, Edward Hicks was also known through his preaching and his published sermons. The artist saw the civil and religious liberties agreed to between the Lenape and the early English and Welsh colonists as a practical realization of the peaceable kingdom on earth. • When Hicks died in 1849, all his personal property, including unfinished paintings, totaled $67.

1 Contemporary illustration shows early dwelling cut into riverside embankment.

> "...to lay out ye sd tract of Land in as uniform a manner as conveniently may be, upon ye west side of Skoolkill river, running three miles upon ye same & two miles backward, & then extend ye parallel wth ye river six miles, and to run westwardly so far as this ye sd quantity of land be Compleately surveyed...Given at Pennsbury, ye 13th 1st mo. 1684."

THE WELSH TRACT.

Did you ever hear a newcomer to our Township try to pronounce "Cynwyd" for the first time? Or "Pencoyd"? Or spell "Bryn Mawr" correctly? We're dealing here with remnants of a very old language that came to rest in the New World with hard-working folk from Wales, descendants of the ancient Britons, the Cymric Celts. These Welsh members of the Society of Friends began to arrive on our ground in 1682 to escape harassment for being Quakers—confiscation of property, fines, sentences to jails of horrible reputation. Friends refused tithes, oaths and worldly courtesies and practiced a plain and direct form of meditative worship for which church and lay officials caused them no end of trouble.

2 William Penn as a young man.

Not long after the Great Charter was delivered to William Penn, a company of seventeen Quaker families in Merionethshire, North Wales, sent two representatives to buy 5000 acres in America for 100 pounds. Seven such companies from various parts of Wales accounted for 30,000 acres, plus individual purchases. Acreage would be

> "sett out as...appointed as neare as may be Land of equall goodness with the rest, or as shall out by Lott."

But there was a flaw in the arrangements. A select group of those First Purchasers met with the Proprietor and were assured, on response to their request, that their land would be surveyed in contiguous acreage so that they might speak their own language and be governed (or at least judged) by persons they would elect, and thus form a "Barony." Indeed, the Proprietor required of Thomas Holmes in 1684:

But there was nothing written to prove and bind the agreement. Part of the land purchased turned out to be in distant Goshen, even in New Castle and Kent counties (now Delaware). Furthermore, several tracts of land in Haverford, Radnor and Merion were assigned English purchasers and some Swedes, all within the hoped-for Barony.

Political animosities arose: Haverford and Radnor townships were declared to be in Chester County (now Delaware County); Merion Township remained in Philadelphia. Despite petitions and protests, hope of a Barony...a County Palatinate...was abandoned.

Three Welsh Quaker meetings remained in close association and built meetinghouses: "Old Haverford" Meeting on Eagle Road, Havertown; Radnor Meeting at Sproul and Conestoga; and Merion Meeting at Meetinghouse Lane and Montgomery Avenue.

These three formed a "Monthly Meeting" to handle disputes, estates, legacies, applications to marry, care of hard-luck cases, reprimands, acknowledge fulfillment of indentured servitude, or hear grievances of servants against their employers. These business meetings met on rotation among the three meetinghouses. As the amount of business increased, the Monthly Meeting created the "Preparative Meeting" to filter some of the items. Merion Meeting was, until the mid-20th century, called a "Preparative Meeting, one that would prepare reports to present to the Monthly Meeting. Today, these three meetings are independent, but are loosely joined via Quarterly Meeting and the Philadelphia Yearly Meeting.

1 *(top)* Merion Friends Meeting (photo c.1888).
2 *(center)* Haverford Friends Meeting (photo c.1890).
3 *(bottom)* Radnor Friends Meeting (late 1800s photo).

IMAGINE

Close your eyes: Picture a modern, palatial cruise ship of 90,000 tons...moonlit night, placid sea, ten decks lighted stem to stern, food and drink provided in twenty elegant locations aboard. Then, think 17th century: a sailing vessel of 90 tons, cabins like coffins, meager meals, bad water, cranky captain, very dark after dark and terrible weather. Twelve weeks of misery, boredom, a baby burial at sea and a threat of smallpox. Such was the voyage of the *Lyon,* the ship that carried the first four families who settled on land in Lower Merion in 1682.

MEMORIES

(Letter from **Dr. Edward Jones,** *the leader of "Company No.1," first settler of Merion, written 13 days after landing here, to John ap Thomas, who died before his family sailed to America in 1683]:*
"Ye name of town [Philadelphia] is now called Wicoco. Here is a Crowd of people striving for ye Country land, for ye town lot is not divided, & therefore we are forced to take up ye Country lots. We had much adoe to get a grant of it, but it cost us 4 or 5 days attendance, besides some score of miles we traveled before we brought it to pass. *[This was locating the 5,000 acre purchase from Penn which became 'Merion,' or (Lower) Merion township].* I hope it will please thee, and the rest yt are concerned, for it hath most rare timber. I have not seen the like in all these parts, there is water enough besides. The end of each lot will be on a river, as large or larger than the Dye at Bala, it is called Skool Kill River.**"**

ON NAMING THE WELSH

Take ten," he said, "and name them **Rice,**
Take another ten, and call them **Price**;
A hundred more and dub them **Hughes,**
Take fifty others, call them **Pughes**;
Now **Roberts** name some hundred score;
And **Williams** name a legion more.
And call," he moaned in languid tones,
"Call all the other thousands **Jones."**
(attributed to the Bishop of Lichfield)

1 This was the scene on the Great Conestoga Road (present Montgomery Avenue) in 1805: the covered wagon is headed eastward toward the General Wayne Inn *(extreme right)*. Merion Friends Meetinghouse is just above the horses and to the right of it are the carriage sheds. (Engraving by Robert Sutcliffs from *Travels in America* published in England in 1815.)

MERION FRIENDS MEETINGHOUSE has stood as a landmark for 300 years. It is the most pictured Quaker meetinghouse in America, was the first public building in the area, and in 1998 was named a National Landmark by the U. S. Department of the Interior. Not only does its age, largely unaltered design and continuous use make it a notable structure, but also the fact that Welsh members of the Society of Friends who built it represent the earliest migration of Celtic-speaking Welsh in the Western Hemisphere. These "Merioneth Adventurers" were not accustomed to building meetinghouses in Wales. In the homeland they were not even permitted to meet for worship in each other's houses when being persecuted as nonconformists. So here in the freedom of America, they built what they knew, something like a barn or a house, with a loft up above to be used as a schoolroom.

In or before 1695, the Welshmen who constituted Merion Meeting contributed labor, materials, loads of stone and wood to construct a meetinghouse. First indication that it was ready for use is found in Monthly Meeting minutes which records that Daniel Humphrey and Hannah Wynne, youngest daughter of Dr. Thomas Wynne, were married "at the public meeting house in Meirion" on October 20, 1695.

Observable evidence suggests that the building was executed as a single unit, according to National Park Service historians, but not until investigative deconstruction or judicious archaeological work under the floor, can more be known.

Minutes of business meetings between 1702 and 1704, and again between 1712 through 1717, record assigned tasks such as "make a cupboard in ye meeting house to the use of ye meeting to keep Friends bookes or papers," or "add hookes and staples to the meeting house windows."

1 *(above)* Contemporary photograph of the meetinghouse entrance.

2 *(below, left)* Interior of Merion Friends.

3 *(below, right)* The loft above the smaller meeting room, generally called the "schoolroom," 1945 *Life* Magazine photo.

(from top):
1- Early 1800s painting, (by Hugh Reinagle?).
2- c.1828 watercolor by W. L. Breton.
3- 1837 French engraving by Boisseau, from a painting by L.Thienon.
4- 1843 from Historical Collections of the State of Pennsylvania by Sherman Day.

In 1702, Griffith John and Robert Jones were appointed to find a carpenter to make benches some of which we believe are still in use, originally made with peg legs and no backs, but now modified for comfort. David Maurice was to "secure the meeting house" presumably against bad weather. With such reference to the meeting house already existing, then why were members requested to "see for stones to build a meeting house in 1703, and were to be reminded to pay their subscriptions toward the building project? Was there thought of creating another, larger meetinghouse?

It may have been at this time the second, larger room was added, wide enough to accommodate two enclosed staircases to a gallery where children sat, strictly divided girls from boys, with access through a low door to the schoolroom. The additional room made the building T-shaped but not cruciform, as is sometimes stated. The roof was a major expense in 1714. The floor, says tradition, was supported by tree stumps.

Analysis reveals that the present chimney was added later, jerry-rigged through the existing roof. Merion may have had a fireplace similar to the one in the Old Haverford meetinghouse (on Eagle Road in Havertown) with openings both inside and outside the building so that fuel could be added from outside without disturbing the silence of the meeting within. On December 16, 1798, we know a stove was in use from a note in Joseph Price's dairy: "Whent (sic) to Meeting, had 4 preachers...no fire in stove yet was prety Passable as to Cold."

In the larger, added room shuttered windows high up above a modern dropped ceiling are visible now from below. Partitions to be lowered when necessary separate the two interior parts, whereby the women's business meeting could be held while the men's was in progress.

(from top):

1- 1851 chalk sketch by Isaac Collins of Philadelphia, published in London, from *Select Miscellanies, Chiefly Illustrative of the History, Christian Principles, and Sufferings of the Society of Friends.*

2- 1860 engraving by T. Elwood Zell from *Retrospect of Early Quakerism* by Isaac Michener.

3- 1871 English print in the Quaker Collection, Haverford College.

4- 1884 engraving from *Enciclopedia Nuova Italiana,* Volume 18.

THREE KINDRED BUILDINGS

About a mile up the trail going west (on Montgomery Avenue), Robert Owen's house, Penn Cottage *(page 29),* was built at the same time as Merion's meetinghouse, probably by the same workmen. An old journal tells of a boy climbing an outside stairway at the Owen house to spy on William Penn saying his prayers in an upper room ..."Penn thanking God for providing comfort "in the wilderness." • From this story we judge it possible that there was an outside stair up the back wall of the meetinghouse for pupils and school-master to use. Jonathan Wynne, only son of Dr. Thomas Wynne...a Quaker minister and physician to William Penn... had a farmhouse built about the same time about a mile and a half east toward the city in the midst of "Wynne's fields" (now Wynnefield), a sturdy house that withstood a Revolutionary War skirmish. Though modified, these three stone buildings, the Owen house, the Friends Meetinghouse, and Wynnestay, *(c.1895 photo below)* bear similarities to one another.

5

(from top):

1- c.1886 oil painting by Isaac L. Williams from the collection of the Historical Society of Pennsylvania.

2- 1912 engraving from *Welsh Settlement in Pensylvania* by Charles H. Browning.

3- c.1910-1920 photograph by Watson Dewees.

4- 1998 pen and ink drawing by Narberth artist, John B. Satterthwaite.

These separate meetings were held until 1883, then combined. A row of nailholes in the wainscoting of the larger room, and hat pegs placed too high, probably mean there once was a higher level of "facing benches" where visiting Public Friends (preachers) and elders sat, men on one side, women on the other.

In 1829 Friends tried to improve the exterior by plastering over the original stonework and scribing lines to resemble cut stone blocks.

At this time, perhaps, a window or door on the east wall of the first room was blocked up for some mysterious reason, the outline still faintly visible under the plaster.

In 1849 an arched vault over a chamber below ground off the east wall was built to hold bodies for burial until graves could be dug.

The existing sheds for horses and equipage were probably built in the 1820s, but "stables" were there in the 1790s, as mentioned in the Price diary. A faint depression of a saw-pit remains where two men could saw beams for the sheds, and pieces of a very dilapidated stone mounting-block lie nearby. A huge sycamore three centuries old stands near the gate to the driveway.

Meetings for worship are still held each Sunday at eleven, unprogrammed and without a pastor or visiting preachers. Silence is broken by occasional spoken ministry by worshipers responding to inspiration of the "Inward Light," principal doctrine of Quakers, the sort of speaking which underscores basic tenets of Friends' faith and practice, namely equality, simplicity, non-violence and peace.

1

2

MERION FRIENDS
BURIAL GROUND

Where there's life there's also death. The subject of a burial ground in each of the four Quaker communities "beyond Schuylkill" (Merion, Haverford, Radnor and, only for awhile, Schuylkill) was broached in 1684. The two men from Merion, Hugh Roberts and Robert Davis, reported that Merion had a burying place, location not described. Possibly Hugh Roberts assigned a portion of his land for burials which may have included the place where Edward ap Rees (Edward son of Rees, eventually, Prees, then Price) buried his young daughter in 1682, just two months after setting foot in the Welsh Tract.

In 1695, Edward Rees sold for five shillings a half acre to trustees of Merion Preparative Meeting for a burial ground and to them leased the adjacent plot where the meetinghouse stands. For 82 years, Merion Friends possessed the only place in today's Lower Merion for burials. Everyone was accepted: Indians, strangers, servants, slaves.

The burial yard was increased in size several times, and now is about 1-1/4 acres and known to contain more than 2100 bodies recorded, and possibly several hundred more never mentioned in writing. About 20% are children.

People died of alcoholism, apoplexy, accidents, bilious fever, burns, childbirth, cholera, consumption, diabetes, drowning, dysentery, freezing, kidney stones, heart attack, hives, lockjaw, murder, palsy, pneumonia, poison, smallpox, suicide, typhus, war wounds, an unidentifiable "white swelling" and yellow fever.

Most of the 246 gravestones still visible in the cemetery date from 1801 and 1804 when John Dickinson sold, for token amounts, two acres to the meeting to extend ground for burials and later, for other buildings. This was the famous John Dickinson, lawyer and statesman who never lived in Lower Merion but owned land here. He represented Pennsylvania in the Stamp Act Congress of 1765 and drafted its declaration of rights and grievances. He encour-

aged the populace by his *Letters from a Farmer in Pennsylvania, to the inhabitants of the British Colonies* to protest harsh British taxation. Yet he did not sign the Declaration of Independence, for which he suffered disapproval, but later served in the patriot militia and most importantly helped draft the Constitution.

A researcher in the early 1900s found some 62 names of militiamen serving in the Revolution who she claimed are buried at Merion Meeting.

Now in the first years of its fourth century, the old "yard" next to the meetinghouse resembles nothing so much as a shady park with only a few standing grave markers (some illegible). Only ashes of Quaker family members may be buried now in Merion Meeting's cemetery, where a peaceful quiet still comforts the bereaved.

3

1 *(left)* This Indenture, a copy done in the 1800s, is an exact copy of the original, signed by William Penn, which acknowledge fhe purchase of 5,000 acres by Dr. Edward Jones of Bala, Wales, and John Thomas, 'gentleman' of Llaithgwon, Wales. This "Welsh Tract," purchased for "one hundred pounds sterling moneys," was then subdivided. John Roberts purchased one of these plots which, when joined with the plot purchased by his bride-to-be, Gaynor Roberts, created a piece of property extending from the Schuylkill River to Conshocken State Road along the city boundary known now as City Avenue.
2 *(right page)* The main house of the Pencoyd estate, c.1860-70.

It was in November of 1683 that John Roberts disembarked from the sailing ship *Morning Star*...near the new community of Philadelphia. John was pleased to discover well-timbered land, a clear spring, plenty of stone for building and soil which was "good and fat."

The following spring, having cleared his land to build a house, John married Gaynor Roberts, who had also purchased ground. They began building a permanent home with the aid of hired carpenters and masons from Philadelphia. The marriage of John and Gaynor in January 1684, was the first such ceremony at the Merion Friends Meeting.

The Pencoyd Farm. The initial crops at Pencoyd were grains: wheat, Indian corn and the principal crop, barley. John Roberts was labelled malster in early records, a grower of barley from which malt is made. John's life was a rich one...he had found freedom and a place to establish a family without the horrors of his homeland where frequent jailings and fines were imposed upon those who wished to be Quakers.

A Heritage Passed. At the end of his successful life, John left the farm to his only son, Robert, who was 40 at the time of his inheritance. By that time, Philadelphia had grown to be a major economic power, second only to London. Robert Roberts, a trustee of Merion Meeting, was known throughout the community as an honest, intelligent man.

He had been operating a ferry which served as a direct connection to the markets of Philadelphia, as

JOHN ROBERTS OF PENCOYD came to the area of Pennsylvania called Merion in 1683. He married a fellow passenger from the ship *Morning Star,* built a stone home, sired children and founded a dynasty in Lower Merion which produced, among other things, a model dairy farm, an iron works, many civic leaders, a physician, a president of the Pennsylvania Railroad and a state senator. John Roberts (1648-1724) became a prominent man in the Welsh settlement of Merion. Because of his fine reputation, he was appointed Justice of the Peace. He was also elected to the Provincial Assembly in 1704. John called his farm *Pencoid* (his spelling) which means in Welsh "head of the woods," an apt name because his large stone farm house was nestled at the top of the rise of land from the Schuylkill River, just about where Saks Fifth Avenue is now on City Avenue.

22

well as keeping an active interest in the farming on his property. Philadelphia's burgeoning population created a greater need for food and, as a result, Roberts abandoned the major crop, barley, in favor of raising beef, suckling pigs, vegetables, butter and eggs.

Surveyor Roberts's Legacy. With expanded use, the property had grown to 180 self-sufficient acres and was passed on to Roberts' son, John Roberts II, known as "the surveyor." Young John had been surveying neighbors' property lines from the time he was a teenager. With his gift for mathematics, he had been put to work early in life laying out roads and the establishing the boundary rights of neighboring land owners. John II married Rebecca Jones with whom he had 12 children.

John and Rebecca's first son, Jonathan, not being interested in farm-ing, became instead a physician and relocated to Kent Island, Maryland. Jonathan's letters home to his parents at Pencoyd give charming and valu-able insights into mid-18th century life. John, the surveyor, died January 13, 1776, not living quite long enough to witness the break with England.

Two Brothers Rebel. However, son Robert Roberts, (the ninth child of John II and Rebecca), and his brother Algernon (the tenth child), went against their Quaker upbringing and trained to fight in the upcoming con-flict. Robert was read out of Merion Meeting on January 26, 1776 for his warlike activities. It is assumed that Algernon met the same fate at Meet-ing as his brother, although docu-mentation is lacking on Algernon's behavior.

Aside from the impending war, another major problem facing the farm was the depletion of nutri-ents in the soil which had seemed so rich to the first John Roberts. Two and a half generations of heavy farming had taken their toll. A friend of the Roberts family, Richard Peters, whose Belmont mansion still stands today in historic Fairmount Park, is credited with introducing the use of gypsum (or "land plaster") to the soil. Peters shared his technique of regenerating the soil with the Roberts family.

At the death of John, the surveyor, son Algernon became the fourth proprietor of Pencoyd. While serving in the army with his brother Robert, Algernon achieved the rank of Lieutenant Colonel of the Seventh Battalion under the command of his future father-in-law, Colonel Isaac Warner. In 1778, he took an oath of allegience to his country which fur-ther estranged him from his Quaker roots.

1 *(top)* The Pencoyd farm, c.1900, showing some of the various buildings on the property with the prized Guernsey herd established by T. Williams and Isaac Warner Roberts. 2 *(center left)* The Pencoyd farmhouse in 1878, with the open porch. 3 *(center right)* An 1882 photo of T. Williams Roberts, age 5 (T. is for Thomas). The boy wrote of his father "Father was a large man over six feet, a clean minded, honest and manly Christian. He had a warm heart & generous nature with a most lovable disposition."

4 *(left)* George Brooke Roberts (1833-1897) was the sixth generation in direct line to own Pencoyd. Roberts had been in railroading since 1851. In 1880 he became president of the Pennsylvania Railroad.

5 On April 13, 1896 the directors of the Pennsylvania honored him on the 50th anniversary of the railroad.

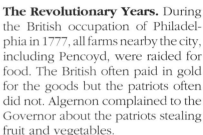

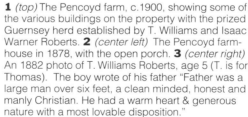

The Revolutionary Years. During the British occupation of Philadelphia in 1777, all farms nearby the city, including Pencoyd, were raided for food. The British often paid in gold for the goods but the patriots often did not. Algernon complained to the Governor about the patriots stealing fruit and vegetables.

After the war, Algernon became a member of Richard Peters' new Philadelphia Society for Promoting Agriculture. By this time, he had changed the focus of the farm once again, concentrating on dairy farming. Algernon provided butter and beef to his main market, Philadelphia. Always an active farmer, he continued to further the cause of farming by writing and spreading the word about new methods and techniques. President Washington, also a good friend of Richard Peters, visited Belmont frequently, so it is quite possible (but not documented) that Algernon Roberts was part of farming conversations which took place at Belmont when the President visited.

Isaac Furthers Agriculture. Algernon reigned as head of Pencoyd for 40 years. When he died in 1815, it was written "none will be more regretted, and few so much missed." His son, Isaac Warner Roberts, took charge of the farm next, promoting many progressive techniques for furthering agriculture and dairying. Isaac's first wife, Emily Thomas, died fairly young after having four daughters. Isaac's second wife, Rosalinda Evans Brooke, bore him two sons, Algernon and George Brooke Roberts.

Isaac enlarged the house with the addition of a large stone wing and maintained the farm successfully for 44 years. However, when Isaac Warner Roberts died, neither George Brooke nor Algernon wished to be farmers in the family tradition. George had graduated from Rensselaer Polytechnic Institute with a degree in civil engineering and a keen interest in railroading. Algernon was drawn to the iron industry which he wished to pursue with his cousin, Percival Roberts. Because both sons were occupied "off the farm," the business of Pencoyd was now managed by their mother, Rosalinda Roberts.

George and Sarah. George pursued and won the hand of Sarah Brinton, whom he married in 1868. Soon after returning from their wedding trip, George's brother Algernon died of a serious infection caused by the lancing of a carbuncle. George was now the new proprietor-to-be of Pencoyd, since his mother, Rosalinda, was still in charge of the farm. When Rosalinda died in 1873, George became the true inheritor and proprietor of the property. George's young bride, Sarah (lovingly called "Sallie"), died in 1869 after giving birth to a son, George Brinton Roberts.

The Railroad Years. George Brooke Roberts married a second time. His new wife, Miriam Pyle Williams, a descendant of both Dr. Thomas Wynne and Dr. Edward Jones, bore him five children. The year of his second marriage saw George's elevation to the position of first vice president of the Pennsylvania Railroad and in 1880 he was elected president. Although not a farmer, George always kept up with the farming business, using the old homestead as a summer home for his family. In the 1890s, he had the farm wired for electricity, 'a modern innovation.'

George was hailed as one of the finest businessmen ever to live,

1 BRINTON'S ALBUM. Eleven year old G. Brinton Roberts took photographs around the Pencoyd estate, starting in 1880. *(top, from left to right):* Greenhouses; "Grandpa Williams' house near Bala Station"; Spring house; Barn; Estate supervisor's home.

2 *(below)* Thomas Williams in carriage (1897 photo) with Archie the horse being driven by Sidney.

being fair and just in all his dealings. His fairness extended to his family as well as business. His will stipulated that each of his children should share in the ownership of Pencoyd so that each could have a house of his/her own. However, all the children were still living in the main house at Pencoyd.

It was some years later that the siblings decided that the third son, T. Williams Roberts, should be the seventh proprietor of Pencoyd. When T. Williams finally took over the running of the farm, he and his brother, Isaac Warner Roberts, decided to establish a herd of Guernsey dairy cattle. In time, they built up the second best producing record in the United States. Their brother, Algernon, became a member of the Pennsylvania Senate but unfortunately developed tuberculosis and died at the age of 34.

Pencoyd in a Time Warp. T. Williams oversaw many changes at Pencoyd. There were new stone chimneys, porches were removed, the entrance was redesigned. Another generation grew up in or near the old farm. However, the time was fast approaching when the growth of the city and suburbs, the demand for housing and new commercial ven-

tures proved too much for the family to endure.

T. Williams' children had to make the painful decision to sell the farm to a developer. Moving the house away from the commercialism was considered but the cost was prohibitive. The peaceful farm atmosphere was already lost to development along City Avenue. Peace and quiet would never surround the old farmhouse again. Pencoyd is now a memory...but what a wonderful memory it is!

1 *(top)* Photo of Pencoyd in 1915, showing additions to the main house over the years.
2 *(right)* Datestone removed from Pencoyd, prior to its razing in 1964.
3 *(below)* Roberts' Pencoyd tract today, on City Avenue, an active commercial strip.

26

1 Castle Bith survives: a sturdy dwelling on Ardmore Avenue, just beyond Haverford Road.

THE LLEWELLYN HOMESTEADS
Castle Bith

Morris Llewellyn (1645-1730), a Welshman from the parish of Castle Booth, purchased 500 acres from William Penn while still in Wales. He, his wife, Ann, and their three children came to Pennsylvania in 1682, a year before Penn. Like many Welshmen, the Llewellyns left their native land on account of their firm Quaker principles. Having claimed their acreage, Morris and Ann built their first shelter (probably a log cabin), cleared the land and began establishing a farm and their livelihood. They were active participants in Haverford Friends Meeting and other civic affairs.

Once their farm was organized, they went about planning a permanent house. Started a year after their arrival, they built a two and a half story stone dwelling and named it Castle Bith after Morris' birthplace in Wales. The homestead sat amidst 150 acres of working farmland and was probably completed in 1699.

Their son, David Llewellyn I, a farmer and surveyor, inherited the home at age 36 and followed the simple agricultural life characteristic of this rural community. He sold the house and two tracts of land to his son, David Llewellyn II (age 19) who kept it for 63 years, until his death in 1794 at 82.

For many years, the home passed through the large Llewellyn clan. William (a son of David II) was an active man; his years at Castle Bith were a time of change and vitality. New machinery and farm equipment increased production and added to the success of their agribusiness. They enlarged the home; extended the house in the back, added one room to each floor and built a huge springhouse (which was later attached to the main house). Subsequent renovations over time have obscured many of the home's original architectural features.

Llewellyn House

Morris Llewellyn, Jr., upon coming of age in the early 1700s, received 400 acres in another area of the Township (now Gladwyne). Called Indian Fields, it was the site of an Indian village at the bend of the Schuylkill River. An agricultural people, they raised corn and beans for their staple diet.

Morris Jr. built himself a dwelling of rough flint rocks gathered from nearby fields. Date stones of 1716, 1750 and 1939 indicated the additions to the house over the years. It had been named Inspiration Farm and Stonehearth by various owners. The home survives (today it is white stucco) along a bend on Conshohocken State Road.

THE LLEWELLYN INSURRECTION

Another Llewellyn...probably the great-grand-son of the first Morris, of Haverford... rose to local fame. A family history, published in 1935, states:
"At the close of the administration of President John Adams [1796-1801], a liberty pole was raised at a small village about ten miles north of Philadelphia, then known as Merion Square. A flag was suspended from it bearing the inscription: 'Down with all tyrants. No gag laws. Liberty or death.' Among the protestants were Captain John Young, Samuel Young and Morris Llewellyn, all from the original Morris family. Word reached the city that the citizens of Lower Merion had planted on their soil the emblem of Liberty and Equality; a squad of troops was sent out to enforce the Sedition Act. Morris Llewellyn was arrested, taken to the city and put in prison. A great crowd attended his trial and promised to attempt his rescue, should he be convicted. But the jury declared him not guilty. He was carried from the court house upon the shoulders of cheering friends. The other parties implicated in the affair are reported to have fled 'to the woods and caves of the Schuylkill hills,' and thus avoided arrest."

2 The Llewellyn homestead in Gladwyne, c.1896.

1 Side view shows three sections, the original 1683 part is at right.

THE HUMPHREYS' PONT READING

Pont Reading, on Haverford Avenue, dates to 1683. The earliest part of the dwelling was built of logs and was home to the Humphreys for over a century. A 1980 photo *(above)* shows three sections, built in 1683, 1746 and 1813. Here lived Charles Humphreys, notable member of the Continental Congress and Joshua Humphreys, who designed the first ships of the United States Navy. His famous warships included the Constitution (Old Ironsides) and the Constellation.

Joshua added the handsome Federal wing of the house in 1813. His grandson, born here in 1810, would gain fame as Chief of Staff to General Meade after the Battle of Gettysburg. So many Humphreys gravitated to the Township that Bryn Mawr was originally named Humphreysville.

2 *(above)* Front, facing Haverford Avenue.

PENN COTTAGE, so-named because William Penn was supposed to have spent time there, was built on land occupied for centuries by a Lenape village. The original building was constructed in 1695 by Robert Owen on 442 acres he purchased for 100 pounds in 1691. Owen was the magistrate in service to William Penn, Justice of the Peace for Merion and a state assemblyman. After the Welsh Quakers settled in 1682, one of their first activities was to build a place of worship, Merion Friends Meeting. Robert Owen, a Quaker member, hired the same stone masons to build his house two miles west on wagon tracks that were to become Old Lancaster Road and then Montgomery Avenue. Upon completion, a gala housewarming was held; venison, purchased from the Indians at sixpence a hind, was served. In 1873, the original modest stone house was altered, then a new wing was added in 1903. All of the original stone walls remain intact. Renovations by the current owners have preserved many aspects of Owen's original "plantation" home, including four working fireplaces.

1 *(top)* William Penn (1644-1718) in an early engraving. **2** *(below)* Datestone, 1695/1873 is on the building. **3** *(right)* Penn Cottage, photo c.1900. **4** *(bottom)* The enlarged home today.

The "plantation" land surrounding Penn Cottage encompassed a major portion of what is now Wynnewood. Robert Owen died in 1697 shortly after the death of his wife, Rebecca (Humphrey). The house became the property of their son, Evan, one of eight children. Evan Owen was a magistrate in Philadelphia.

The house next passed to Jonathan Jones, grandson of Dr. Thomas Wynne after whom Wynnewood was named. Jones was married to Evan's sister, Gainor. The following owner was *their* son, also named Jonathan, who died in 1747. In 1770, the house came under the ownership of the first female owners, Gainor Jones and Mary Jones, granddaughters of the first Jonathan.

At some point, the house was said to have been occupied by Gen. John Cadwalader, who married Martha Jones at Merion Meeting. Martha was a daughter of Edward Jones, founder of Wynnewood. Cadwalader taught at the Friends school in Philadelphia, then moved to the city where he was chosen a member of City Council and the Pennsylvania Assembly.

For the next 150 years, the home passed through a succession of Joneses. The historical list of owners may not always allude to the occupants of the house at any given time, since, apparently, the house was also known as the "bride's cottage" and the brides who occupied it may not have been the owners.

The Toland family (cousins of Mary R. Jones) lived there for 34 years. The first non-familial owners were the Evanses, who purchased the home in 1923.

In 1979, Penn Cottage, one of the oldest residences in Pennsylvania, was included in the Pennsylvania Inventory of Historic Places. In 1997, a bronze plaque was placed in front of the old house by the Welcome Society of Pennsylvania, so-named for the ship that carried William Penn to America in 1682.

GREEN HILL

Like other Welshmen who were persecuted for their Quaker faith, brothers Charles and Thomas Lloyd were members of a landed aristocratic family, the Lloyds of Dolobran. In 1682, the Lloyd brothers, along with Welsh Quaker leader John ap John, gained ownership of a sizeable portion of the 40,000 acre Welsh Tract. Their rectangular parcel included the southeast corner of Lower Merion, and south and west of the corner of Lancaster Pike and City Avenue.

Thomas Lloyd, his wife, and their children arrived in Pennsylvania in June 1683 after an eight-week journey on the ship *America*. Lloyd's wife, Mary, died shortly after their arrival. Three of Lloyd's daughters would later marry men who would each serve as mayor of Philadelphia. Educated at Oxford, Lloyd's rare qualities became apparent in the developing city of Philadelphia. William Penn appointed Lloyd, only a year after his arrival, president of the Provincial Council. (When Penn returned to England, he put his wigs in Lloyd's care with the stipulation that he could use them if he wished).

Upon Lloyd's death at age 54, an unimproved 118 acre tract was sold to **David Price,** Yoeman, of Merion, who immediately settled on the farmland in 1694. On land, identified from then on as the Greenhill tract, Price built a solid stone house, known for 269 years as the Old Homestead. Over the next dozen years, Price added adjacent land until he owned almost 300 acres.

In 1731, Price conveyed 207 of those acres to his son Issachar, a carpenter: "...houses, outhouses, Edifices and Buildings." For almost 30 years the property was leased to a succession of farmers: **John Hughes, John Evans** (who owned land northwest of the Hughes farm), and **Ludwig Knoll.**

John Hughes was active in colonial affairs, member of the Pennsylvania Assembly, and friend of Benjamin Franklin (who appointed him Stamp Distributor for the Provinces). Upon his death in 1772, Hughes' land was inherited by his son, John, Jr.

John Hughes, Jr. married Margaret Pashall, the great granddaughter of one of the original Lower Merion settlers, Dr. Thomas Wynne. Both John and Margaret died in their twenties, leaving two daughters. The orphaned sisters were raised at Greenhill by a cousin, **Mary Hollingsworth.** But the Hughes girls, unmarried, both died in *their* twenties.

In 1799 Mary married **Israel W. Morris,** a well-to-do broker and commission merchant, and son of Captain Samuel Morris of Revolutionary War fame. About 12 years later, the couple moved from Philadelphia to Mary's farm at Greenhill.

From 1815 to 1835, the Morris' leased the farmland section (..."except for Mansion, lawns, raspberry patch, bath house, old barns, orchard, fields & meadows...") to **John Esray.** At Mary Morris' early death, the Greenhill tract was inherited by Israel and their children, Wistar, Han-

1 *(above)* Rare photo (c.1940s) of the Old Homestead, built in 1695 by David Price. It was demolished in 1964 to make way for the Green Hill apartments. **2** *(center)* Israel W. Morris, photographed by his son, Wistar. **3** *(below)* Israel Morris' residence, built in 1862.

nah and Jane, all born at the Old Homestead.

Wistar Morris, founder of Morris, Tasker & Company in Philadelphia, held many positions of importance in Philadelphia. He was also a director of the Pennsylvania Railroad, president of the Board of Pennsylvania Hospital and trustee of Haverford College.

In 1863, Wistar married Mary Harris and built a large stone mansion 300 yards west of Old Homestead. Their only daughter, Holly, was born the following year. Thirty years later, Wistar remodeled the spacious country house and built a copy of a castle in Scotland of granite, designed by Mantle Fielding, and trimmed with fossiliferous limestone.

Holly married Rev. Charles

Wood but died eight years later, also leaving two small children, Margaret Paschal and Charles Morris, who were raised by their grandmother, Mary Harris Morris, in the mansion. Margaret married Logan McCoy; Charles managed the Green Hill Farms Hotel. Wistar Morris' elaborate Green Hill Farm, with 18 acres, was sold to Friends' Central School in 1925.

1 *(top)* Wistar and Mary Morris with their daughter, Holly. **2** *(above)* Wistar Morris' Green Hill estate, purchased by Friends' Central School in 1925.

SOME OTHER EARLY NOTABLES

Dr. Edward Jones (1657-1737), barber-surgeon; trustee for the seventeen Merioneth Adventurers who, with John ap Thomas, purchased 5000 acres to be divided among them. His wife Mary was a daughter of Dr. Thomas Wynne. Landed in America in August 1682 on the ship *Lyon.*

Edward ap Rees (c.1645-1728) came to America on the *Lyon,* August 1682. First married Mably (Mabby), second Rebecca Humphrey. Sold and gave land for Merion Friends Meetinghouse and burial plot; owned most of what is now Narberth.

Robert ap David (1645-1732) came to America on the *Lyon;* one of the original four founders of Merion Friends Meeting, having been first to arrive in 1682. Lived as a gentleman farmer near the Schuylkill for 50 years.

William ap Edward (died 1714); first wife was Hugh and Gainor Roberts' sister, Katherine (died 1676). Second wife, Jane, came with him on the *Lyon.* Bought from other settlers parcel of land which later became the George estate, now Overbrook.

Rees ap John ap William, yeoman (died 1697-98) "...was plaine, serious, and honest and his wife Hannah likewise a good honest plaine Loving tender-hearted woman, Serviceable and faithfull in her place and calling..." She was a sister of Edward ap Rees.

Hugh Roberts (1644-1702) from Bala environs of Merionethshire; with wife, Jane, (died 1686) and five children arrived in America in 1683. A traveling minister among Friends, muchly persecuted in Wales. Here he became a member of Provincial Council.

Cadwalader Morgan (died 1711). His wife, Jane, was a sister of Edward ap Rees; son, Morgan Cadwalader, died at age 19, an invalid, but an ardent minister. His celebrated statement as to why he did not buy a slave was an early indication of Quaker anti-slavery sentiment.

John ap Edward, enterprising member of the Society of Free Traders of London; brought four or more servants with him; died soon after arrival, 1683.

Robert Owen (c.1657-1697) brother-in-law of Hugh Roberts, with whom he was jailed for failure to attend Anglican church services in Wales, and later fined for holding a Quaker meeting. Came to Pennsylvania in 1690; bought from Thomas Lloyd 442 acres in today's Wynnewood.

John ap Evan (Bevan), (c.1646-1726) a trustee for a company buying 2,000 acres; came to Pennsylvania in 1683, "grave and solid in his deportment." Elected member of Assembly four times; Justice of the Peace.

John Cadwalader, "Schoolmaster of Merion," son of Cadwalader ap Thomas, brother of the co-trustee for the Merioneth Adventurers, John ap Thomas. He married Martha Jones, granddaughter of Dr. Thomas Wynne, in 1699. Their daughter Mary became Mrs. Samuel Dickinson whose son was John Dickinson, author and statesman who assisted in writing the Constitution.

Jonathan Wynne (1669-1720). Only son and heir of Dr. Thomas Wynne, physician and personal friend of William Penn. Jonathan's farmhouse, "Wynnestay," still stands in today's Wynnefield (formerly Blockley); occupied for eight generations by Wynne descendants.

HARRITON HOUSE. Americans often search for their heritage in the homes of their patriots. Harriton House in Bryn Mawr is no exception. Charles Thomson, first and only Secretary to the Continental Congresses, was Harriton's most famous occupant, but the story of the house and estate encompasses more than 300 years beginning with the settlement of Merion by Welsh Quakers. The property was originally a 700 acre land grant from William Penn in 1682 and part of a much larger tract of land known as the Welsh Barony or Welsh Tract. Today the restored 1704 house and surrounding 16-1/2 acre park are open to the public as a cultural resource owned by Lower Merion Township and administered privately by the Harriton Association, a not-for-profit membership corporation.

1 *(top)* Photo, c.1890, by the well-known 19th/early 20th century photographer, S. Fisher Corlies.

2 *(above)* 1897 sketch of Harriton House.

Bryn Mawr. The house we know as Harriton was built by Welsh Quaker Rowland Ellis (1650-1731) in 1704 and called Bryn Mawr (meaning "high hill") after Ellis's ancestral farmstead in Wales. The three-story, T-shaped stone house with its flaring eaves and tall brick chimneys is a unique survivor of substantial early domestic architecture in southeastern Pennsylvania. Interior paneling and the closed-string staircase endure in the house from this early period.

Prominent Quaker. Rowland Ellis was a substantial member of his Welsh community, serving as a member of the Pennsylvania Assembly, tax assessor, tax commissioner, justice of the peace, overseer of Radnor Meeting and overseer of the Quaker public schools in Philadelphia. Ellis served his Welsh neighbors as a translator in the marketplace and courts.

He first arrived from Dolgellau, Merionethshire, northwest Wales, in 1687 and settled here ten years later on his 700 acre estate. He experienced financial difficulties and was forced to sell his beloved home in 1719.

The Harrison Era. The name change of the house and estate came in 1719 with the sale of the property to Maryland tobacco planter Richard Harrison. Harrison had married Philadelphian Hannah Norris in 1717; some of the vast Norris family holdings were known as Norriton, thus their land became known as Harriton.

Though a Quaker, Harrison brought tobacco culture and black slaves with him from Maryland, and the Harriton estate is believed to be the northernmost tobacco plantation on the southern slave economy in the colonies prior to the American Revolution.

Harrison ran into some controversy with his fellow Quakers at Merion Meeting and was chastised not for owning slaves but for owning too many. At the time of his death in 1746, Negro slaves represented better than half of his personal estate, (690 pounds sterling), while all of his household goods, wearing apparel and implements of husbandry represented only about 25% of his estate (390 pounds sterling). Tobacco was grown successfully and profitably at Harriton at least until Harrison's death.

1 c.1908 view of Harriton House when the house was the dairyman's home for the Harriton Guernsey Dairy.

The Thomson Occupancy. Charles Thomson was Harriton's most famous occupant. He came to Lower Merion and Harriton by his marriage to Richard Harrison's daughter Hannah. Hannah had inherited the property the same year as her marriage to Thomson, just four days prior to his election as the first and ultimately only Secretary to the Continental Congresses.

Thomson would be most quickly remembered as the designer of the Great Seal of the United States as well as the man who attested to the Declaration of Independence as an official resolution of Congress.

Thomson spent his retirement years at Harriton, from 1789 until his death in 1824, after 15 years (1774-1789) of public service. Thomson had two major interests in his retirement. The first was America's principal industry after the Revolution, agriculture. He experimented with new agricultural techniques and crops, and he was an avid beekeeper.

Thomson was an ardent abolitionist, and he managed his farm not with slaves but by letting out on "shares" with his workers. His second interest was the completion of the first translation of the Bible from Greek to English, to be published on the North American continent in 1808.

Tenant Farmers. The Thomsons had no children, and the estate eventually descended through a blood relative of Hannah's sister, a young woman named Naomi McClenachan who married Levi Morris (for whom Morris Avenue is named).

After Thomson's death, the substantial stone house was the home of Naomi's tenant farmers through the 19th century. The huge Harriton estate was divided essentially in half in 1901 with the sale of a parcel of ground to William Austin, who built his manor house known as Beau-

mont. Harriton House was last used as a tenant farmhouse by the dairy manager, Frederick Huggler, for the Harriton Guernsey Dairy (1908-1927) which provided milk and cream to the growing suburban Lower Merion community.

An Historic Treasure. The house was sold out of the family in 1927 and purchased by Lower Merion Township as an historic site in 1969 through the efforts of the Harriton Association. Today, the house has been faithfully restored to the period of Charles Thomson's occupancy and is open to the public on a regular basis. It is furnished with a fine collection of 18th-century American decorative arts, including objects owned and used by the first and only Secretary to the Continental Congresses, Charles Thomson.

1 *(top left)* Rowland Ellis' "great hall" or common parlour at Harriton, used by Charles Thomson as his study. The closet bookcases were described by a c.1820 visitor: "with the doors standing open and the books and papers tumbling out"!

2 *(top right)* Charles and Hannah Thomson's formal parlour at Harriton House.

3 *(below)* The restored exterior of Harriton House as it appears today complete with pent eave and balcony across its front.

Historic plaque **1** *(above)* erected by the Lower Merion Historical Society in 1998. **2** *(right)* A small section of Price's diary.

Price's daily records of 40 years of local life were known to exist, but where were they? The diary turned up at the Historical Society of Pennsylvania after a search by three members of the Lower Merion Society. A microfilm reel was purchased and Mary Keim spent three years painstakingly transcribing Price's diary onto computer.The convoluted script, the phonetic spelling and archaic phrasing was a test of her tenacity and skills. Mrs. Keim reports:

"Joseph Price starts every day with a weather report...where the wind was, whether it was cold, hot, wet or dry. He only mentions a thermometer once in 40 years so he apparently had no access to one. It was quiet. It was dark. He mentioned the Northern Lights many times; how they would wait after evenings meetings until the moon came up.

He was a builder and a carpenter... a good reason for operating a saw mill. And as a coffin maker, he attended to the burials (often at Merion Friends Cemetery).

Price was an active citizen, held a number of not-so-important posts in Lower Merion, and was trusted by his neighbors. He helped them with wills and helped to resolve disputes.

We find out a lot about money, food, recreation and the position of married women (all property belonged to the husbands). There were detailed reports on weddings, daily work, education, crime and punishment and various social problems.

Health and mortality fascinated him. He reported treatment methods: bleeding, plasters, laxatives. Alcoholism was something that carried many men off. There were many arguments at harvest time and a lot of drinking (and fights). He talks about many suicides and, surprisingly, depression.

During the project I became so close to Price and his world that, at the end, I felt I lost a personal friend. "

JOSEPH PRICE, (1753-1828), was the fourth generation of that Quaker family to live in Lower Merion. His great grandfather, Edward ap Rees ("ap" is Welsh for "son of"), came from Wales in 1682. He purchased 156 acres from William Penn and then an additional 49 acres. The Price holdings by 1780 included what is now Narberth and a large part of Wynnewood.

Over the years, the name Rees became Prees, and then finally, Price. Joseph Price was one of the Township's important citizens...a Renaissance man. As a plaque outside of the house he built in 1803 on Lancaster Avenue (near Meetinghouse Lane) attests: "Quaker Farmer, Innkeeper, Undertaker, Militiaman, Diarist, Saw Mill Operator, Milestone Installer, Carpenter, Turnpike Supervisor, Patriot, Concerned Citizen."

Price married Mary Walter when he was 44; she was 27. He and Mary had eight children. Remarkably, all eight lived at least to adolescence, and six reached their majority. So many babies died in infancy, often in summertime, probably from infections due to bad drinking water, or measles, or smallpox.

The Prices lived first at "Locust Hill" on Montgomery Avenue, across from what is now Merion Mercy Academy in Merion. While Price was building a saw mill on Indian Creek (in today's Shortridge Park), he moved his family into temporary quarters next to the mill, called his "forest hut." A few months later they moved into the just-completed William Penn Inn (Montgomery Avenue and Clover Hill Road in Wynnewood).

The William Penn Inn was completed by Price in 1799, who lived there with his family for only three and a half years. Price (a Quaker) noted that he "felt ashamed to tend tavern." However he energetically embarked, laying in his equipment...candles, dishes, tumblers, rush-bottom chairs; food and drink ...quarters of beef, turkeys, half barrels of salmon and other fish; casks of wine, barrels of cider, gin, beer and whiskey. At the same time, he farmed, continued work on improving the inn, operated a saw mill and carried on his many civic duties.

Price's patrons were mostly "wagoners" carrying goods on the pike from Lancaster to Philadelphia. They were not the big spenders. In mild weather they slept in their wagons, and, in the cold, on the floor of the inn. Many carried their own food and spent only for oats for their horses and drinks for themselves.

Records show especially good days, when there were 12 wagons and the inn served 10 breakfasts and 5 suppers.

Price attempted to attract patrons by holding small game hunts, fox hunts and magic shows. But these did not appeal to his rowdy clientele. The work load got to him; he tired being awakened in the middle of the night and Mary resented being pressed into service. Joseph decided to sell.

The new tenant was Samuel Drake who ran it as boarding school for boys until his death five years later. It reverted to an inn and Price thereafter referred to the property in his diary entries as Penn's Hill.

Later in the 1800s, the owner was Nathan Parker Shortridge, a prosperous dry goods merchant and bank president.

1 1890s photos *(above and below)*, showing Shortridge's Victorian embellishments.The building **2, 3** *(below)* survives today as apartments.

An important building job for Price, in 1803, was a home for his first cousin, Rees, a prosperous farmer. The house, **1** *(below)*, still standing, is on Montgomery Avenue near the northwest corner of Meetinghouse Lane in Narberth.

The house featured intricate woodwork, a trademark found in all of Price's creations. Helping to raise the roof was Thomas Adams, son of ex-president Adams. He lived in Philadelphia at the time and came out here to enjoy the roof-raising, a great social occasion for men. It was a good excuse to get together, have a jolly time...plenty to drink and plenty to eat. They had a wonderful feast, probably drinking all the way through. Alcoholism was discussed in his diary and, one suspects, it was a problem

Price shared with others.

Reese Price and his wife stayed in the home for two months. His wife hated the place and became very depressed. The couple moved back to their original home and their son, Thomas, and his wife occupied it.

In 1805, Price was commissioned to build the Merion Friends caretaker's house, **2** *(at right)*, just east of the meetinghouse. A relatively small structure, it was built on land given to the Merion Friends by John Dickinson, author of "Letter from an American Farmer."

According to Price's diary, he received $800 to build the house but after he paid for all the materials and wages of the masons and other workers, he only cleared about $175.

Joseph Price's formal education was minimal but, for his time, he was well-educated. He had great respect for learning and was a great reader: Alexander Pope, John Milton's "Paradise Lost," William Penn's "No Cross No Crown." On his forays into Philadelphia he would buy books for his children.

Price began his diary when he was 35 and the last entry was three days before his death at age 75. His daily entries were made on odd scraps of paper (over 3,000) that he carried around with him, loosely fastened together with string. This extraordinary 40-year document offers a treasure trove of details of Lower Merion life in that era and a testament to the varied skills and interests of an extraordinary ordinary man.

2 *(above)* Horse mounting blocks, close to the road, in front of the Price House. **3** *(right)* Milestone number 9 "planted" by Price.

In 1795, the opening of the Lancaster Turnpike was a big event. Price was contracted to cut and place milestones along the new highway. Number 9 was nine miles from Philadelphia and still is on Montgomery Avenue near Wister Road in Wynnewood. Price reported in his diary he "planted eight in one day" and eight more the next day. The Pike was now a toll road. An interesting piece of trivia: the first toll paid in the United States was by a local stonecutter named North. If one looks carefully, a number of milestones can be spotted along the old roadways.

In June of 1812, the Trustees of the Lower Merion Academy, **1** *(above)* selected Joseph Price and Nathan Lewis contractors "for Building Lower Merion Benevolent School house." The memo stated that the Trustees would pay them $5,700 which the builders would use to pay for the materials and wages for the workmen. The "architects" were to find the materials for building "a good and substantial stone house for a school and the accommodation of a Family, fifty five feet front and thirty six deep, three stories high in the front and two stories and a Cellar back."

An insurance survey done in October 1814 placed a valuation of $4,600 (1814 dollars) on the schoolhouse. It is a unique example of public architecture for its time. It sits majestically on high land along Bryn Mawr Avenue in Bala Cynwyd, still used for educational purposes by the local school system.

39

1 *(below)* Pencil sketch of Katherine Thomas' log cabin drawn by Jonathan Jones, one of her descendants, from a description given to him many years before.

2 *(above)* 1910 photo of 303 acre farm with barn on the right. At left, what appears to be one house is actually two...Grove of the Red Patridge is at the rear.
3,4 *(below)* Two views of the house today.

ROBERT JONES' GROVE OF THE RED PARTRIDGE

Grove of The Red Partridge was built in or before 1742, as proved by a coin found in the chimneypiece. (It was said to be the custom of concealing a newly minted coin in the wall of a new dwelling).

The owner-builder was Robert Jones, son of John ap Thomas, a Welsh Quaker who purchased land from William Penn in England but died before he could sail to America in 1683. John's widow, Katherine, brought her family and servants (the party numbered 20) on the *Morning Star.* Two of her children died on the long voyage and were buried at sea.

Her 612 acre tract in Merion was called Geilli yr Cochiaid (Grove of the Red Partridge) because coveys of the game favored the spot.

Like most Welsh arrivals in the new territory, the family resided in a log cabin until a small home was built. The 1742 house consisted of a basement with dirt floor, two rooms on the first floor and two on the second. An enclosed staircase leads from the basement to the third floor attic.

In 1791, Isaac Lewis ("tailor") added rooms including a fireplace where all household cooking took place. Nearby was a bake oven, now plastered over. Initials "IL" are carved into a stone at eye level just left of the front door.

Beginning about 1850, James and Michael Magee owned the house and a large portion of Penn Valley. Mr. Stretch, dairy famer, was a tenant of the house for a number of years.

In 1921, Daniel Newhall bought the house and about 12 acres from the Magee estate and more than doubled the size of the house. Stones from a barn on the property were used in the new addition so that the facade would be of matching material, but seams between the 1742, 1791 and 1921 parts of the house are clearly seen. After additions, the house had 9 bedrooms and 5 baths. Newhall's initial "N" and the date, 1921, are carved in a stone to the right of the front door.

COLONEL OWEN JONES' WYNNE WOOD

1 Engraving of Wynne Wood.

Joseph Price's *Diary* notes the May 1803 raising of rafters for a substantial house that was the nucleus of one of the two mansion houses...probably the main dwelling...on the large estate thought to have received its name Wynne Wood at mid-century during Colonel Jones' ownership. This property had been part of the 446 acre plantation established in the late 17th century by Welsh Quaker Robert Owen. Owen's son-in-law Jonathan Jones (a grandson of William Penn's physician Thomas Wynne) took the place over after his marriage to Gainor Owen.

This large tract remained substantially intact in that family for over two centuries. One notable resident was the couple's son Owen Jones (1711-1793), the last provincial treasurer of Pennsylvania before the Revolution.

Another was his grandson and namesake, the prominent soldier-politician Colonel Owen Jones (1819-1878), a University of Pennsylvania graduate admitted to the bar in 1842. He is thought responsible for calling attention to the early link between the Wynne and Jones families by introducing the name Wynne Wood first for his own property, then seeing the name Wynnewood used for the nearby railroad station, and the surrounding community.

Made rich by wise investments and a political maverick, he cut his old family ties with the Federalists, Whigs and Republicans for a lifelong interest in Democratic politics. Colonel Owen Jones served as a county commissioner and was elected to Congress in 1856.

This son-in-law of a Continental Army veteran quickly responded to the Civil War's outbreak by raising a company of cavalry among his friends in Lower Merion and nearby townships which became the 44th Regiment Pennsylvania Cavalry. He served with distinction as a Colonel of this regiment at Fredericksburg, Manassas, Cold Harbor and many other campaigns that often decimated his troops.

His Wynne Wood mansion was destroyed by fire in 1858, its contents saved and the house rebuilt as a 2-1/2 story mansard-roof dwelling with lateral wings and a parapet. Its handsome three-bay southerly prospect featured a portico with cornice and four tall columns. Its style reminiscent of traditional Virginia plantation houses, this dwelling with its wide sweep of lawn abutting the Main Line rail tracks, became a 19th century showplace.

It was next owned by the Colonel's son, J. Aubrey Jones. Wynne Wood stood on just 100 acres in 1900, and in 1908 passed to the Joneses' cousins, the Tolands, who demolished it soon afterward.

OLD ROADS AND TRAVEL. From 1750 to 1840, the roads heading out of Philadelphia, especially the western routes, were the main pathways of commerce and frontier expansion in the colonies and early republic. Pennsylvania was one of the most important gateways to the west, with the rush really beginning after the French and Indian Wars. The Delaware Valley and south central Pennsylvania were also the gateways to the Shenandoah and Blue Ridge regions of the south. It is no wonder then that historians writing in the early twentieth century remarked that the Main Line possessed the greatest number of "colonial relics" of any of the former colonies. The typical colonial roads were narrow two-lane affairs that followed old Indian trails that previously followed animal paths.

LANCASTER TURNPIKE: EARLY HISTORY

The first roads followed ridgelines where drainage was good, or watercourses where grades were more even. Nonetheless, they were muddy and dangerous in bad weather.

The Lancaster Turnpike was revolutionary when it opened in 1794 for both its width and surface. The 24-foot wide right of way was Macadamized, covered with densely packed fine gravel laid over a deep foundation of coarser stone. Just as with highways todays, there were load restrictions meant to protect the pavement. Wagon wheels had to be a certain width, and heavy loads were not permitted at all in the winter when the surface was more fragile.

Many contemporary drivers curse the convoluted routes of roads such as Conshohocken State Road, or Conestoga Road, or deplore the traffic on Lancaster Avenue. These were also the most important east-west routes of the 18th and 19th centuries, for both people and freight.

STAGE COACH TRAVEL

A stagecoach was a carriage, drawn by four or six horses, used to carry passengers and mail on a regular route. The first stage lines were established in colonial America in the mid-1700s, based on a London system started 80 years before. They operated chiefly between Boston, New York and Philadelphia.

The coaches bounced along at a brisk ten miles an hour, lucky to make 30 or 40 miles a day, weather permitting. Horses were changed at relay stations every 15 or 20 miles.

In 1818, a stage line ran through Merion from Chestnut and 6th Streets in Philadelphia. It passed through Merion, Gulph Mills, King of Prussia, Valley Forge and Phoenix Iron Works to French Creek Boarding School...one day's trip. The stage ran, outbound, on Tuesdays, Thursday, and Saturdays and returned to Philadelphia on Mondays, Wednesdays, and Fridays. The fare was $1.75...or 6 cents a mile.

The fast stages imposed great stresses upon the narrow, rutted roads, as there were schedules to be maintained and prestige for cutting time off a run. Different stages also raced between stops, to be the first to arrive at a wayside inn.

There was a hierarchy of the establishments: the inns served the stage traffic and other places served the drovers of the mammoth Conestoga wagons. Innkeepers jealously guarded their reputations, since losing the patronage of one of the stage lines could lead to ruin in the competitive marketplace.

1 Stage coach of 1795 from "Weld's Travels."

CONESTOGA WAGONS

A Conestoga wagon was a sturdy, colorful covered wagon named for the Lancaster county town where it was first built. 25 feet long, its canvas top supported by huge hoops 11 feet high, the vehicle weighed over 3,000 pounds. The massive wagons were made of white oak and poplar with a sag in the middle to take the strain off the ends. Sturdy iron wheels and axles were needed for the rough roads to be traveled and the streams to be crossed.

A wagon cost $250, but the six powerful horses that drew it were worth $1,000. Each horse sported colored headbands and ribbons and a set of vari-toned bells which heralded the rumbling approach of the Conestoga.

It is not difficult to imagine the strain of pulling heavy loads up and down the numerous hills of the area. Many teams had at least one lame or sick animal, and the casualties along the road were many. Furthermore, the cost for stabling a horse overnight was the same as lodging for a person, so it was not uncommon for the teams to be left out in all kinds of weather.

Wagonmasters were a tough, hard-bitten, resourceful class of men: seasoned by weather and experience, ready to fight for a load, not hesitant to force another wagon off the road in a right-of-way dispute.

Unlike the more stylish stagecoach drivers, these men wore rough homespun and leather and a flat wide-brimmed hat to give some protection from sun and rain. Pockets would bulge with cheap cigars called "stogies," presumably a corruption of Conestoga.

This rough era came to an end when steam locomotives ushered in a new age of progress.

1, 2 *(above)* Conestoga wagon teams.

GYPSIES

Gypsy campers were known to aggravate adults and delight children early in this century. One campsite was on the bank of the Schuylkill beside Rudolph's Row, today underneath the Expressway and beside the Green Lane/Belmont bridge in Belmont Hills. A Rudolph family member objected when gypsies flaunted propriety by washing clothes in the river on Sunday. • The second campground was in today's Gladwyne near Old Gulph Road, then empty space. Jenny Haley, a child in 1900, recalled gypsies begging corn or fruit from farmers' wives in exchange for fortune telling. They traveled in covered wagons drawn by poor, thin horses...arrived in May and departed in October.

TO MARKET, TO MARKET

Once upon a time, before the Revolution, women from Lower Merion rode horseback and carried butter, eggs and vegetables packed in saddlebags to market in Philadelphia. Later came the introduction of two-wheel carts with muslin covers fastened with strings "like a sun bonnet"...miniature Conestoga wagons. Ladies could ride in these modern inventions instead of horseback.

SHOES FOR SOLDIERS

Jacob Latch, who lived on Old Lancaster Road at today's Latch's Lane in Merion, obtained a furlough from service at Valley Forge and occupied his time making shoes for his barefoot comrades at arms.

HIGHWAY ROBBERY

An old lady of the Stadelman family, who operated the Black Horse Inn at City Line and Old Lancaster Road, remembered once coming upon passengers of a mail coach. They were tied to trees at 16th and Market Streets in Philadelphia, having been robbed by highwaymen.

Old Lancaster #7
By the entrance to the municipal parking lot near the intersection with Levering Mill Road.
Old Lancaster #8
By the front door of Beneficial Savings Bank near the intersection with Gordon Ave.
Old Lancaster #9
At 349 East Montgomery Ave. which is between Wister and Owen Roads.
Old Lancaster #10
At 111 West Montgomery Ave. near the intersection with Woodside Ave.

THE MILESTONES: Ancient Landmarks. As a unit of measure, the mile dates back to Roman times. The Latin is "milia passuum," meaning a thousand paces. The Romans also erected stone markers at mile intervals to notify the passerby of distances covered or the number of miles to go to reach their destination. These markers were conveniently called milestones. Distances from Rome were measured from the "gilded column" in the Forum which was inscribed with the names of the principal roads and the distances of the major cities.

Remove not the ancient landmark, which thy fathers have set."
–Proverbs 22.28

Colonial Landmarks. Early in American history, Philadelphia was a major city in Pennsylvania. Roads radiated in all directions like a spider's web to the surrounding towns. Philadelphia's equivalent of the Roman "gilded column" was located at the old Philadelphia Court House which stood on Market and Second Streets.

It was Benjamin Franklin, the Colonial Postmaster, who insisted on having milestones erected, because they expedited mail delivery by keeping the postal riders on schedule. These milestones also became popular as a way of identifying the location of a property. For example, on the 1752 Scull and Heap Map, under the "Table of Distances," we find the Merion Meeting House listed as hav-

ing the address of 7–5 (7 miles and 5 furlongs). Many inns were intentionally located near these markers because the innkeepers thought milestones brought them good luck and fortune. Finally, along the turnpike roads, these markers were a means for seeing that no person was charged for more miles than he traveled.

As a note of interest, Benjamin Franklin is credited with the invention of the "odometre." This ingenious mechanical device was used to determine the exact location for each milestone. The "odometer" was attached to a carriage wheel and as it passed over the road it recorded the distance of a mile.

The Three Roadways. Granite milestones continue to mark the distance to Philadelphia along the rights-of-way of our three local roadways: the Old Lancaster Road (now Montgomery Avenue), Old Gulph Road and Lancaster Road. There are a total of fourteen milestone sites that exist in Lower Merion. Let's take a brief look…

Old Lancaster Road. One of the oldest roadways in the state, Old Lancaster Road began as an Lenape foot path. After the arrival of the Welsh, the Religious Society of Friends (Quakers) established their Merion Meeting House and used this path to link them to their fellow Quakers who lived and worshipped at the Great Meeting House at Second and High (Market) in Philadelphia. A short time later this path was extended in a westwardly direction to connect to the Radnor Meeting House.

There is no clear documentation when milestones 7 through 10 were installed, but they were probably in place by c.1740. They were erected on the north side of this roadway and were inscribed with the appropriate mileage numeral on the front side.

Old Gulph Road. Old Gulph Road, an extension of Old Lancaster Road, was constructed to enable the Welsh Quakers easy access into the Mill Creek Valley region. In the valley or gulph (a hollow place in the ground), they constructed their mills along Mill Creek which was used to power their grist, lumber, woolen, paper and powder mills.

Milestones 9 through 13 were erected on the north side of this roadway c.1793 by the Mutual Assurance Fire Company of Philadelphia as a price for their charter from the Penn family. Because of their unique design, this group of milestones is commonly referred to as "William Penn Milestones." On the front side, which faces the roadway, there appears the appropriate mileage numeral, while on the back side are three raised cannon-balls on a bar within a shield which is the coat-of-arms of Admiral Sir William Penn.

Lancaster Road. The War for Independence was over and the country was focused on opening up new territories to the west. Traffic was so heavy on the Old Lancaster Road that there was a demand for an additional road between Philadelphia and Lancaster. This led to the construction of the Lancaster Road (Route 30), which was completed in 1794 and called "The Great Road to the West."

Milestones 5 through 9 were erected on the north side of this roadway in 1795 by Joseph Price who was awarded the contract by the State of Pennsylvania. It's important to note that the Lancaster Road milestones used a different starting point of reference from the other two roadways. These marked the distance to the Market Street Bridge (30th Street) at the Schuylkill River. Therefore, there is a difference of two miles in their measurement to Philadelphia. On the front side, which faces the roadway, appears the appropriate mileage numeral followed by "M to P" or "Miles to Philadelphia."

Old Gulph #9
At 201 Old Gulph Road across from the entrance to the Friends' Central Lower School.
Old Gulph #10
By the entrance to the ford at the intersection with Williamson Road..
Old Gulph #11
At 703 Old Gulph Road near the intersection with Morris Ave.
Old Gulph #12
Near the gatehouse at Beaumont Retirement Community between Great Springs Rd. and Ithan Ave.
Old Gulph #13
On Old Gulph Road at the corner property of 104 Mt. Moro Rd.

Lancaster Ave. #5
At St. Charles Seminary across from the main entrance to Lankenau Hospital.
Lancaster Ave. #6
Between Stanford Drive and Clover Hill Road.
Lancaster Ave. #7
At the intersection with exit roadway from the Township Administration Building.
Lancaster Ave. #8
At 423 Lancaster Ave. at the intersection with Llanalew Road.
Lancaster Ave. #9
On the south side of the road in front of Ludington Library.

1 *(left)* The Black Horse Inn, built c.1720, stood at the entrance to Lower Merion at City Avenue and Old Lancaster Road.

TAVERNS AND INNS served many purposes other than as bars and hotels. A farmer did not have to be able to read. He could recognize a Red Lion, George Washington, William Penn, a Spread Eagle, the Turk's Head...painted on the sign outside. They were like street signs and information booths for visitors seeking directions to relatives or locations of houses, farms, blacksmiths, lumber yards. Most patrons were male. Taverns were the living rooms for most neighbors because houses were small, ill-heated, crowded with children, and bereft of extra food and drink. A host would naturally entertain his cronies at the local tavern. Courtesies were exchanged in the form of drinks, and deals sealed by beverage. The taverns also served as spaces for serious business: voting place, post office, general store.

The Drovers. There were many kinds of taverns. Drovers of cattle had favorites, which had pasture land behind, or nearby, to accommodate huge numbers of animals with water and fodder available...enough to keep up the weight of every animal destined for stockyards in Philadelphia. These were the "long roaders" and the Red Lion in Athensville (Ardmore) was especially favored with its original 30 acres.

When the animals were gathered in for the night, wagonloads of hay moved through the herd with a man pitching fodder right and left; water troughs were kept full. Fortunately, properties surrounding such lots were spacious, houses scattered, and the owners not too fussy about smells. If you made the trip to town behind either a drove of cattle or a 100-mule packtrain, yours was not a journey in a rose garden.

The "Ordinary." Well before the Revolution, the "Ordinary" supplied a menu at a fixed price, as well as a warming drink. Some catered to a better class of customer than the "long roaders." In many cases, a blacksmith and wheelwright opened shop close by. The Conestoga wagons would pull into a tavern (or "stand") for the night. Drivers would have dinner and companionship for awhile, but in good weather, to avoid room rent, retire to sleep in their wagons. Joseph Price, diarist, in his short tavern-keeping career, deplored this custom.

65 Choices. There were "tap" houses run by Irishmen beginning in the 19th century. These catered to farmhands, immigrants, and roustabouts. A slug of "red-eye" with a seegar (cigar) thrown in, cost three cents, wrote Josiah Pearce of Ardmore. Between Philadelphia and Lancaster, 61 miles, there were 65 taverns. "The traveller never was faced with a horrible death by thirst" (Josiah again).

Houses of refreshment along the Schuylkill's canal catered especially to the muleteers responsible for driving mules to pull canal boats. Brawls, murders, and intense domino games characterized some of the river taverns. Wagoneers also participated. They traveled in from farms, used Ridge Pike, then came down to cross the Schuylkill and go into Philadelphia via River Road.

Some confusion as to names of these taverns results from the innkeepers moving from place to place, carrying the tavern signs with them: Robin Hood and Samson and Delilah, for instance.

2,3 *(below)* Further west, beyond Lower Merion Township, is the famous King of Prussia Inn and its distinctive sign, reputed to have been painted by Gilbert Stuart. British spies were known to congregate there seeking information about the troops at Valley Forge. Swallowed up between bustling highways, the inn's demolition was halted by action of an historical society in 1953, and moved to a nearby location.

1 *(above)* Earliest photo of the General Wayne, c.1880, shows the arrival of the brewery truck, welcomed by a line of regulars.
2 *(below)* The inn sign on the roadside shed.

THE GENERAL WAYNE INN

The First Owners. Myths overlaid facts about this special gathering place for more than 250 years. Somewhere in or under the building stand remnants of original walls built in 1709 for Robert Jones (Robert ap John), second of four sons of John ap Thomas, Quaker leader and co-purchaser of land directly from William Penn, who died before the family sailed to America.

Robert was a member of the Provincial Assembly and a justice of the peace in colonial times, but never an innkeeper. When he died in 1746, he left the property to grandson Silas Jones of Darby who rented it to Anthony Tunis. Tunis, so far as is known, was the first to operate an "Ordinary," serving meals at a fixed price.

By this time the country road passing the Tunis Ordinary and the Quaker meetinghouse next door had

become an important route west, the King's Highway or the Great Conestoga Road.

Came the Revolution. The road, which in less than 100 years had lengthened the link between Philadelphia, Lancaster and towns beyond the Susquehanna River, provided a way for both British and patriots to march. It carried coaches filled with Continental Congressmen fleeing to York, and regularly accommodated long packtrains carrying provisions to feed the city.

In 1775, Abraham Streaper (also Streeper) bought the inn, probably enlarged it, and continued the establishment as a place of rest and refreshment. Streaper's wife, Hannah, was a great, great granddaughter of Dr. Thomas Wynne, William Penn's compatriot.

Washington's Encampment. On Sunday September 14, 1777, Washington's army crossed from the Roxborough side of the Schuylkill to the Lower Merion side, via Levering's ford. Journals of participants describe: "the water being nearly up to the waist" and before dark "(we) reached the great road to Lancaster at Merion Meeting House, and proceeded up that road, when we encamped in an open field..."

Perhaps Washington had a bowl of soup at the Streepers, but proof is lacking. The next day, from the Buck Tavern about three miles

47

west along the Lancaster Road, the General sent a plea to Congress for blankets and provisions "the season becoming cold..." Washington took his army west to prevent the British from reaching an American supply depot at Reading; meanwhile Cornwallis took Philadelphia on September 26. Three months would go by before weary Americans settled into winter camp at Valley Forge.

Naming the Inn. When did the tavern get its name? Probably after Mad Anthony's triumph at Stony Point, New York in 1779. In 1790, an appeal was advertised for a stolen horse to be returned to "Abraham Streeper, living at the sign of General Wayne."

Although much repeated, the story is not true that on February 6 or 9, 1795, three troops of Philadelphia Light Horse came out to Streeper's to celebrate General Anthony Wayne's return from victory in the Battle of Fallen Timbers. A neighbor, Joseph Price who frequented Streeper's bar and was "sparking" Mary Streeper, kept a diary. For the days mentioned

1 *(above)* The General Wayne, c.1900. Then operated by James Baird, the workers line up out front for a photo.
2 *(center)* An unusual side view shows the narrow dirt Montgomery Avenue.
3 *(below)* Turn-of-the-century view, then operated by Edward O'Dell.

as the time of welcome for General Wayne, Joseph records nothing more exciting than a bit of fox hunting, coffin making and attending Merion Meeting next door.

On February 10, Joseph set off in the snow for Norristown, on behalf of Mary to obtain a court order to sell Streeper's Tavern to pay debts. It was hardly a time of wild celebration at the tavern; no feasting on "assorted pastries and baked goods brought in by the farm wives from far around the Merion area" as one romantic wrote.

Edward Price bought the inn and the next day deeded it back to Mary Streeper, now cleared of debt. Alas, she married Titus Yerkes, not J. Price, and the public called it Yerkes from then on.

Politics and Postal Service. In 1806, the inn became the polling place for the district. On election day a horse and wagon shuttled back and forth between Ardmore and the General Wayne, for Democrats only. Libations poured freely at both ends of the line "as an accessory to hilarity following success, or as a solace to the regret of defeat" according to the recollections of Josiah Pearce. "On certain occasions the Democratic majorities were so heavy the messenger from the Wayne really staggered under their weight when he reached the boss' office."

The General Wayne post office was established February 5, 1830, closed on July 10; re-established February 8, 1850, then moved to another location as Academy Post Office in 1882.

In 1854, Yerkes' daughter sold the inn for $13,500 to David Young with an added acre, presum-

ably across the road. James Baird owned it from 1883, and Timothy Murphy bought a part to build a blacksmith shop in 1885. Edward O'Dell bought the General Wayne in 1897 about the time Belmont Driving Park, just up Meeting House Lane, became a harness-racing mecca, with fans of fast horses taking sides, trotters vs. pacers. In 1936, a sheriff's sale delivered the Wayne into the hands of I. Newton Smith who ultimately sold it to Barton Johnson, landlord for many years.

An Historic District. Concerned about the preservation of the building and the meetinghouse, a group petitioned The Pennsylvania Historical and Museum Commission in 1998 to include the two buildings in a small historic district. In September of that year, the Merion Friends Meeting/ General Wayne Inn Historic District was created, thus honoring two important buildings and protecting the inn from inappropriate changes in the future.

1 *(above)* The General Wayne, c.1912.
2 *(below)* The famous inn today.

THE BUCK INN

Location, location, location...the real estate people tell us...is all important. The old Buck Inn of Haverford was blessed with a prime site, just where Old Lancaster Road and the New Lancaster Turnpike intersected and briefly overlapped. Currently, a car dealership occupies the place.

Popular Meeting Place. The Buck enjoyed the custom of stage coach travelers and gentlemen on horseback, or local men serious about their farming, namely the Society for Promoting Agriculture; their meetings rotated among local taverns. Drovers of large herds and "long roaders," those rough fellows who hauled loads in the 3,000 or more Conestoga wagons plying the route between Pittsburgh and Philadelphia, usually used the Red Lion, down the Pike.

Some say the Buck was built in 1730 or 1735, but records were burned so no proof is available. Others have written that either John (the American) Penn or his brother Thomas had a hand in the establishment, but proof is hard to come by. What is absolutely certain, however, is that General Washington stopped at the Buck long enough to write a letter to Congress (September 15, 1777) begging supplies for his already threadbare troops, depleted by the lost Battle of Brandywine, and still months away from winter quarters at Valley Forge.

Many innkeepers occupied the landmark: Griffith Evans, Samuel Rees, William Bell, Patrick Miller, John Gregory, Joe Miller, Jonathan Miller and Edward Siter.

Subsequent Changes. The property became a residence in 1844 after purchase by a member of the Martin family whose descendants continued to own it for more than 100 years. From about 1950 offices occupied the building until a national food chain proposed to buy it for $200,000 and build a modern place to offer their own style of refreshment.

Neighbors flew to the defense of the historic former tavern, but Friends of the Inn failed in their efforts and the old Buck was demolished in 1964.

1 *(above)* Old postcard of Haverford's Buck Inn. **2** *(below)* Neighbors, in 1964, protest the demolition of the historic tavern to make way for a fast food restaurant.

RED LION INN

(The building stood very close to today's Greenfield Avenue on Lancaster Avenue, facing Ardmore West shopping plaza.)

After the American Revolution, the new Lancaster Turnpike was built straight through Lower Merion, eight miles from center Philadelphia.

1 A c.1890s photograph records the patrons and the delivery carriages in front of the popular Red Lion Inn. Believed to have been built in 1796, it was demolished in 1941.

The Green Tree. Malcome Guinn first began to dispense refreshment at the Sign of the Green Tree in what is now the middle of Ardmore, then Athensville. In 1808, Green Tree was sold to John Siter (Sider) who, we believe, changed the sign to depict a Red Lion. Historian William Buck, writing in 1859, claimed that the old building was torn down and the "present fine three story hotel...erected in 1855" and kept by Horatio (Rash) Litzenberg, who retained the name Red Lion.

The Litzenberg Era. This "stand" was more than a tavern with rooms to rent upstairs and 30 acres out in back for herds of cattle en route to Philadelphia stock pens. Its east wing housed a general store where village necessities were stocked and drovers swapped yarns around the stove; in a corner there was a bar, open til 10 o'clock, closed on Sundays. Three times a week a wagon pulled by two horses made a trip to the wharves on the Delaware River to replenish merchandise. Later, back in Athensville,

willing hands unloaded goods in exchange for "many a sarsaparilla, etc., particularly the etc." wrote Josiah S. Pearce who himself may have rolled a barrel of mackerel or two for Mr. Litzenberg.

This proprietor was, 1855-1875, the most important man in the village: businessman, farmer, banker and mainstay of the Lower Merion Baptist Church...a man small in stature but filled with energy, integrity, willing and able to toss a man twice his weight into the turnpike if it

seemed to him "a good, honest, Christian necessity."

Failing health forced Horatio Litzenberg into retirement; others ran the store, and eventually a son-in-law was landlord of the entire enterprise after Horatio died in 1880.

The Pennsylvania Railroad advertised rates for summer guests at the Red Lion at $8 and $10 per week in 1884, when 700 people called Ardmore home.

Years rolled by and Prohibition and progress spelled the end for the Red Lion as an inn. By early 1900s, the Autocar Company, Lower Merion's only heavy industry, all but surrounded the old inn and finally occupied it as office space. The building was demolished in 1941.

1 *(top)* One presumes that is proprietor John J. Dallas standing in front of his Red Lion Inn, c.1915. **2** *(center)* The building housed offices of the Autocar Company in the 1920s. **3** *(below)* The historic tavern looked sad at the end of its days in the mid-1930s.

TOLL GATES

Toll houses were established along the township's public roads in 1791. Lancaster Pike was a busy narrow dirt road over which passengers, freight, the mail, and farmers' produce were transported. The Philadelphia and Lancaster Turnpike Company was formed to care for the 62 miles between Philadelphia and Lancaster. By 1795, there were nine toll gates along the route. Many warehouses and shops were dotted along the way to deal with provisions and repairs. The Pike prospered as a tollroad until the canal and railroad took away its business and it became a broken-down, disreputable route.

In 1876, the Pennsylvania Railroad, to prevent the extension of street car lines from the city into the suburbs, bought Lancaster Pike from 52nd Street to Paoli for $20,000. The Lancaster Avenue Improvement Company was established with A.J. Cassatt as president. A second company, the Philadelphia, Bala and Bryn Mawr Turnpike Company, was formed to control what is now Montgomery Avenue. No toll houses remain.

1 *(top)* Early photo of the busy toll house at Lancaster Avenue and City Avenue. Built c.1871, it operated there until c.1914.

2 *(above)* This toll gate was at Montgomery Avenue and Old Lancaster Road, across from Merion Meetinghouse.

3 The toll house at Church Road in Ardmore was built in 1875.
4 On an April evening in 1909, an auto crashed into the front.

OLD WILLIAM PENN

It was a popular misconception of struggling householders in the 18th and 19th centuries that tavern-keeping was a good way to make money. Quaker Joseph Price, hard-working and gregarious, a farmer, carpenter, coffin-maker, sawmill operator, major in the militia, was chronically short of cash, an affliction often mentioned in his 40-year diary.

Four years after he finished several tasks for the new Lancaster Pike construction...he placed the milestones, for instance...he decided to build an inn at the six-mile stone on the southwest edge of his own land. This building is still in use and is 200 years old in July 2000.

A Patriotic Place. In building the inn, Joseph Price hired stone masons but most of the work in wood was his, and the final touch was the obligatory sign, Old William Penn, painted by a man named Drinker. Price named rooms for heroes: Washington, Adams, Jefferson and the entrance hall, The Nation. A lesser room he named for Gov. Thomas McKean of Pennsylvania, "as unfinished as his Brane."

Transients, arriving late and leaving early, demanding meals at odd hours, put a strain on Mrs. Price. "A French Gentleman Left his Lady and 2 Little Girls to board" at $10 a week. Oyster suppers brought customers but the general hilarity "made the Dredfullest dirty house perhaps Ever was Seen..." Finally the diary, two years later, recorded: "too many taverns, we Cant Live by it...I have been at too much Expence."

When an Englishman named Drake offered to lease the Old William Penn in 1802, Price readily agreed, and the inn became a boarding school for boys until 1807, then returned to being a tavern and hotel.

1 *(top)* The inn, c.1910, had become the residence of Parker Shortridge, **2** *(center)* Somewhat later view from the front. **3** *(below)* The building survives today as an apartment dwelling.

The Shortridge Estate. In the 1880s Parker Shortridge, wealthy Philadelphian, bought 75 acres and lived in the house he called Penngrove, then added adjacent Clover Hill farm of 100 acres. A long driveway from Wynnewood station ran straight to Penngrove across fields, where later the Wanamaker store would operate. Price's building still stands, an apartment dwelling today.

THE THREE TUNS/ ST. GEORGE'S

Before 1730, Richard Hughes built a building sufficiently large to advertise as the Three Tuns Tavern...a "tun" being a large cask or barrel...situated on the road that eventually led to Lancaster. He sold 45 acres to Francis Houlton in 1760 who renamed the inn Prince of Wales where he or a tenant served the passing parade of wagons, pack-animals, stage coaches and drovers pushing their herds toward Philadelphia. (This road-of-many-names is known today as Old Lancaster, Montgomery Avenue, Conestoga Road, and Lancaster Pike.)

The Syng Residence. In 1772, a master silversmith of renown... vestryman of Christ Church, treasurer of Philadelphia, trustee of the College of Philadelphia (University of Pennsylvania) and charter member of the Library Company...came out to the country to live and bought the tavern for his home.

He was Philip Syng, Jr., son of a silversmith, father of eighteen children, and especially remembered for his inkstand used at the signing of the Declaration of Independence. He was also a watchmaker, a maker of electrostatic machines, inventor of the first lawnmower, and assistant to Benjamin Franklin in developing the lightning rod.

Philip Syng died in 1789, age 85. If the next date is correct, we surmise Mr. Syng did not die on his plantation in Lower Merion, for it was sold in 1783 to Captain Robert McAfee, famous for his capture of the renegade Capt. Fitz.

McAfee presumably again operated the house as a tavern. Landlords came and went until 1811 when James Anderson, M.D. purchased the property then serving the public under the sign of St. George, probably short for St. George and the Dragon, always a popular tavern title.

The Anderson Home. Dr. Joseph Anderson had fifteen children, was strict, thrifty, litigious, and a classics scholar. The village around him he named Athens and was distressed when the populace added -ville to it. His son,

Dr. Joseph Anderson never married, lived at St. George's with a brother and sister. They passed the house on to nephew Dr. Joseph W. Anderson, also unmarried. The dynasty ended in 1957 with his death. The last Dr. Anderson is fondly remembered, and the family name is perpetuated by nearby Anderson Avenue that connects Montgomery and Lancaster Avenues. Some say it was originally a bypass for teamsters to avoid the toll booth below Athensville on the new Lancaster Pike.

With the death of this respected doctor, the house, surrounded by great old trees, home to Andersons for 146 years, was doomed despite pleas of neighbors to save it. Apartments and the YMCA now occupy the land at the corner of Mill Creek Road and Montgomery Avenue.

1 *(below)* The former tavern, winter 1911, after it had become the home of the Anderson family for 100 years.

1 *(top)* Croft Kettle Mill at left and the Roberts Grist Mill in the right distance.

2 *(left)* Croft Kettle Mill on the Mill Creek and Old Gulph Roads corner. The mill was built in 1840 and is seen here during its use as a residence in the early 20th century.

3 *(right)* The Roberts Mill remains c.1910.

THE MILLS OF LOWER MERION

The Rise and Fall of the Mills. The largest waterway running through Lower Merion Township is Mill Creek, a source that bubbles up in Villanova, runs southeast through Bryn Mawr, spills into Dove Lake in Gladwyne, and then proceeds over various falls until it links with a tributary just east of Ardmore. There it turns sharply eastward, and with new replenishment meanders through the lush Mill Creek Valley, separating Penn Valley and Gladwyne, until it empties into the Schuylkill River at Flat Rock Park. For over two hundred years the power of the water in Mill Creek fostered mill industries unmatched anywhere in the Township. The many different mills supplied both local residents and Philadelphians with grain, paper and cardboard, guns and gun powder, lumber, sheet metal, woolen fabric, cotton and woolen threads, and candle and lamp wick.

The paper produced by the mills served for America's earliest documents, currency, and cartridge paper and can be identified by watermarks in archives throughout the country. At least twenty different mill sites along the creek have been identified by documents, standing buildings, ruins, or archaeological remains. For each one a mill pond, dam, raceway, sluices and mill buildings, wheel houses, and intricate mechanisms had to be constructed and maintained by owners and workers. Mill Creek Valley was a bustling industrial site through much of the 19th-century. Mill ownership expanded beyond the original Welsh settlers to include families from Germany, Switzerland, and England.

Certain mills, such as paper, grist, and saw mills became uneconomical by the 1850s due to advancing technologies. These closed or were converted to textile mills. More influential in changing the industries was the power of the water that drove the wheels, stampers, mill stones, saws or spindles. It had devastating effects when uncontrolled. Storms and floods frequently destroyed dams and mills, wiping out entire businesses. The flood of 1893 brought the final destruction of most remaining mills on the creek. The one exception was the former Nippes gun factory that had been converted to the Barker Woolen Mill. With a conversion to a water turbine, this mill produced woolen thread into the 1950s and still stands.

Maps and advertisements tell us that at least a textile and paper company retained their land and warehouses into the second decade of the 20th century. But by then Mill Creek Valley had begun to shift from an active mill community with worker tenements, small, stuccoed twin homes, a store and post office at Rose Glen, and the neighboring Reading Railroad line to a quieter, suburban residential community.

As industry moved elsewhere, properties were purchased by wealthy financiers and industrialists for suburban living. New homes were built by turn-of-the-century architects on the hilltops. Mill structures, mill owners' homes, and modest workers' housing were converted into serviceable residences for staff.

In the 1920s, for example, James Crosby Brown's estate grew to 185 acres of former industrial land. After Brown's death in 1930, the restricted and sensitive development of his estate into three-acre lots helped protect the natural environment and established minimal and compatible new residences in Mill Creek Valley.

More recent protection has come through Lower Merion Township's purchase in 1994 of Walter C. Pew's 103-acre estate to create Rolling Hill Park. Within this natural parkland, stone building ruins along the waterway remain as architectural testament to Lower Merion's industrial past.

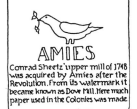

Watermark from paper made at Wᵐ Hagy's mill-1769-later Humphries Shoddy Mill-"Fairview"

In 1762 Frederick Bicking, a Germantown paper maker, built a mill near the mouth of the creek

Fred'k Sheetz, son of Conrad,operated the lower paper mill at the 10mi stone-1788· The plow, huntinghorn, bell etc, were popular watermarks

Conrad Sheetz'upper mill of 1748 was acquired by Amies after the Revolution. From its watermark it became known as Dove Mill.Here much paper used in the Colonies was made

1 Samples of watermarks found in papers made by the papermakers of Mill Creek. Watermarks were symbols, names or initials used to identify the manufacturer, the type of paper, or the person for whom it was made. They are visible in fine papers when a sheet is held up to the light *Drawings by John M. Nugent.*

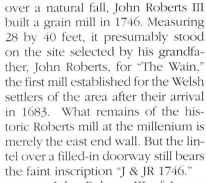

THE EARLIEST MILL

Roberts Mill. On Old Gulph Road in Gladwyne, where Mill Creek spills over a natural fall, John Roberts III built a grain mill in 1746. Measuring 28 by 40 feet, it presumably stood on the site selected by his grandfather, John Roberts, for "The Wain," the first mill established for the Welsh settlers of the area after their arrival in 1683. What remains of the historic Roberts mill at the millenium is merely the east end wall. But the lintel over a filled-in doorway still bears the faint inscription "J & JR 1746."

John Roberts III of Lower Merion and Jane Downing of East Caln Township in Chester County married at a Quaker public meeting at Uwchlan on the first day of the fourth month of 1743. Their years of success in marriage and business is marked by the birth of 12 children between 1743 and 1768 and the growth of John Roberts' land holdings along Mill Creek to the Schuylkill. By 1774 these amounted to 420 acres, and taxation that year was on one grist and saw mill and one paper mill.

To accommodate his family, in 1752 he built a large, stone addition in a typical Welsh architectural tradition to the existing small stone house on the hillside above the mill started by his grandfather. The Revolution and Roberts' role as a Quaker pacifist brought the flourishing career and life of this wealthy citizen to a sad end in November 1778. Roberts was tried and hanged for treason in Philadelphia, having been accused of assisting General Howe's army. His mill sites were confiscated and sold to new owners, but they established the industrial network for another 100 years of milling on the creek.

1 *(top)* The Roberts Grist Mill as it appeared at the end of the 19th century.

2 *(center left)* The east end of the Roberts Mill showing the gable side where the date stone remains.

3 *(bottom left)* By the early 1930s, most of the upper walls of the mill had collapsed.

4 *(center right)* These small stone vernacular buildings neighboring Roberts Mill and residence constitute the purest 18th-century architecture derived from Welsh

traditions that remains in the Township. In 1980 they became part of the Mill Creek National Register Historic District.

5 *(bottom right)* The Roberts Mill wall fragment still remains along Old Gulph Road.

THE PAPERMAKERS

Conrad Scheetz. The earliest Lower Merion mill noted on a map is labeled the "Schultz Mill," which appears on the 1750 Scull and Heap *Plan of the City and Environs of Philadelphia*. The location northwest of Merion Meeting verifies this mill as that of the Schütz family, Protestant papermakers who settled in Germantown from Crefeld, Germany in 1733. Their name eventually became anglicized to Scheetz.

In 1748 Conrad Scheetz purchased from a Donald Davis 100 acres with an existing fulling mill (such mills processed woven or knitted woolen into a tight fabric) on Mill Creek. The site is now along Dove Lake Road, but neither the road or the lake existed at that time.

Scheetz converted the mill to a paper mill known as the Upper Mill. His accounts with Benjamin Franklin show the purchase of rags for paper production and the sale of many types of paper to Franklin for his press. Some were personalized with watermarks bearing Franklin's initials and symbols rather than those of the Scheetz mill.

By 1768, Scheetz had constructed a second mill downstream where a lesser quality paper was produced. It stood on the west side of the creek adjoined by a residence below where Old Gulph Road fords the stream in the vicinity of the 10 mile marker. This mill became known as the Lower Mill and it remained in the family until the end of the 19th century.

Scheetz had eight children who worked or married within the papermaking trade. Their family residence (redesigned during the Colonial Revival period), a spring house, and stone portions of a much altered barn are all that remain of the Upper Scheetz Mill today.

Dove Mill. The Scheetz Upper Mill took on new acclaim in 1798 when it was sold to Thomas Amies from Switzerland. He brought the name Dove Mill and the watermark of a dove to this site. Amies' deed for the purchase

3 *(above)* This ream wrapper for writing paper at the Montgomery County Historical Society depicts an image of the Dove Mill in Lower Merion. The building in the foreground with the large vertical windows is presumably the drying house. The mill building where the stampers, driven by water power, beat the cotton pulp into shreds stands to the right.

1 *(left)* The Dove Lake Mill was photographed by John Browne, an amateur photographer from Philadelphia, from the west side of the lake. The lake was formed when Samuel Croft, a new owner, dammed the creek in 1873 for a brass rolling mill further down stream. By then a fire had already destroyed some of the buildings, which are seen partially flooded. Oil paintings of the mill buildings under Croft's ownership are exhibited in the Gladwyne Library.

2 *(below)* In 1884, painter Thomas Eakins took a group of his students from the Pennsylvania Academy of Fine Arts to Dove Lake where they were photographed in the nude as a scientific study for Eakins' projected painting *Swimming*.

3 The painting of the swimmers *(bottom)*, including Eakins and his dog, was exhibited in 1885. Within six months, Eakins was forced to resign from his prestigious position as Director of the Academy for using students as models and offending Victorian sensibilities.

of the Scheetz Mill identifies him as a cordwainer or shoemaker from Philadelphia.

Amies' papermaking skills were presumably learned in his homeland (the Swiss produced some of the highest quality paper in Europe), and then furthered in America by a tenure at the Wilcox Ivy Mill in Chester. The watermark of a dove with an olive branch in its beak may have been derived from that mill, but for Amies it was intended to exemplify paper that could not be counterfeited.

The manufactory census of 1820 provides critical statistics on Amies' business. He employed 12 men, 18 women, and 4 boys costing annual wages of $5,000. The fine paper produced annually had a value of $19,000. His mill investment reached $25,000 with paper stock valued at $12,000. Despite these figures that imply success, twice before Amies died (in 1849) bankruptcy was declared at his mill. Importation and industrialized papermaking processes gradually put Mill Creek's handmade papermakers out of business.

4 Thomas Eakins' self portrait.

Bicking's Mill. Another German papermaker who settled in Lower Merion and established not just a paper mill but also a saw mill, a fishery on the Schuylkill, and a family cemetery was John Frederick Bicking of Winterburg, Germany. His original purchase in 1762 of a mill site upstream from the extant Barker's Mill rapidly expanded to 255 acres, and reached the Schuylkill by 1798. At that time he was taxed for a 40 by 50 foot mill, a 23 by 60 foot barn, a one-story 24 by 30 foot stone house, a spring house, two log houses, and a cart house on pillars.

During the Revolution Bicking co-authored a petition labeled "Memorial of the Paper Makers of Philadelphia" sent to the Committee of Safety for Pennsylvania, explaining that if every man from 16 to 50 was conscripted to fill military ranks, all the paper mills on the continent would be shut down and no paper for printing offices or ammunition would be produced. The papermakers' appeal for exemption was honored and papermakers were even called home from military service.

Bicking died in 1809 at the age of 79, and he and his family are buried in their cemetery that remains in a backyard on Fairview Road. His son David took over the mill, which prospered until his death in 1832.

Deringer's Mill. The next notable owner of the Bicking Mill was Henry Deringer, pistol manufacturer from Northern Liberties, who purchased the site in 1840. By that time a "tenement" for workers' families is listed on the deed. The largest roofless structure that stands now in Rolling Hill Park (back from the creek) was apparently this building.

Little evidence exists to indicate considerable manufacturing of Deringer weapons was carried out at this mill. The site may have been an investment opportunity, for in 1849 Deringer sold it to his son-in-law, William H. Todd, a Kentucky planter for $7,444.50 plus an annuity to the widow of a former owner.

1 *(top)* Early photo (c. 1905) of Toddstown. The Mill Creek Reading Room and Chapel are in the foreground. The mill workers' tenement house (with four dwelling units), built before 1840, is seen to the left.

2 *(below)* William Todd's mill building was constructed upstream from Nippes/Barker's Mill. Todd's mill produced cotton thread until 1878, when it was sold to Gilbert Fox and run as Glencairn Mill.

The value of the real estate was more accurately defined by the 1850 Census, appraising the mill at $50,000. Todd at the time was 44 years old, his wife Amanda 28, and they had an eleven year old son and three daughters under seven. They converted the paper mill to a cotton yarn manufactory with additional structures added to the site. The number of workers involved became so numerous that the community was called Toddstown. Nearly thirty years later, in 1878, litigation for debts forced Todd to sell his mill at a sheriff's sale. The next owner, Gilbert Fox, carried on the business successfully under the name Glencairn Mill.

Walover's Mill. After the Revolution Peter Walover, an immigrant from Menz, Germany, settled in Lower Merion. He was trained in papermaking in America at the Paul Jones Mill in Manayunk after serving as an indentured servant to Henry Drinker. The mill and miller's house he purchased in 1807 was one of John Roberts' original paper mills. The buildings were located at the current hairpin turn in Mill Creek Road at the narrow bridge.

For nearly ten years Walover apparently ran an efficient and immaculate mill, but the economic recession that occurred after the War of 1812 forced him into debt. His 33 acres of land with three "messuages" and a paper mill were sold at a sheriff's sale in 1818. These buildings remain today serving as suburban residences.

The millers' early-18th-century home is known as "Tayr Pont" and is characterized by a second-story porch. The mill building itself, along the side of the road, was run as a paper mill until 1848 by the new owners, Horatius G. Jones and Evan Jones. At that time Evan Jones renovated it to a cotton and woolen mill. Later he converted it to a flour mill called Merion Flour Mills. A date stone stating "E J 1848 Remodelled by Edw. S. Murray 1890" indicates a later conversion by Edward Murray, whose business was known as the Merion Roller Flour Mills.

Mill Creek became the locus for mills established by many other papermakers, but unfortunately remnants of these buildings are hard to find today. Family names that were prominent throughout the 18th and 19th century were William Hagy, another Swiss papermaker, John Robeson, whose family owned both paper and saw mills, and John Righter whose paper mills were located along Righter's Ford Road. Of these three manufacturers, the Righter mills were the least enduring. The Hagy mill site was eventually converted to the Chadwick textile mill, which prospered until the end of the 19th century. The Robeson mill also was converted to textile manufacturing, producing materials into this century. Levi Morris founded the Harriton Flour Mill on Old Gulph Road below Pyle's Dam and Morris Road in Bryn Mawr during the late 19th century. Some buildings converted to residences and a wheel house still remain.

POWDER MILLS AND GUN AND METAL WORKS

One of the most difficult mills to locate in the landscape are gun powder manufactories. Maps and deeds identify owners; newspaper reports of the times tell sad tales of explosions and deaths, but none of these fully identifies the locales.

During the Revolution a Jacob Losch, powder maker of Lower Merion, wrote the Council of Safety on March 14, 1777 that following an agreement made with the state to manufacture gunpowder, he had completed a mill and works at the cost of 400 pounds.

1 *(top)* Edward S. Murray's Merion Roller Flour Mills. **2** *(center)* Transport wagons are seen in front of the mill. After 1914, James Crosby Brown began purchasing property along Mill Creek to protect his estate. Brown had the mill converted to apartments for his staff in the 1920s. **3** *(below)* After 1935, it became a private residence.

He complains the government has not supplied him with sufficient funds to relieve his debt, and that he has "the mortification that now when the water is plenty he has not a sufficiency of salt peter and brimstone – That he has been and laid himself under great expenses in building said Mill – has a large family to maintain who as well as himself must be great sufferers unless some assistance shall be given him." No results for his request nor his mill have been found.

Nippes Mill. Another powder maker was George Keyser. His site has been identified by eventually becoming the Nippes rifle manufacturing mill. In 1800 Keyser purchased acreage for 1,400 pounds from the John Roberts' estate along Mill Creek from a Benjamin Brooke, forge owner in Gulph Mills. Within a year the site was sold back to Brooke at a sheriff's sale for only 1,000 pounds. A residence and mill are listed in the deed, but one wonders if an explosion may not have occurred to reduce the price and force such a quick sale.

The subsequent sale of this property by Brooke to J. Abraham Nippes, gunsmith of Northern Liberties for $4,000 in 1807 established the beginning of a long tenure of manufacturing at this mill just west of the intersection of Rose Glen and Mill Creek Roads. The site developed into the long-functioning Barker's Woolen Mill. Today most buildings still stand serving various businesses and light industry.

The Nippes family (J. Abraham, Anna, and son David) began the production of guns for the U.S. Government here as early as 1807. In 1823, after Abraham had died, the mill was sold to son David. The Nippes' manufactory produced guns with the initials of D.N. through 1865 when David died.

Associated with this mill site are three significant, roofless stone buildings now part of Rolling Hill Park. One is east of the mill near the creek and may well have been the dwelling house for the owner. The other two are west of the mill, set on a raised earthen and terraced platform. The oldest building is a two-story double unit,

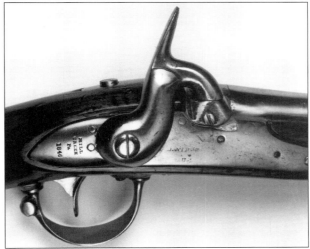

1 Early 20th-century photo *(above)* of the Nippes Mill where rifles were produced for the U.S. Government. The main brick building purportedly dates from 1814. Additions were made after 1865 when the mill was converted to a woolen manufactory. **2** *(right)* The action of a Nippes rifle manufactured on Mill Creek between 1807 and 1865.

each with an attached one-story kitchen. The second building is a later double dwelling.

Daniel Nippes' estate was settled in 1881 by selling 65 acres of his property with the mill at an auction. The buyer was William Booth who ran the mill with his half brother, Thomas H. Barker, and converted it to a carpet and rug yarn manufactory. The date stone on the creek facade of the mill states "Wm. Booth Roseglen Mill 1886." In 1924 the mill was sold to William A.L. Barker who died two years later. Thomas H. Barker II purchased the mill and ran it as the Thomas H. Barker & Co. Inc, Carpet Yarn Mill until 1956. The success of the mill, run by over 60 employees, has been attributed to the use of a metal water wheel or turbine installed in 1890.

Croft Mill. Another manufacturer of metal products on Mill Creek was Samuel Croft, from Birmingham, England. His Philadelphia gilt button business was so successful that he used the capital to build a rolling mill for the production of sheet brass and German silver across from the Roberts Grist Mill. The year 1840 carved on a stone gate post of Croft's Kettle Mill identifies its construction date. The mill building is now a residence.

Croft also owned the Dove Mill site. Here, in 1873, he built a dam that impounded the creek to form Dove Lake. Today the original sluice and stone waterway to the mill pond for the Croft Kettle Mill still function, receiving water from the fall at Roberts Mill, the site where the mill industry started over three hundred years ago.

At the intersection of Mill Creek and Old Gulph Roads stands a house known in local lore as "The 1690 House," the first dwelling of the first John Roberts. Remnants of a log cabin are enclosed within a wall; a plaque, of questionable accuracy, is beneath its peak.

1 *(left)* In the earliest known photo of the house, a log section is visible, but there is no plaque at its peak (at the left).

2 *(below)* By the time this c.1920 photo was taken, a plaque had appeared at that peak, but the logs were gone.

JOHN ROBERTS OF THE MILL. At the intersection of Old Gulph and Mill Creek Roads is a small group of pre-Revolutionary buildings. Now the Mill Creek Historic District and listed on the National Register of Historic Places, its development was begun by John Roberts, a "yeoman and millwright" from Denbighshire, Wales. In the 317 years since his arrival, much intrigue and innuendo have swirled about the site and its first family. On November 20, 1683 the ship *Morning Star* landed "upstream" (in Philadelphia) carrying a group of Welsh settlers. John Roberts "of the Mill" or "of the Wain" (wagon) had purchased the rights to 500 acres in 1682 from Penn; he received a warrant on 250 acres in 1702; the patent on the property was granted to his grandson in 1743.

3 *(below)* The house as it appears today with sympathetic additions built after approval by the Township's Historical Architectural Review Board.

A rushing creek coursed through Roberts' acreage; a natural waterfall provided power for the mill he would build. No documentation has been found of Roberts' exact arrival to his land, what his first buildings were or where they were located. Possibly he first constructed his gristmill, lived first in a lean-to against a hillside, then built a more substantial dwelling.

1690 House. Downstream from the mill site stands a house enclosing remnants of a log building. By local tradition called the "1690 House," a plaque under its peak is of questionable accuracy. An article from a 1905 *Chronicle* noted that a plaque, appeared "this year" when a log cabin on Mill Creek was "transformed" into a "modern dwelling".

1 *(left)* A recent photo of the John Roberts House, at the corner of Old Gulph Road and Dodds Lane. It is now believed the earliest section (front left) was built by the first John Roberts when he married in 1690. In 1752, his grandson, John Roberts III, created the addition (front right) which originally had pent eaves and a balcony over the front door. The roof of the c.1690 section was raised c.1905 and the rooms of the house, which had become derelict, were rearranged.

Some assume this was Roberts' first home; others question the logic and practicality of his having selected this site. It is 500 feet from his mill, too far downstream by colonists' standards, and also lies in the floodplain of Mill Creek.

The proximity of the "1690 House" to the 1840 Croft Kettle Mill, directly across the creek, suggests a more likely possibility of its association with that mill. A small double unit is shown on a 1900 atlas of the area. The real history of this building may never be known...and local lore will undoubtedly persist.

Roberts Marries. In 1690 at Haverford Meeting, John Roberts, "bachelor of Wain," believed to be 60 years of age, married Elizabeth Owen, said to be 18, an age difference not uncommon in those days. As Welsh settlers traditionally built more substantial homes when they married, it is now thought that Roberts built a typical Welsh 1-1/2 story stone house, c.1690, on a hillside near the mill.

John Roberts sired four children. Roberts' wife might have died in childbirth in 1699, the reason that no mention of her was made in his will of 1704, the year he died.

John Roberts II. John and Elizabeth's eldest son, John, took title to his inheritance in 1716 and he married Hannah Lloyd in 1720. Sadly, this young man "sound of mind and memory, but frail of body," died a year later...four months before the birth of their son, also named John.

John Roberts III. It was this John Roberts who became very prosperous and active in community affairs as the Revolutionary War approached. Roberts III inherited his property in 1742. A year later, he married Jane Dowling and, over the next 25 years, fathered twelve children, of whom ten survived past infancy.

Roberts III amassed extraordinary holdings of over 700 acres. Records show that he owned mills and land in neighboring townships and, with partners, had other mills in Maryland.

A New Mill. By 1746, the year he replaced the earlier mill of his grandfather, Roberts had a virtual monopoly on milling in Lower Merion. His mills made flour, lumber, paper, oil and gunpowder. Also, he owned or-

2 *(below left)* The Roberts grist mill in an early 20th century photograph.
3 *(below right)* In 1999, the Township received a grant for stabilization of this last fragment of the Roberts mill wall beside Old Gulph Road. Joe Forrest, a master stonemason, recently completed the arduous work.

c.1700   c.1905   c.1690 + c.1905   1752   1752   c.1690 + c.1905

chards, woodland and watered meadows for his abundant livestock. He would have employed many workers and servants.

An Enlarged Residence. In 1752, John and Jane Roberts built a fine 3-1/2 story addition to the small stone dwelling of his grandfather. It boasted large windows, pent eaves and a balcony sheltering the front door. The original datestone, inscribed "J&JR 1752," is beneath its east peak.

The earlier, c.1690 house, likely one room with a loft, then became the kitchen, possibly also housing servants. Some dozen rooms held fine furnishings and the necessities of daily living.

This manor house overlooking Mill Creek, was a lovely setting for a family of privilege.

Activism. John Roberts III became a highly respected citizen in the greater community. A Quaker, he was named a trustee in 1763 for purchasing land for the Merion Meeting. By 1758 he had become active in public affairs. Roberts was appointed to a commission overseeing improvement of the Schuylkill River in 1760 and 1773. In 1774 he became a member of the Committee of Correspondence to protest the British government's Port Bill. In 1775, in opposition to the slave trade, he was a delegate to the Convention for the Province of Pennsylvania.

Unsettling Times. In the years leading up to the Revolutionary War, increasing desire for independence from Britain spurred political maneuverings and personal jealousies. It

was a trying time for Quakers, an affluent minority group which opposed war. In late 1777, predominently Quaker Lower Merion was overrun by foraging parties of both the British and American armies, sent to ransack farms and mills for provisions. John Roberts, miller, sustained the greatest losses.

1 *(above)* An illustration of the John Roberts House showing its evolution.

2 *(center)* Two c.1900 photos of the abandoned John Roberts House ...which might have started the "haunted house" stories. Later, it became a two-family house.

HAUNTED HOUSE?

• In the late 1800s, a man approaching the abandoned house wrote, "It's haunted, they say."

• Artifacts in the house have reportedly been "rearranged" overnight.

• In the 1940s, a young couple, alone in the house, claimed that they heard mysterious footsteps.

• In 1984, a roofer's helper, climbing to the attic, turned and asked, "Is this house supposed to be haunted?" He "felt a presence" up there.

• In 1994, a man servicing the oil burner told of strangely frigid air moving around him, then a gentle icy touch on his arm.

(Neither knew the house's history.)

1 *(right)* Across Old Gulph Road from the last fragment of the John Roberts Mill on Mill Creek in Gladwyne, this double house was built in two stages. The original house, recessed to the right, was built c.1790 for a miller after Roberts; the left section was added c.1820-1840.

Roberts' Imprisonment. By 1777, Roberts had received frequent threats "by some malicious Persons in my Neighborhood" claiming he was a Tory. Denying any involvement, he fled to British-held Philadelphia for safety.

Roberts later wrote that American soldiers then appeared at his "Plantation," threatened and abused his family and stole 64 animals. He said he intended to return home but his family, "who thought my Life in Danger, deterred me."

While in Philadelphia, Roberts helped imprisoned Americans and did other good deeds. He wrote of threats and abusive treatment by the British army.

At some point he was forced to guide British soldiers on foraging raids in Lower Merion...his only assistance to the British.

Roberts surrendered to the Americans after the British left Philadelphia. On June 19 he affirmed allegiance to the state. It is thought that he aided George Washington about this time by informing him of pending British movement.

Nevertheless, on July 27, based on oaths of neighbors, the Smiths, with whom he purportedly had a land dispute, a warrant was issued for Roberts' arrest. The charges: high treason.

Perhaps Roberts expected acquittal based on his many good works. But he was arrested with others on August 10 and jailed in the Walnut Street prison. Only Abraham Carlisle and John Roberts were made to stand trial, rapidly convicted and sentenced to die by hanging.

Public Protests. An outcry followed. Petitions were sent to the Supreme Executive Council seeking a stay of execution and leniency for Roberts. The nearly thousand names included prominent Friends, 26 military officers and three signers of the Declaration of Independence.

The entire jury on his trial favored a stay; even Chief Justice Thomas McKean, who presided at Roberts' trial and vehemently denounced him, asked postponement. Roberts' children and wife pleaded on their knees for his life.

But the Council was adamant. John Roberts was executed on November 4, 1778.

Lingering Questions. It is said that Roberts' hanging was "political murder"...he was made an example to discourage loyalists. Certainly he was put to death on slight charges.

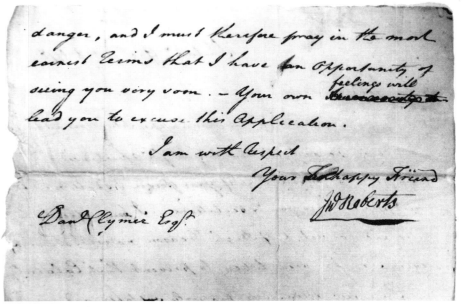

2 *(center)* and **3** *(above)* Portions of a letter written by John Roberts III as he awaited execution. Even from jail, while pleading for help, he tried to aid others.

Interestingly, pertinent documents, including Justice McKean's notes of the trial, were soon "missing."

All of Roberts' estate was confiscated except those items his widow could prove were in her dowry. Its dispersal suggests ulterior motives, too. Four days after purchasing the property, Edward Milner quietly sold it to John Nesbitt and his two partners. Well-known to Justice McKean, the three were advocates of the Revolution. Roberts' estate would seem a coveted "reward."

By 1792, an act was passed returning to Jane Roberts any unsold portions of Roberts' estate and giving her a small pension.

John Roberts' religious beliefs, great wealth and attempts to hold a middle course in the war probably led to his persecution and death.

Roberts best described his plight in his sad description of himself as "an unfortunate Man, born down by popular prejudice."

FICTION, NOT FACT

For years myths have surrounded John Roberts' execution, but...

• Roberts was <u>not</u> hanged by an irate mob in his yard. Neither did a mob, unable to find him, hang a worker there,

• Roberts was <u>not</u> buried beneath the hanging-tree, but in the cemetery at Merion Meeting

• Roberts did <u>not</u> escape through a a tunnel from the cellar.

• Roberts did <u>not</u> add ground glass to flour meant for American soldiers. This fantasy first appeared about 1850, possibly when it was noted that a mill worker in Maryland was hanged for poisoning flour...near the time of John Roberts' execution.

1 (above) A view of the Roberts House from the hillside across Dodds Lane. The garage (at left) might have been a springhouse.

2 (below) The dining room is in the original section of the house. The present owners greatly simplified the interiors to reflect the Quaker origins of the house, yet comfortable for 20th century living.

THE PHILADELPHIA & COLUMBIA RAILWAY

A Train for the Accommodation of Way Passengers will leave

COLUMBIA for PHILADELPHIA

Every Morning at **11** o'clock, and a like Train will *Leave Philadelphia* each Morning at the same hour, stopping at the following named points:

EASTERN TRAIN.

	H. M.			H. M.
Leave Basin at	1 P	Arrive at Coatesville	3	
Arrive at Mountville	11 50	" Gallagherville	3 20	
" Hempfield	12 15	" Downingtown	3 40	
" Lancaster (dine)	12 30	" Oakland	4	
" Bird-in-Hand	1 30	" Steamboat	4 15	
" Leaman's	1 50	" Paoli	4 45	
" Kinsor's	2	" Eagle	5	
" Gap	2 10	" Brookeville	5 20	
" Pennington's	2 30	" Whitehall	5 40	
" Parkesburg	2 45	" Philadelphia	6 30	

WESTERN TRAIN.

	H. M.			H. M.
Leave Philadelphia at	11	Arrive at Parkesburg	3 15	
Arrive at Whitehall at	12 20	" Pennington's	3 35	
" Brookeville	12 40	" Gap,	4 10	
" Eagle	1	" Kinsor's	4 25	
" Paoli (to dine)	1 20	" Leaman's	4 35	
" Steamboat	1 50	" Bird-in-Hand	5 10	
" Oakland	2 10	" Lancaster	5 40	
" Downingtown	2 25	" Hempfield	6	
" Gallagherville	2 35	" Mountville	6 20	
" Coatesville	3	" Columbia	7	

A. MEHAFFEY,

Sup't Col. & Phila. R. R.

Alex. Knox, Printer, 96½ Chesnut street, Philadelphia

A Ride on The Main Line. The War of 1812 had ended and the country was expanding by extending its borders westward. New York, Baltimore and Philadelphia were the major seaports which stood to benefit the most in trade to the west. The road system could not handle the increased traffic so we entered into the age of canals, which offered faster service and were cheaper to operate.

New York built the Erie Canal which joined the Hudson River with Lake Erie, thus providing a through waterway from New York City to the Great Lakes. The Erie Canal opened in 1825.

Maryland, replacing their National Road, began the construction of the Chesapeake and Ohio Canal which connected Baltimore with the Ohio River.

As a counter measure, Pennsylvania decided that it wanted to develop its own canal system linking Philadelphia to the frontier city of Pittsburgh and authorized its construction. But when the survey was made, it was found that there was not enough water in the right places for a canal between the Delaware and the Susquehanna Rivers.

In March 1823, the Pennsylvania State Legislature issued a charter for the first railroad in the state. It authorized the construction of an 82 mile railway, from Philadelphia through Lancaster, terminating at Columbia (on the Susquehanna River), as part of the "Main Line of Public Works of the State of Pennsylvania." The nickname, "The Main Line," derived from this early Pennsylvania railroad.

A Government Venture. The Philadelphia & Columbia Railway was one of the earliest railroads in America and the first in the world to be built by a government rather than by private enterprise. The contracts for the work were granted by the Canal Commission, under whose supervision the line was operated. Considered a public toll road, individuals and companies paid tolls to the Commission for use of the rails. They also supplied their own horses, rolling stock and passenger or freight facilities.

1 A timetable dated April 1, 1837. In this schedule, provision was made for "tarrying" for from five to thirty minutes at each of the stations. These intervals provided time for buying refreshments.

The Philadelphia & Columbia Railway finally became operational on September 1832, with carts and wagons dragged by horse power on a 20-mile section which began in Philadelphia (at Broad and Vine Streets) and ended at Green Tree Inn, west of Paoli.

The first passenger cars were constructed on the same general design as the stage coaches and were nicknamed "fireflies," so designated because of their brilliant red color. They were drawn by two horses, recruited from the Conestoga wagon traffic.

When the idea of locomotives

2 The original Paoli Local, which first ran September 20, 1832.

1 A view of the "Incline Plane" from the top of the Belmont Plateau (north of the Belmont Mansion) looking down towards the Schuylkill River with the Columbia Bridge in the background. The "Incline Plane" was 2,805 feet long, with a rise of 187 feet. Stationary steam engines raised and lowered the trains with cables and winches.

was first conceived, there was great opposition on the part of those who either used the railway or lived near it. They declared that the engines would destroy the value of their property, and that the sparks from them would set fire to their houses and barns. It was not until April 1834 that the first train was drawn from Philadelphia to Lancaster by a locomotive, named the "Black Hawk." Not until 1836 did locomotives finally displace horsepower. The Baldwin locomotives worked the best. The English ones, while well built, were found too light for the heavily curved and graded American tracks.

Eventually, "The Main Line" expanded from the Philadelphia & Columbia Railway to include the Eastern Division of the Canal (from Columbia to Hollidaysburg, 172 miles); the Allegheny Portage Railway (from Hollidaysburg to Johnstown, 36 miles, crossing the Allegheny Mountains); and the Western Division of the Canal (from Johnstown to Pittsburgh, 104 miles). This network carried passengers, but its primary purpose was freight.

The Railway Route. The railroad began in Philadelphia and headed in a westerly direction:

- It crossed the Schuylkill River at the Columbia Bridge and proceeded up the "Incline Plane" at Belmont Plateau.
- There it turned right and paralleled Belmont Avenue and then followed Conshohocken State Road into Lower Merion.
- Still paralleling Conshohocken State Road, it passed through the Cynwyd train station, up Bala Avenue and Bentley Road and crossed behind the fire house.

- It then crossed over to the south side of Montgomery Avenue (Bowman's Bridge).
- At All Saints Church, it crossed back over to the north side of Montgomery Avenue and went in front of the Lower Merion High School.
- From there it curved left onto Church Road and onto Coulter Avenue to the Athensville (Ardmore) train station.
- It followed the tracks of the R5 until Haverford where it again curved left onto (Old) Railroad Avenue to the intersection of Bryn Mawr Avenue and County Line Road.
- Here it followed Glenbrook Avenue until it crossed County Line Road, then Lancaster Avenue, then up Montrose Avenue and rejoined the R5 line at the Rosemont station where it continued west and left the Lower Merion area.

A New Direction. Shortly after the railroad opened, it became obvious that the "Incline Plane" at the Belmont Plateau was inefficient. Hauling cars up and down the grade created significant delays both to passengers and to freight. It wasn't until October 1850 that the Broad & Vine to Athensville (Ardmore) line was abandoned and replaced with the 30th & Market Street to Athensville (Ardmore) line which remains today the route of the Paoli Local (R5).

In 1851, the abandoned line was purchased by the Philadelphia & Reading Railroad. The tracks from Broad and Vine to the Columbia Bridge were used by the Reading; the tracks from the "Incline Plane" west to Athensville were kept open for awhile as a possible detour route, but were eventually dismantled.

Development of the railroad locomotive marked the beginning of

the decline of the canal system. Also, the builders thought that once the system was open, the receipts would pour into the state's coffers. They failed to foresee the huge ongoing maintenance and operational cost required. Therefore, the state decided it wanted to get out of the railroad business. In 1857, the Pennsylvania Railroad, whose original charter was to construct a line from Harrisburg to Pittsburgh only, bought the Philadelphia & Columbia Railway for $7.5 million. To save money, the Pennsylvania Railroad merely upgraded the Philadelphia & Columbia Railway line tracks and the PRR now had a continuous route from Philadelphia all the way to Pittsburgh.

2 Since transport was accomplished by connecting systems of railroads and canals, the boats were constructed in sections. They could be coupled together when afloat and disconnected and placed on suitably designed eight-wheeled cars for transport over the railroad. In this way, freight was carried over the entire systems without transferring from cars to boats, or vice versa.

On leaving Philadelphia, the first stop was at the White Hall station, located at the corner of Glenbrook and County Line Roads in Bryn Mawr. Old lithograph **1** *(above)* shows the White Hall depot at left *(now The Bryn Mawr Hospital Thrift Shop).* The White Hall Hotel on the right was built during the railroad expansion years. The hotel **2** *(right)* in 1905. The depot **3** *(below)* seen in Civil War-era photo.

THE WHITE HALL HOTEL

Between 1870 and 1900, the White Hall was the fashionable hotel of choice for summer residents when the Philadelphia & Columbia Railway passed under its rear windows and brought city folk from the overheated town to the country breezes of Bryn Mawr.

• The genial host and part owner of the hotel, Charlie Arthur, was a popular figure, no doubt greeting all whose carriages stopped in front of his long porch or who arrived at the railway station across the intersection.

• Guests reserved their rooms year after year, even though there were no "sanitary arrangements and no water in the building." A pump in the yard provided water, candles and lamps served for illumination and chamber pots came with the rooms. Yet the atmosphere was that of a big house party. Everyone knew everyone else. A nearby ice cream parlor did brisk business and, behind the hotel, across the tracks, was a pleasant grove where children could play and all ages could sit and enjoy summer days. In the late afternoon husbands came by train from their city offices to join their wives, waiting for them dressed in their best. • But alas, the glory faded. The Pennsylvania Railroad relocated the mainline tracks, eliminating the curve where the White Hall stood, and its summer gaiety declined. Furthermore, the Pennsy built a magnificent rival beside its new tracks, the great Bryn Mawr Hotel. That hostelry lured the beautiful ladies in their long white dresses away and horse shows, dances and elegant socials created new diversions.

• The White Hall slowly sank into oblivion and utlimately to "boarding house" status. The faithful planned one last party to mark its passing. This end-of-the-19th century event welcomed more than 300 people. The sitting rooms were jammed with merrymakers and 150 guests at a time were served dinner by butlers lent for the occasion. They played games, "Going to Jerusalem," "Drop the Handkerchief"; a fiddler was found who struck up the "Virginia Reel." The aging building held together throughout the evening.

Writing in 1922, W. Townsend recalled the great changes that had occured during his lifetime. Here is his description of train service in the 1860s:
"The Pennsylvania Railroad did not cater much to commuters in the Sixties. There were only six trains a day each way. If the 6 pm was missed, there was nothing till the 'Emigrant' at midnight, which was a through train for arriving foreigners and it stopped for each destination they were booked for. The cars were lighted by oil lamps and in cold weather, red hot coal stoves stood at each end."

THE PENNSYLVANIA RAILROAD
AND THE DEVELOPMENT OF THE MAIN LINE

More than any other person or entity, it was the Pennsylvania Railroad that built the Main Line. For 111 years, its trains linked Lower Merion with Philadelphia and the nation. Even today, three decades after the railroad merged with a rival, the Pennsylvania's legacy continues to shape life in the township.

The Pennsylvania Railroad began its long association with the Main Line when it purchased the Philadelphia & Columbia Railroad from the state in 1857. At that time, there were only three stops in Lower Merion: Libertyville (serving modern Narberth and Wynnewood), Athensville (now Ardmore) and White Hall (Bryn Mawr). For a little over a decade, the Pennsylvania concentrated on rebuilding the line and developing long distance traffic. As late as 1869, the railroad operated only a handful of local trains along the Main Line.

1 The original Philadelphia & Columbia Railroad was a curvy, hilly line, ill-suited for the Pennsylvania's planned high speed line to the West. Throughout the township, the Pennsylvania rehabilitated the old line and the photograph above shows its well-maintained tracks at modern Wynnewood in 1861.

1 The Bryn Mawr depot, the pride of the Pennsylvania's Main Line stations, is seen in a 1876 engraving.

As part of the process of relocating its line, the Pennsylvania acquired a number of farms in what was then Humphreysville. The railroad decided to develop this land as both an elite residential community and a summer resort. The railroad renamed the station (and effectively the town) Bryn Mawr.

The creation of Bryn Mawr as a haven for the city's wealthiest residents reflected national trends. A little after mid-century, the railroads serving Boston, New York and other large cities began to encourage elite residential development along their lines. The Pennsylvania was a decade (or more) behind the creation of similar railroad suburbs, both nationally and in the Philadelphia region. Although not the first, the Main Line soon came to

symbolize the quintessential railroad suburb.

The railroad not only encouraged the construction "of homes of more than ordinary architectural taste" but it also built a large hotel to cater to summer boarders. Escaping the heat of a Philadelphia summer by staying in the rural hinterland had been common for the city's elite since the Colonial period. The Pennsylvania Railroad's Bryn Mawr Hotel served this market.

In Bryn Mawr, the Pennsylvania took a direct part in suburban development. Throughout most of Lower Merion, the railroad played a secondary role. Private developers (many with ties to the Pennsylvania, however) purchased farms and subdivided them. To encourage these

DEVELOPMENT

As was the case in many upmarket suburbs, the Pennsylvania Railroad sold its lots in Bryn Mawr subject to strict rules. The following were listed in an 1874 promotional brochure for the Main Line:

1st. All buildings must be set back from the lines of the streets such distance as shall be designated in the deed.
2d. The improvements on the lots fronting on Montgomery Avenue must be of not less than $8000; and upon other avenues, streets, or lanes, of not less than $5000.

3d. The erection of buildings must be commenced within two years, and completed, so far as to render the same habitable, within three years of the date of purchase.
4th. The erection of any buildings included in the following classifications will be expressly prohibited, namely: – Hotels, taverns, drinking saloons, blacksmith, carpenter or wheelwright shops, steam mills, tanneries, slaughter-houses, skin-dressing establishments, livery stables, glue, candle, soap or starch manufactories or other buildings of offensive occupation.

2 *(left)* The Pennsylvania Railroad built a 250 room hotel within walking distance of its Bryn Mawr depot in 1871. It was destroyed by fire in 1889 and replaced by a larger and more elaborate structure designed by the well-known Philadelphia architectural firm of Furness, Evans and Co. After the Main Line declined as a summer resort, the railroad first rented and later sold the new building to the Baldwin School. Ironically, this decline in popularity was caued in part by the growth of high speed train travel to more distant resorts, such as Cape May and Maine.

WORKING NEIGHBORS

It would be easy to view the history of Lower Merion during the late-nineteenth and early-twentieth centuries as the tale of wealthy families and their expensive mansions. But that would be far from the whole story. Even at the peak of conspicuous consumption, the majority of people who resided in the township lived much less extravagant lives. The large homes were built by teams of workers ranging from local laborers to artisans in brick and stone who came from Europe to practice their crafts. Many would make Lower Merion their home. • Once built, these stately homes required legions of employees to serve the families and to maintain the structures and grounds. Many of these people were migrants to the area; some from Pennsylvania's rural hinterland, others from the American South and many from Europe. In addition to those whose livelihoods depended directly on the mansions, scores of workers providing a range of services lived in more humble houses in virtually all the communities along the Main Line. Without these shopkeepers and craftsmen supplying the necessities of everyday life, the suburbanization of Lower Merion Township could not have taken place.

activities, the railroad built stations and added passenger trains. By the 1880s, the Main Line's depots were models of Victorian architecture. Passenger service along the Main Line increased rapidly in the late-nineteenth century from six locals in 1869 to fifteen in 1874 to over thirty from 1884 onward.

Pennsylvania trains serving Lower Merion carried more than just passengers. In the late-nineteenth and early-twentieth centuries, railroads had a virtual monopoly on land transport. The same trains that hauled passengers also conveyed mail and "express" (a railroad-operated private package service). Pennsylvania freight trains brought coal for heat, lumber for building and nearly everything else to the township for decades.

Starting in the late 1880s, the nature of suburban development in Lower Merion changed. Although large and expensive estates for the wealthy continued to be built, much of the new construction was for middle-class families. These new

suburbs were products of combined technological and economic changes in the late nineteenth century that made it possible to extend the full range of city amenities to nearby communities. The Pennsylvania Railroad recognized the importance of these services when it declared in a 1913 promotional brochure: "The charm of this suburban life, with its pure air, pure water and healthful surroundings, combined with the educational advantages provided, churches, stores and excellent transit facilities to and from the city, is manifest."

Although pockets of middle-class development dotted the township, Bala and Cynwyd on the Pennsylvania's branch to Reading perhaps best represent this new type of suburb. Within a few decades of the start of train service in 1884, developers had converted sparsely settled farmland into thriving suburbs.

Not everything the Pennsylvania Railroad did benefitted Lower Merion. Following the introduction of electric trolleys in the 1890s, the

1 The Athensville depot, now **Ardmore,** was typical of the first generation of train stations built in Lower Merion. (This 1858 photo is the oldest in the society's photo archives.) The small frame structure met both the railroad's and the community's needs until the suburban development began in the 1870s.

1 After the end of the Civil War, the Pennsylvania constructed a number of commuter stations on the Main Line. Built by Wilson Brothers, they included **Ardmore** *(above)*, Bryn Mawr and Villanova.

Alexander J. Cassatt (1839-1906) was a Haverford resident and President of the Pennsylvania Railroad at the peak of its influence and power. Cassatt came from a wealthy Pittsburgh family and joined the railroad in 1861. He rose quickly through the organization and became the railroad's first Vice-President at the age of forty-one. He retired from active management two years later but soon returned as a director. He served as the Pennsylvania's seventh President (1899-1906). Cassatt's major accomplishment was the construction of the great Pennsylvania Station in New York City with its elaborate system of tunnels and yards in both New York and New Jersey. • As Lower Merion's Supervisor of Roads for nineteen years,

Cassatt promoted a system of paved roads with granite curbstones. His commitment to good highways reflected his hobbies. A noted horse breeder, Cassatt was also well-known for driving his carriage at high speeds over township roads, accompanied by bugle-blowing coachmen. • At the corner of Montgomery Avenue and Grays Lane in Haverford is a small monument to Cassatt's role in providing Lower Merion with a system of good roads.

2 Alexander Cassatt.

railroad fought hard to keep this new form of transport from the township. The railroad even purchased part of the route of the Philadelphia and Lancaster Turnpike and installed Alexander J. Cassatt as president of this subsidiary in order to forestall the installation of trolleys along the road. The Pennsylvania was not completely successful, as a trolley line was built to Ardmore through Delaware County in 1902.

In 1915, the railroad electrified its line between Philadelphia and Paoli. The engineering used on this route became the model for the Pennsylvania's other electrification projects. Eventually these stretched from New York to Washington and west to Harrisburg. The short, red electric cars (known to the railroad as MP-54s) served the township for over sixty years, grinding their way back and forth between Center City and Paoli.

Passenger service on the Main Line outlasted the Pennsylvania Railroad. In 1968, the once-mighty Pennsylvania merged with its arch rival, the New York Central, to form the ill-fated Penn Central. The only change this consolidation brought to the Paoli line was the repainting of some of the MP-54s in green. Following the bankrupcy of the Penn Central in 1970, service on the line began to deteriorate. After initially funding the trains, the South Eastern Pennsylvania Transportation Authority eventually took over direct operation of the Main Line in the 1980s. Today, the Main Line is one-half of SEPTA's R5 line, the region's busiest commuter route. Thousands of people still use the trains every day to travel to and from Lower Merion for business, shopping and pleasure.

This mnemonic device has helped generations of riders remember the order of the stations on the Main Line. The first nine depots serve Lower Merion Township:

- **OLD**
  Overbrook ("over a brook")
- **MAIDS**
  Merion (Merioneth, a county in Wales)
- **NEVER**
  Narberth (town in Wales: sacred place)
- **WED**
  Wynnewood (Dr. Thomas Wynne)
- **AND**
  Ardmore (small town in Ireland)
- **HAVE**
  Haverford (town in Wales: goat's ford)
- **BABIES**
  Bryn Mawr (town in Wales: great hill)

- **REALLY**
  Rosemont (1683 farm of Rees Thomas)
- **VICIOUS**
  Villanova (St. Thomas, 16th c. bishop)
- **RETRIEVERS**
  Radnor (Radnorshire, a county in Wales)
- **SNAP**
  St. Davids (Welsh saint)
- **WILLINGLY**
  Wayne (General "Mad" Anthony Wayne)
- **SNARL**
  Strafford (Earl of Strafford)
- **DANGEROUSLY**
  Devon (English tourist resort)
- **BEAGLES**
  Berwyn (town in Wales)
- **DON'T**
  Daylesford (tourist resort in Australia)
- **. PERIOD**
  Paoli (Pasquale Paoli, Corsican general)

1 Overbrook *(top)*, 5.6 miles west of Center City, is located on the Montgomery County-Philadelphia boundary and is the first stop on the Main Line serving Lower Merion. The core of the station is a frame structure that initially looked more like an American Gothic farmhouse than a depot. This engraving dates from the 1870s.

2 Merion. Less than a mile west of Overbrook, stands the Merion station. This view shows the original frame depot in the 1890s. The surviving complex at Merion today is probably one of the most complete examples of a "typical" early-twentieth-century suburban station in the region. The buildings are standard Pennsylvania Railroad designs executed in brick and stucco. On the outbound platform are the small waiting room and an express building (used to house packages sent out by the Center City stores).

TRAIN STATIONS

A wide range of stations has served Lower Merion Township from the 1840s to the present. The early structures built by the Philadelphia & Columbia and the Pennsylvania were small and utilitarian; they reflected both railroads' emphasis on long haul traffic. As the Pennsylvania Railroad actively began to court commuters in the 1870s, the station buildings grew larger and more elaborate. Finally, there was a return to simpler structures in the 1950s, when Victorian depots needed replacement.

During the 1870s and 1880s, the Pennsylvania built or rebuilt eleven stations to serve the township on the railroad's main line and its branch to Reading. These structures ranged from standard designs (replicated in many locations throughout the massive system) executed in wood or brick at Bala, Cynwyd and Merion to individually designed depots of stone at Narberth, Wynnewood, Ardmore, Haverford and Bryn Mawr.

1 The **Elm** depot (now **Narberth**, 7 miles from Center City) was one of the Pennsylvania's stone-built Main Line structures from the 1870s and predates by over twenty years the establishment of Narberth borough.

2 The depot at **Wynnewood** dates from the early-1870s and is perhaps the best preserved of the once ubiquitous stone stations built by the Pennsylvania Railroad along the Main Line. In addition to the structure at Elm, larger buildings in the same idiom were built at Ardmore, Haverford, Bryn Mawr and Villanova. Wynnewood station was famous for having one of the Pennsylvania's few female station masters. For nearly fifty years (1903-1952), Mary Jefferis served both the railroad and the community.

3 An 1874 guide gave **Ardmore** and its station a glowing description: **"**The advantages presented by this locality have caused the erection of a number of elegant residences in the vicinity, and the demand for building-sites is active. No station in the neighborhood of Philadelphia has greater promise. The railroad company erected here one of the most beautiful and convenient passenger stations on their line.**"**

4 This photograph shows the second station to serve **Haverford,** c.1890, when the stop was still named Haverford College. The original depot was on the portion of the old Philladelphia & Columbia that was abandoned in 1870 when the Pennsylvania eliminated the White Hall curve. This stop was named after the nearby Quaker college and was the only station on the Main Line to have a Welsh name prior to the Pennsylvania's renaming exercise of the 1870s and 1880s.

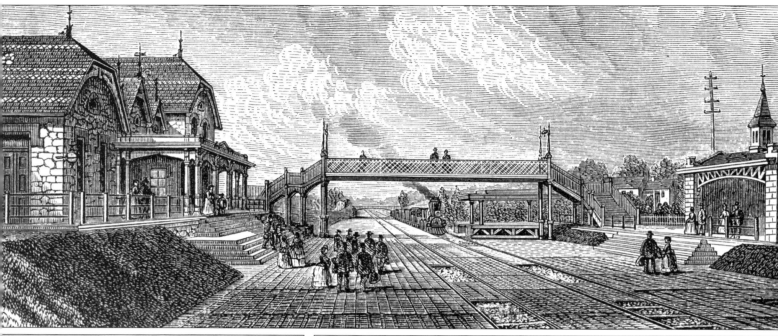

The **Bryn Mawr** station **1** *(top), in the late 1800s, and* **2** *(above),* about 1905, was the showplace of the Pennsylvania's Main Line stations. The largest and busiest of the line's depots, it served the only suburb that the railroad took a direct role in developing. This Victorian depot, like its counterpart in Ardmore, was replaced by a more spartan brick structure in the early 1960s.

3 Bala *(center)* is the first station in the township on the Pennsylvania's Schuylkill Division to Reading and Pottsville. This neat frame structure was based on a standard design used by the railroad throughout its system. One prominent early passenger was Pennsylvania Railroad president George Roberts who lived in nearby Pencoyd Farms.

4 Cynwyd *(bottom)* is an example of a Pennsylvania Railroad standard design executed in both brick and frame. The station building remains today largely unchanged; it is the only surviving Schuylkill Division depot in the township. Interestingly, Cynwyd was not listed as a stop on the first timetable issued for the line in 1884.

1 One of the more interesting stations in the township was the depot at **West Laurel Hill,** later named Barmouth *(above).* It was the last stop in Lower Merion on the Schuylkill Division and was built to serve the nearby cemetery of the same name. Visiting cemeteries was a popular activity for Victorians and the location of this station near one of the region's largest generated much weekend traffic for the line for the first few decades of its existence.

2 This recent photograph of **Rosemont** station, the furthest west stop in Lower Merion, illustrates SEPTA's program of leasing portions of its train stations. In this case, the majority of the structure is used by a real estate firm.

NAMING NAMES

The Main Line today is full of Welsh (and other Celtic) place and street names and many people assume that this nomenclature is a legacy of the early Welsh Quaker settlements. Although this is true of some names, such as the townships of Lower Merion, Haverford and Radnor, most were the creation of the Pennsylvania Railroad in the late nineteenth century. When the Pennsylvania began developing the area as an elite suburb, it found many of the existing place names too plebian for its aristocratic plans. In common with suburban real estate speculators nationwide during the period, the railroad wanted more sylvan names. It chose a series of Welsh and Celtic names for its stations and streets. Subsequently other developers followed suit, giving the Main Line its distinctive identity.

1850s	**1870s**
Athensville	Ardmore
Humphreysville	Bryn Mawr

When the Pennsylvania built its line to Reading through Lower Merion in the 1880s, it continued to name stations after Welsh locations. Sarah Brinton Roberts, wife of the railroad's president, is credited with choosing the names Bala and Cynwyd for the two main stops.

Two other charming frame depots, further out on the line, are shown in these c.1890 photographs: **3 St. David's** *(top)* and **4 Wayne** *(above).* A sign posted at St. David's station read: "Phila. 13.2 miles / Pittsburgh 339 miles."

1 A fanciful engraving from an 1874 booklet published by the Pennsylvania Railroad promoting the bucolic Bryn Mawr area and selling lots for real estate development.

THE BRYN MAWR HOTEL

At the heart of Bryn Mawr was the genteel Bryn Mawr Hotel (or Keystone Hotel, as it was first called), a grand summer resort constructed and operated by the Pennsylvania Railroad Company. Conveniently located in the rural countryside only half a mile from the Bryn Mawr train station, the picturesque resort provided summer fun and social activities to the well-heeled from Philadelphia and other cities beyond.

A Careful Plan. The creation of a resort locale, just outside of Philadelphia, was a deliberate move by the railroad's management to entice riders to use their Main Line passenger

2 The original Keystone Hotel in Bryn Mawr was built in 1871. The popular summer resort burned to the ground 16 years later.

service. Toward this end, they purchased an adjoining 25-acre tract in the late 1860s and built an elaborate train station and the resort hotel. The remaining land was sudivided into lots and sold to those desiring to escape the over-crowded, hot, noisy city in favor of the healthier bucolic countryside of Bryn Mawr.

Designed by the Pennsylvania Railroad-favored architect Joseph Miller Wilson, the four-story, stone masonry Keystone Hotel building boasted 350 rooms, a very fashionable polychromed slate mansard roof, and a verandah to rival any other resort hotel verandah.

The Keystone first opened its doors for the summer season of 1872. Healthy profits enabled management to construct additions and improvements to the hotel after only its first year. The first few summers were so successful that, after the 1876 Centennial Exhibition, the management determined to keep the hotel open into the winter. Failed attempts to draw enough reservations after September, however, proved that Philadelphia society preferred to winter in the city.

Hotel High Living. Equipped with every convenience and luxury for its guests' comfort and delight, the

Keystone's amenities included gas light, bathtubs, the first elevator on the Main Line, a "ten-pin alley," first-quality mattresses, and the location of one bathroom on every floor! No expense was spared with the interiors either...the furniture was valued at $75,000 in 1887.

Social life of all Bryn Mawr centered around activities at the Keystone. Both locals and hotel guests eagerly awaited the event of the season, the Bryn Mawr Assemblies, which would draw more than 500 people. Equestrian activities were popular as well as carriage riding and horseback riding. Baseball, tennis, and cricket were also favorites.

The Keystone Hotel would not stand forever. Amidst (and probably because of) declining popularity and a decrease in net profits, the building was suddenly destroyed by fire in October, 1887.

The Resort Rebuilds. Apparently still a promising resort location, Bryn Mawr would soon see another hotel on the same site. The Bryn Mawr Hotel Company, whose board of directors included Philadelphia industry and railroad leaders of the day, was incorporated in 1890 for the sole purpose of constructing a first-class hotel. The group commissioned the

1 From 1896 to 1913, the Bryn Mawr Hotel boasted its own annual horse show. The "Who's Who" of Philadelphia society attended, and the event drew people from the New Jersey shore area, New York, Connecticut and Boston. This early 1900s photograph shows an equestrian show at the popular Bryn Mawr Assemblies.

well-connected Philadelphia architectural firm of Furness, Evans and Company to design its new building. Not to be outdone by the fanciful, picturesque architecture of other resorts, the hotel was reportedly inspired by the restored 16th century Chateau de Pierrefonds in France.

The impressive, four-story granite structure was built with the latest conveniences, including a hydraulic elevator, the latest in plumbing fixtures, extensive ventilation and drainage systems, a steam heating system, and electric light.

Croquet and golf were popular activities and were played on the expansive front lawn. The first hole of the nine-hole golf course was located right in front of the main entrance. Clay tennis courts were located in the rear, directly below the verandah. Balls, dances, fund-raisers, and nightly card games provided indoor amusements for the hotel guests in this flambouyant hostelry.

Miss Baldwin's School. Florence Baldwin brought her Preparatory School for Girls to the Bryn Mawr Hotel in 1896 when she leased the building and one-third of the grounds during the fall and winter months to conduct her classes. The hotel continued to operate during the summer months until finally, in 1913, the owners signed a year-round lease with Miss Baldwin for her boarding school. In 1922, the Baldwin School purchased the 25 acre lot. The building still stands today ...an architectural treasure from another era.

2 Florence Baldwin opened her school in her mother's home (the northwest corner of Morris and Montgomery Avenues) in 1888. She then leased the hotel for the winter season and bought the building 17 years later. It has housed the Baldwin School for over 100 years. Today, the distinctive architecture remains intact.

MEMORIES

"I grew up on the 'wrong' side of the tracks in Bryn Mawr but I made it. We were the only black family between the Pennsy Railroad station and Bryn Mawr College, having been born and raised in the Bryn Mawr Courts Apartments on the corner of Morris and Montgomery Avenues. My father was the janitor and we lived in the basement apartment. My brother, Joe, and I attended Bryn Mawr Grammar School from kindergarten through 7th, and during that entire period I do not recall once being invited to the home of any of my white classmates. Early-on, social segregation was the rule. Blacks sat in the front left section of the one movie house on Lancaster Avenue. The adults frequented different bars and social clubs...all segregated. Churches and the private schools (Bryn Mawr College, Harcum, Shipley and Baldwin) were all places that blacks visited as employees, but never as members. The public schools, libraries and hospitals were the exception to segregation. • Bryn Mawr Grammar, Ardmore Junior High and Lower Merion High were basically integrated, i.e., the classroom and certain athletic teams such as football, basketball, baseball, track and soccer. However we were *not* encouraged to join the golf, tennis, swimming, gymnastic or fencing teams. If we had wanted to, I'm not too sure we would have been allowed. Never did I experience any overt racism within the schoolhouse. • I graduated as a college prep student in 1944 and immediately entered active duty in the Army Air Corps as a pre-aviation cadet at Keesler Field in Biloxi, Mississippi, a 'great' place for a young black from Lower Merion Township to be sent on his initial assignment. While an astigmatism terminated my quest to become a pilot, the Army Infantry's Officer Candidate School afforded me the opportunity to receive a commission as a second lieutenant of Infantry at the tender age of 19."

Gen. Julius W. Becton, Jr.

[During the next 38 years, while the Army achieved full integration, Becton served in three wars. He retired in 1983 as a Lieutenant General. He served as Director of the Federal Emergency Management Agency (FEMA); next became a university president; then CEO/Superintendent of the District of Columbia Public School System. He has retired (again) and enjoys life with his wife of 50 years, Louise Thornton Becton (Radnor class of '44).]

1 The Autocar plant and offices occupied many tracts along Lancaster Avenue in Ardmore and down the connecting Greenfield Avenue. This c.1909 photo is looking east from Holland Avenue. The Red Lion Inn building is on the right.

2 (*center*) Autocar factory at left, Merion Fire Company at right.

3 (*above*) View of Lancaster Avenue looking west, c.1915-20.

4 (*right*) Original Autocar building, c.1900, on Lancaster Avenue.

THE AUTOMOBILE REVOLUTION.

The early part of the twentieth century produced a prodigious number of automotive ventures. Many of these early pioneers did not make it past the prototype stage before disappearing forever. Of the three automobile makers within the Lower Merion borders, one continues today, one achieved great fame in the 1920s before closing virtually forgotten in 1971, and the other disappeared after just a brief four year period.

AUTOCAR

The first manufacturer of motorized conveyances in the area was Autocar, founded in April 1900. The first year of production, 1901, saw 27 one-cylinder vehicles roll from their shops. In 1902, they introduced a two-cylinder model, believed to be the first produced in the United States. They also pioneered the modern spark plug, shaft drive (replacing chain drive) and engine timing controls for the steering wheel. In 1907, they introduced their first truck, and found their niche among manufacturers. So popular were their heavy trucks, that in 1912, they ceased manufacture of passenger cars entirely.

During World War I, they supplied personnel carriers, ambulances and heavy trucks for the war effort. In 1920, they introduced a 4-cylinder

1,2 *(above)* The first Autocar, 1901, the first American shaft-driven auto and a circulating oil systems. Only the first 800 cars had steering levers instead of wheels.

model producing 29.6 horsepower and capable of operating their heaviest capacity truck, which sported a payload of 6,700 pounds. In 1921, they introduced an even larger 12,000 pound payload truck painted in your choice of color, so long as it was "Autocar red."

Between 1923 and 1927, they offered an electric vehicle in addition to their gasoline-powered units, but top speed was limited to 12mph and only found buyers in major cities.

1928 brought a 6-cylinder engine with 46 horsepower for their ever-larger vehicles. 1930 brought the famous "Blue Streak" engine, which was to be used for the next 20 years in various sizes. During the depression, they introduced tractor-trailers which could haul to up 73,000 pounds.

For World War II, they built over 10,000 military vehicles, armored half-tracks and trucks for the war effort. One market niche they achieved was the development of a tractor to transport airplanes and tanks.

3 *(center)* Advertisement in 1916 issue of *Literary Digest* shows Autocar fleet used by Chicago firm hauling coal and building materials. **4** *(below)* Autocar managers and directors pose for their annual group photo, pre-World War I.

Chassis $1650

THE AUTOCAR COMPANY, ARDMORE, PA.

Motor Delivery Car Specialists   Established 1897

Write for Autocar Catalog and List of Users

FLEET OF AUTOCARS USED BY WILCOX COMPANY, CHICAGO, FOR HAULING COAL AND BUILDING MATERIALS

1 *(above)* Louis S. Clarke, builder of the first Autocar, drives Autocar No. 2 on the grounds of his home, c.1950.

Post-war interstate road construction proved to be a boon to Autocar, with ever-increasing sales. With the new 1952 V8 engine, Autocar trucks became the choice for construction, mining, refuse and specialized heavy hauling industries.

In 1953, White Motor Company purchased Autocar and, in 1954, the Autocar plant was moved to a new, much larger facility in Exton. On July 31, 1956 the now-vacant factory was being torn down by Cleveland Wrecking when a workman's torch caused an oil line to explode, igniting the oil-soaked floors and turning the entire factory into an inferno which burned fiercely for 12 hours. Bringing the fire under control required the service of 44 firetrucks, 300 firefighters and over 6 million gallons of water. An interesting side note is that many firetrucks used to fight this fire were built upon Autocar chassis.

White/Autocar was purchased by Volvo in 1981. Autocar expanded under the new owners to produce construction and heavy trucks with modern styling to attract owner-operators, a successful venture. Today, production of Autocar trucks continues in Volvo's Dublin, Virginia plant. The next time you see a big construction dump truck, look for the Autocar "bow tie" on the front fender and remember its origin in Ardmore.

AN AUTOCAR IN THE SERVICE OF STRAWBRIDGE & CLOTHIER

"Used in every line of Business"

AUTOCARS have gained the confidence of the leading concerns of the country, many of whom have extended their delivery territories fifty per cent. by their use. Begin your motor delivery service with a car that is endorsed by every owner. In economy, service and lasting qualities the Autocar is the leading delivery car of America. Write for list of users and Catalog No. 4 N.

2 Autocar manufactured delivery trucks used by local merchants such as Strawbridge & Clothier.

Advertisement from the 1912-13 *Bala Cynwyd Directory*. Haverford Hotel is in the background.

3 The Autocar factory in flames, July 31, 1956. in the foreground, a La France-powered ladder truck, owned by Merion Fire Company, was one of many to "return" home to fight the blaze.

NOTICE!

Agreeable to an Act of the Legislature, we the undersigned, Commissioners of

LOWER MERION TOWNSHIP

WILL OFFER

AT PUBLIC SALE,

THE REPAIRING, to the Lowest Bidder, the following Sections of PUBLIC ROADS, in said Township:

Section 1. Conshohocken or State Road from Conshohocken to the Spring Mill Road.

Sect. 2. Spring Mill Road from Schuylkill to the State Road, including Stillwagon's Road.

Sect. 3. Boyd's Road to Mount Pleasant School House, by way of Isaac Priest's smith shop.

Sect. 4. Gulf Road from the Upper Merion Line, to Ramsey's Inn.

Sect. 5. County line Road from Upper Merion line, to the Spring Mill Road.

Sect. 6. Spring Mill Road from the State Road, to the Gulf Road, Ramsey's Inn.

Sect. 7. Spring Mill Road from Ramsey's, to the County line, down the County line to the Rail Road.

Sect. 8. Gulf Road from Ramsey's, to the Baptist Church.

Sect. 9. Gulf Road, from the Baptist Church, to Old Lancaster Road.

Sect. 10. Roberts' Road from the Baptist Church, to Delaware County line, by way of Ashbridge's farm.

Sect. 11. Anderson New Road, from John Neason's, to the Pike, and all southwest of the Gulf Road, including the Lancaster Road.

Sect. 12. Stony Lane Road, from Spring Mill Road, to Llewellyn Cemetery.

Sect. 13. Taylor's Road, from Young's Ford Road to Stony Lane Road.

Sect. 14. Young's Ford Road, from Schuylkill, to Llewellyn Cemetery.

Sect. 15. Hagy's Ford Road, from Schuylkill to Young's Ford Road.

Sect. 16. Soap Stone Road from Schuylkill to Hagy's Ford Road.

Sect. 17. Young's Ford Road from Llewellyn Cemetery, to Merion Square.

Sect. 18. State Road from Spring Mill Road, to Merion Square.

Sect. 19. State Road from Merion Square, to Mill Creek.

Sect. 20. Judge Jones' Road from Spring Mill Road, at Mount Pleasant School House, to Robeson's smith shop, by way of Lloyd Barr's.

Sect. 21. Black Rock Road from Merion Square, to the Roberts' Road.

Sect. 22. Robert's Road from Fisher's Road, to the Baptist Meeting

Sect. 23. Fisher's Road from the Robert's Road, to the Gulf Road.

Sect. 24. From Merion Square to Robeson's saw mill, by way of Joseph Haley's Sr., and Mill Creek Road.

Sect. 25. Robert's Road from Mill Creek, to Fisher's Road, by way of Sheet's Hill.

Sect. 26. Righter's Road from Merion Square, to Mill Creek.

Sect. 27. Rozell Valley Road from Young's Ford Road, to Mill Creek.

Sect. 28. Gray's Road from Anderson Lane, to the Lancaster Road.

Sect. 29. Anderson Lane from Mill Creek Road, to the Lancaster Pike.

Sect. 30. Mill Creek Road from Schuylkill, to Robeson's saw mill.

Sect. 31. Schuylkill Road from Mill Creek, to Spring Mill, at the Rail Road Crossing.

Sect. 32. Schuylkill Road from Spring Mill, at Rail Road Crossing, to Conshohocken.

Sect. 33. Schuylkill Road from City Line to Belmont Road.

Sect. 34. Belmont Road from Manayunk Bridge to City Line.

Sect. 35. Clegg's Road from Belmont Road to Schuylkill.

Sect. 36. Righter's Ferry Road from Schuylkill to the Lancaster Road including Levering Mill Road to City Line.

Sec. 37. State Road from the City Line to the Jones' Road.

Sec. 38 State Road from Jones' Road to Flat Rock Road.

Sec. 39. State Road from Flat Rock Road to Mill Creek.

Sec. 40. Schuylkill Road from Manayunk Bridge to Mill Creek.

Sec. 41. Jones' Road from the Schuylkill Road to the State Road.

Sec. 42. Jones' Road from the State Road to the Lancaster Road. including the Academy Road to Manayunk Road.

Sec. 43. Manayunk Road from the Belmont Road to Jones' Road, including the Meeting House Road.

Sec. 44. Leedom's Road from Schuylkill to Jones' Road, including Hubbel's Road to the Flat Rock Road.

Sec. 45. Sibley's Road from the State Road to Flat Rock Road.

Sec. 46. Flat Rock Road from the State Road to the Lancaster Road.

Sec. 47. Flat Rock Road from Hubbel's Road to the State Road.

Sec. 48. Hollow Road from Schuylkill to the Flat Rock Road.

Sec. 49. Eli K. Price Road from Mill Creek to the Hollow Road.

Sec. 50. Fairview Road from Mill Creek to the Flat Rock Road, including Fisher's to Righter's Road.

Sec. 51. Righter's Road from Mill Creek, to Flat Rock Road.

Sec. 52. McClenachan Hill Road from Mill Creek Road to the Flat Rock Road.

Sec. 53. McClenachan New Road from the foot of the Hill, to the Lancaster Road.

Sec. 54. Joseph K. Ayres' Road from Anderson's Lane, to the Lancaster Road.

Sec. 55. Lancaster Road from the junction of the Merion Plank Road, to the Church Road.

Sec. 56. Lancaster Road from the Church Road, to the Gulf Road.

Sec. 57. Church Road from the Lancaster Road to the Haverford Road.

Sec. 58. Paskill Road from the Lancaster Road to the Lancaster Pike.

Sec. 59. Knox's Road by way of the Lutheran Church to Delaware County Line.

Sec. 60. Haverford Road from the City Line to Delaware County Line.

Sec. 61. Kelly's Lane from Haverford Road to the County Line.

Sec. 62. Merion Avenue from the Lancaster Road to the City Line, including Union Avenue.

Sec. 63. City Avenue from the east line of John Mann's Land in Montgomery County to the Belmont Road.

The Sale of Sections No. 1 to No. 32 will take place, at the Merion Square Hotel, ON WEDNESDAY, April 18, 1866. *Sale to commence at 12 o'clock, M.*

The Sale of Sections No. 33 to No. 63 will take place, at the General Wayne Hotel, ON THURSDAY, April 19, 1866. *Sale to commence at 12 o'clock, M.*

Lower Merion, April 2, 1866.

JOSEPH KEECH,
WM. G. SMITH,
THOS. G. LODGE,
Commissioners.

SLOAN Printer, 4369 Cresson St. opposite Railroad Depot, Manayunk.

1 Bidding poster.

GLADWYNE, Lower Merion's first town, evolved at the intersection of the roads now called Youngsford and Righters Mill. It is still a quiet, walkable country village, until 1890 known as Merion Square. Mill Creek flows through Gladwyne; most of the many mills have vanished or are in ruins. By 1880, the village had 35 houses, a few stores, and 207 inhabitants. Area residents depended on a stage that operated from Gladwyne to Ardmore, or on the Philadelphia & Reading Railroad which had a station, Rose Glen, near the banks of the Schuylkill River. The Merion Square Hotel (now the Old Guard House Inn) was built on land that was once part of a 250-acre tract of Welshman Richard Walter. It was built in three stages, the earliest dates from about 1810-1817, completely surrounded by farm land. Although there is no evidence that the building was in existence earlier, there is a legend that during the Revolution colonial troops stopped there to quench their thirst.

1 *(top)* The Merion Square Hotel in an 1896 photo. The inn's owner, Jesse Johnson, is standing to the right of the corner post with his family. **2** *(above)* Johnson in later years.

The hotel's next proprietor was Thomas Haley, Johnson's his son-in-law, who ran the establishment for some years.

1 Haley *(above)* is to the right of the post with Merrill Haggerty, who is handling the horse and buggy. The hand pump may be seen today on the Youngsford Road side near the entrance.

2 Haley's son, Roy *(right)* and the boy's pet goat. The inn was encircled by farms with cows, horses and domestic fowl.

3,4 *(below)* The charming Old Guard House has enjoyed a fine reputation as a gourmet restaurant for over 20 years.

1 *(top left)* The commercial building and residence (1913 photo) opposite the Guard House was built in 1798 (date stone at east end of building) by Henry Hemboldt. The next owner, in 1802, was Harmon Yerkes who added a store. 2 *(top right)* The east end was once known as the War Office, the Saturday night center in the 19th century for discussions by mill workers. David Egbert, also a storekeeper, bought the property in 1822 and the family ran it for 60 years. It also served as the village post office from 1850-1898. 3 Isaac Cornman was the next owner (1915 photo) and it was in the family for over 50 years. 4 After that, it was a hardware store owned by Conrad Barker *(below)*. The building photographed in 1980.

The Merion Square settlement, in early years, became known as War Office because John Rawlins, a captain of a volunteer rifle company, recruited soldiers there for the War of 1812. Years before, John Young, a prominent landowner, was appointed by the Pennsylvania War Office to confiscate flour and other supplies in the area during the Revolution. Later, as the hamlet grew, a new owner, David N. Egbert, changed the village name to the less bellicose Merion Square. Egbert's store *(left page)* later became Cornman's, then a hardware store. Gladwyne is a contrived name and was probably first used by the Reading Railroad for its stop at Mill Creek to avoid confusion with other Merions in the township.

1 *(above)* John Breen's General Store in 1895, once known as Davis' in the heart of the village. The building, after more than a century, looks the same except for the absence of a porch. It houses the Delaware Market, a gourmet grocery catering to the carriage trade.

2 *(top)* Once nicknamed Tammany Hall because of meetings of Democrats at the butcher shop, this small house next to the Gladwyne Free Library had also been a grocery store and tea room. It is now an attractive private home.

1 *(right)* Arnold's birthplace, on the corner of Youngsford and Conshocken State Roads in Gladwyne, c.1902 photo. It now serves as the rectory of St. John Vianney Catholic Church.

2 *(top)* "Hap," on right, with his sister Betty and brother Tom, photo c.1888-89.

3 *(below)* 1945 formal photo; five stars. Note Military Avaitor Badge on his pocket... only about a dozen were ever awarded. Arnold's grandson, Robert, recalls: "He never wore all the medals he had...they would have gone from his shoulder on down!" "Hap" is regarded as the father of the United States Air Force.

HENRY HARLEY "HAP" ARNOLD

"Hap" Arnold (1886-1950) was born on a farm in Gladwyne in 1886. His parents were Mennonites, stern authority figures, who imbued their children with "hard work, no play." A serious child, "Hap" had a permanent grin ...hence, "Hap." Shortly after the boy was born, his family moved to Ardmore. Dr. Arnold sold the family home to the Barkers.

Educated locally, he participated in sports and graduated from Lower Merion High School in 1903.

When brother Tom refused his father's edict to attend West Point, "Hap" took the order and found life delightfully liberating there and gained a major reputation as a prankster.

Since his high school days, "Hap" was interested in the experimental flights of the Wright Brothers. His ambition was to be in the cavalry, but he was assigned to the infantry. There were several mapping assignments in the Phillipines. On one trip he was billeted next to George Marshall, which proved important to both men during World War II.

Deciding that flying was the way out of the infantry, "Hap" enrolled in an exciting new flight training program offered by the Army Signal Corps. The instructors: Wilbur and Orville Wright! In 1912, he was almost killed in a dangerous tail spin which so shattered his nerves that he

1 *(top)* "Hap," standing second from left, with some of his Lower Merion High classmates. **2** *(bottom)* On General Arnold's last trip to the area in May 1947, he visited students at Ardmore Junior High.

did not fly again for four years. Major Billy Mitchell, the aviation visionary, encouraged "Hap" back into flying.

When home on a leave, his sister introduced him to a local girl, Eleanor (Bea) Pool. He shyly pursued her, as did dozens of other Ardmore boys. Bea and "Hap" wed on September 10, 1912.

When the United States joined the war in 1917, "Hap," to his chagrin, was assigned to Washington, D.C. Though unhappy at not being on combat duty, he made great contacts, learned about mobilization...all of which served him well later in his celebrated career.

By 1938, he was Chief of the Air Corps and struggled to bring that branch into the first rank. He lobbied for increased aircraft production, more

air bases and improved pilot training. After the U.S. entered the war in 1941, "Hap's" vision led to victories in Europe (he insisted on daylight bombings to hit German supply depots) and Japan (initiating fire storms across that country). He foresaw the future of rockets in conflicts and worked with the scientific community and industry in their early explorations.

Victory took its toll...three heart attacks. "Hap" retired in 1946, wrote three books, (including his 1949 autobiography, *Global Mission*) and visited Lower Merion in 1947. He died a few years later. One of only nine men ever to achieve 5-star rank, "Hap" was a hero here...and a hero to his nation.

[Adapted from "The Sky Warrior," an A&E Biography, produced by Lou Reda]

(from top) **3** Training with the Wright Brothers, 1912.

4 "Hap's" wedding to Bea Pool in Ardmore on September 10, 1912.

5 Normandy, June 1944, Arnold (left) briefs generals: Ike, King and Marshall.

1 The Gladwyne Methodist Church *(above left,* 1913 photo*), originally the Merion Square Methodist Episcopal Church, on Righters Mill Road, dates from 1838 when it was organized. The first part, now the Sunday School, was built in 1840, rebuilt in 1865-66 and improved between 1943-1950. An addition was completed in 1961.

2 Next door is the Independent Order of Odd Fellows *(above right,* 1912 photo), constructed in 1852. Its cemetery, behind the building, blends into the cemetery of the Methodist Church and contains the graves of many of Merion Square's (Gladwyne) first residents.

3 After the Civil War, the small clapboard building *(right)* was erected to be both the post office and home of the wounded veteran, William Snell, who became the postmaster of Merion Square, the only post office in Lower Merion. During those years it was used for storage for the hardware store next door; then a barber shop. Now the Gladwyne Lunch, a popular place for breakfast and mid-day meals, it is one of the few restaurants in the township where outdoor eating is permitted.

4 The solid stone building *(right)* built in 1921 by All Saints Episcopal Church, was the Gladwyne Community Hall with a basketball court, a stage and, at one time, was the post office. One room was for Maud Bell's books that evolved into the Gladwyne Free Library by 1930. The modern addition and glassed exterior stairwell were added in the 1960s and the building was completely renovated in 1992. The Community Room is the setting for meetings ranging from the Civic Association, Story Hour for youngsters and the Library League's annual Craft Show. The library is the "Heart of the Village."

A walk through the Gladwyne (Merion Square) Historic District, established in 1980, reveals an amazing variety of residences: **1** converted mill workers' houses *(top);* simple homes with Victorian, Stick Style and Gothic Revival embellishments; cottages and double-houses from the 1920s; small, elegant estates. **2** The charming home *(above)* was likely a section of a state pavilion removed from Fairmount Park at the end of the Philadelphia Centennial. **3** Stores *(below)* have a small-town look and pride themselves on their friendly service. In two short blocks one finds: a gas station, two banks, a big super-market and several small groceries, drug store, dry cleaner, florist, veterinarian, real estate agencies and other specialty businesses.

4 The Claypool home as it appears today.

MEMORIES

"My father moved to Gladwyne in 1900 and worked for the Reading Railroad as a station agent down by the river. It was called Rose Glen. Later, he bought a coal yard right back of the station from a man named Wightman. My brother, Elmer, and I used to haul the coal by wagon and a team of horses. We could put a ton and a half of coal in a wagon, and had to shovel all the anthracite coal ...either that or bag it. In the wintertime, we had to hitch four horses to that same wagon to pull the coal to Ardmore. Three trips a day. • They tell me that years ago there used to be shad in the river as far as Norristown and the river was beautiful and blue. In the winter-time it would freeze over...I walked down it. One winter it was so cold it froze over and Mr. Claypool went across the river with a team of horses to one of the mills over there and got a load of cinders to cinder the roads here in Gladwyne. The ice was anywhere from 12 to 14 inches thick. Mr. Claypool used to run a stagecoach into Ardmore. He would haul people to Ardmore for 15¢. Then he had horse cabs that would cost you 25¢. He would try to get two or three people in a cab before he would start. • He lived at the corner of Rose Glen and Youngsford. There was a show there at Claypool's being filmed ...moving picture people...no one knows for sure whether it was Mary Pickford in that show, *Rebecca of Sunnybrook Farm* I think it was called. Mrs. Harvey remembers seeing smoke coming out of the windows at Claypool's on her way home from school. My brother broke horses for the moving picture people. Headquarters were up at Betzwood. Oh, I guess I was eight or nine years old at the time they were making movies. My brother used to ride for Buffalo Bill, later on in the *Buffalo Bill Show*." **Warren B. Althouse**

[Lubin Studios, the motion picture firm in Betzwood, made many films locally in the early years of the 20th century. One was about a young woman in distress in a simulated burning building, the Claypool House *(above).* The town's children watched the filming and the rumor started (and persisted!) that the blonde actress was Mary Pickford, one of Hollywood's most famous stars. The movie, said to be one of her best known, *Rebecca of Sunnybrook Farm* (1917), was actually filmed in California...and the setting had nothing to do with Gladwyne.]

1 *(left)* Robert Chadwick, c.1880, proprietor of Merion Mills **2** *(below, left)* that was located on the northeast corner of Rose Glen Road where it meets Mill Creek.

It was built in 1836 by Chadwick's father for the manufacture of cotton goods. The building became came part of the Gladwyne Colony c.1910. It was demolished in 1968.

3 *(top right)* A small double house for mill workers at Egbert's Mill, c.1900, shown in the distance.

4 *(middle right)* The same mill workers' house as it appears today, greatly modified with a large northern wing added. The original front doors facing the street have been made into windows, a porch added on the east to shield the new front door, above which two of the upper windows were sealed.

5 *(below right)* Egbert's Mill, now a private residence as it is today, basically unchanged except for a garage addition to the north joined to the house by a second story ramp. Little is known of Egbert's Mill, noted as a lamp-wick factory on old maps. The two houses, the most eastwardly on Rose Glen Road, became part of Dr. Ludlum's Gladwyne Colony. The water wheel (not shown) at the tenant house was a 1980s addition to generate electricity.

Seymour DeWitt Ludlum stumbled across the almost deserted village of Rose Glen on a horseback ride from his home in Merion. The setting was perfect for a sanitarium for the mentally ill that the young psychiatrist planned to found. Most of the industry that had thrived along Mill Creek a half century before was gone, but the buildings were intact. It was isolated, calm and beautiful, an ideal location. Dr. Ludlum bought the buildings that had been a little hamlet: the post office and store, the Merion Mills across the stream and nearby houses.

Over the years they were turned into hospital wards, laboratories, doctors' offices and living quarters. Called The Gladwyne Colony, to the passerby it seemed to be a "little village out of yesterday."

Dr. Ludlum died at 80. His son, S. DeWitt Ludlum, Jr., who had assisted for many years, became the director of the Colony and ran it for another decade. By this time the newly built Schuylkill Expressway made all of Gladwyne accessible, the land values higher and brought more people to live there.

Ensuing changes in medical standards, increased fees and public attitude made the Colony increasingly difficult to run. It was sold and only Ludlum's house, Fernside, remains.

1 *(top)* The Gladwyne Colony. **2** *(above)* Young DeWitt, seated in front with his Great Dane, his mother, Berta Höerle Ludlum and his maternal grandparents. They all lived at Fernside. **3** *(below)* Dr. Ludlum in later years, on the porch.

MEMORIES

"I was born in Lower Merion in 1914. No brothers or sisters, just me. My father, **Dr. Seymour DeWitt Ludlum** (1876-1956), was a psychiatrist. On a ride in 1912, he found the valley and said, 'This is what I want.' I was born in a building called Chadwick... very close to the stream and Rose Glen Road. Father built a number of buildings. One was his hospital...he wanted a place he could put patients according to their ability to live under supervision for a week. He often had one hundred patients! I lived in what was called "the laboratory." It was father's office, where he worked. Eventually, there were about 13 buildings on 30 acres. • My parents were divorced when I was four, so I lived with my mother in North Jersey. Mother was a pretty high-handed person. I didn't get to meet people, except the ones she liked. Therefore, I wasn't a mixer. She was always taking me out of school... I went to 14 schools...it wasn't too pleasant. I traveled with her on many trips to Europe. We lived abroad for a while... Rome, Paris, Vienna. • Back home, I went to Solebury School for a year. Father wanted me to go to Hoosac, so I transferred. Then on to Penn. Then into the Army. From '46 to '52, I started working for my father in the managerial part of the hospital. Then over to Bryn Mawr Hospital. In the Army I had learned how to do electro-spectroscopy. I was at Bryn Mawr for 30 years in the EEG department. When I retired in '82, I went back the next day as a volunteer, two days a week. Been there 15 years. The hospital has been my second home for 45 years. They can't get rid of me!" **S. DeWitt Ludlum, Jr.**

2 (below) Dr. Ludlum's house, Fernside, in a early photo, the only Colony building that survived. It has recently undergone a sensational rehab. 3 (bottom); the original stone facade fronts a very modern wing.

1 (above) Formerly a post office during the time of Chadwick's Mill. The Inn was The Gladwyne Colony's main office on Mill Creek Road at the foot of Rose Glen.

4 (top) The Gladwyne Colony in winter: the former Chadwick Mill at left and the administration building and offices at right. When able, patients were encouraged to work on the grounds, plant gardens, care for the many animals at the Colony and also participate in therapeutic crafts 5 (below).

Clement A. Griscom, president of International Navigation Company, lived in Haverford at his estate, Dolobran. He invested in Soapstone Farm, a 130 acre quarry in Gladwyne, **1** (1919 photo) off Monk Road. Soapstone and sandstone pits had been there near the river since Lenape times. The Indians used soapstone for jewelry and tradition claims that the steps at Independence Hall came from that quarry. **2** *(above)* The house of a tenant farmer and his family.

3 *(left)* Dam on Mill Creek Road that pumped water to the Clement Griscom home, later to John T. Dorrance's hilltop estate.

The dam was demolished in a 1953 flood. **4** *(right)* House and store along River Road in Gladwyne, date of photo unknown.

5 Dr. Eckert at UNIVAC, 1962.

NOTABLE NEIGHBOR:

J. Presper Eckert (1919-1995) was the co-inventor, in 1946, of the world's first electronic digital computer, ENIAC. • The only son of a prominent Philadelphia family of real-estate developers and builders, Eckert proved to be an electronic whiz kid. At age 8, he built his own crystal radio on top of a lead pencil; at 12, he designed remote-controlled toys and played complicated numbers games with his father; as a teenager, he constructed the forerunner of today's portable radio and built hi-fi amplifiers that he installed in his school (Penn Charter). He scored second highest in the country on the college entrance examinations. • After graduation in 1937, he entered the Wharton School of Business. "I lasted three days," Eckert recalled with a laugh. "They were putting me to sleep. They took simple ideas and took forever to explain them." Thwarted in his longing to go into physics, he enrolled at U. Penn's Moore School of Electrical Engineering. Pres Eckert got his Master's in 1943 and soon was brainstorming with Prof. John W. Mauchly, a Penn research instructor 12 years older than he. It was an association that would bring fame to both men. • During World War II, the Army had given a $150,000 grant to the Moore School to find a way to speed up ballistics calculations needed to aim its big guns. To plot the flight of a projectile that might last 60 seconds took one person about 20 hours. The project began on April 9, 1943...Pres' 24th birthday. 200 people, many working 16 or 20 hours a day (Eckert and Mauchly often slept on cots at school), spent two and a half years on the development of the Electronic Numerical Integrator and Calculator. • That first computer was a 30-ton monster: 80 feet long and 8 feet high, a mass of hundreds of thousands of wires, tubes, resistors and capacitors. In 1946, ENIAC was moved to the Aberdeen Proving Grounds in Maryland to work its miracles. • Long after the war, the behemoth was dismantled. In 1955, a large section was sent to the Smithsonian, parts to West Point and one panel to Eckert's home in Gladwyne. Pres delighted, at parties, to pull aside the living room drapes to dramatically reveal a homely black panel...his "baby."

1 The former Dorrance estate in Gladwyne.

NOTABLE NEIGHBOR

A notable Lower Merion resident who lived in Gladwyne but worked in Camden, was **John T. Dorrance,** chairman of the board of the Campbell Soup Company. He died of a heart attack at the Bryn Mawr Hospital in 1989 at the age of 70. At the time he was a trustee and heavily involved with the Philadelphia Museum of Art, one of his many charitable interests. A shy and unassuming man, Dorrance grew up in Radnor, attended the Montgomery School in Wynnewood, St. George's School in Rhode Island, then Princeton University. After his graduation in 1941, Dorrance was drafted into the Army as a private but rose to become a lieutenant with the OSS during World War II. He served in China. • Jack Dorrance, as he was called, is well-remembered in Lower Merion because of his contributions to every honorable charitable organization in the Township, from hospitals to libraries to fire companies as well as the larger organizations in the city and nationally. Dorrance served on the boards of a number of institutions including the Wistar Institute, Princeton University, the Church Farm School, Hampton University in Virginia, the Eisenhower Exchange Fellowships, the Academy of Natural Sciences, the Philadelphia Maritime Museum, the PennJerDel Corporation and the World Wildlife Fund... proof that people of means can make significant commitments to the world about them.

THE PEW FAMILY, an extraordinary clan (mainly based in Lower Merion) made important early contributions to American industry. Their plans eventually made an influential impact on a local, national and worldwide scale. Their founding of the Sun Oil Company led to a sensational business success which, in turn, was able to support the family's beliefs in contributing to the community's needs. That goal funded The Pew Charitable Trusts, which continues the family's commitment to support nonprofit organizations working in the areas of culture, education, the environment, health and human services, public policy and religion.

2 Rocky Crest, Gladwyne estate of Joseph Pew, Jr

JOSEPH NEWTON PEW

(1848-1912) Raised on a farm in western Pennsylvania, he was the youngest of ten children. When Pew was 11, America's first oil well gushed forth in Titusville, not far from his home. In the 1870s he went forth to seek his fortune in real estate and insurance.

After his marriage to Mary Catherine Anderson, he applied hard work and enterprise to develop the Keystone Gas Company, which used the by-products of oil (natural gas) to provide local heat and light.

In the late 1880s, the growth of the enterprise led to the founding of the Sun Oil Company. During this period, J.N. Pew and his wife began to raise a family and to pass along those values that they believed were essential to leading a productive and faithful life.

In 1902, Pew entered into a partnership to build a refinery along the Delaware River (an 82 acre site at Mar-

cus Hook). The first ocean-borne crude oil was shipped there that year.

By this time, J.N. Pew was the father of five. In 1908, he moved his family to Glenmede, the former Graham estate on Old Gulph Road and Morris Roads in Bryn Mawr. At his death in 1912, Joseph's second son, John Howard Pew, age 30, became president of Sun Oil Company.

J. HOWARD PEW

(1882-1971) Under J. Howard's regime, the Sun Oil volume was estimated to have multiplied forty times. His earliest contributions were scientific. During his regime, he expanded the company into shipbuilding and was proud of Sun Oil's contribution during two world wars. He was known throughout the organization for his personal interest in his thousands of employees and often made the rounds to check in with workers on all levels.

His 67-acre estate, Knollbrook on Grays Lane, was a short distance from his brother Joseph's place. Unlike Joe, J. Howard led a plain life, disliked entertaining and enjoyed long walks around his estate. During World War II, he ignored his cars and chauffeurs and took the train to work each day. Deeply religious, he participated in the affairs of the Presbyterian Church on local and national levels. J. Howard Pew died just short of his 90th birthday.

JOSEPH N. PEW, JR.

(1886-1963) Joseph, a Cornell graduate, was the more worldly, outgoing brother. As vice-president of Sun Oil, he was a visionary in both science and commerce...the company's "idea man." He devised a pipe line from Marcus Hook to the Great Lakes; he innovated the custom blending of gasolines; he introduced Blue Sunoco.

At the end of World War II, Sun Oil was one of the few American industries owned and managed by the founding family after five decades. He continued a lifelong commitment to the concept of free competition in the marketplace.

Like his brother, J. Howard, he shared the social responsibility of support for the Presbyterian Church and was a liberal donor to the national Republican Party. He died at 77.

MARY ETHEL PEW

(1884-1979) graduated with honors from Bryn Mawr College. Her mother's death in 1935 led to a determination to devote her personal life and inheritance to the support of cancer research.

Mary Ethel made her home at the family's estate, Glenmede. Her interest in health care prompted her to volunteer at a small hospital run by Lutheran sisters, called Lankenau, which has become an important medical institution in the area.

Ms. Pew, in 1953, gave Skylands, her 26-acre estate in Gladwyne, to the Philadelphia Motherhouse of Deaconesses. Upon her death at the venerable age of 95, her ancestral home, Glenmede, was willed to Bryn Mawr College as its Graduate Center.

MABEL PEW MYRIN

(1889-1972) The youngest of J.N.'s children, Mabel devoted her life to "issues of survival," the improvement of the educational process and the problems of caring for and educating the handicapped.

Like her brothers and sister, she was deeply involved in the support of health service institiutions. Scheie Eye Institute and Presbyterian-University of Pennsylvania Medical Center were two institutions that benefitted from her dedication. She was also a

2 J. Howard Pew

longtime benefactor of Saunders House, a care facility for the elderly in Wynnewood.

ALBERTA HENSEL PEW

Joseph's wife, Alberta, is a fascinating character in the family tree. Though she embodied many of the principles of a priviledged life, she ignored the trappings of advantage in order to pursue her individual course. An avid sportswoman (especially devoted to salmon and trout fishing) she participated in golf, tennis, swimming, sailing, horseback riding and shooting. She was a champion markswoman...a student of Annie Oakley!

Her interest in gardening and the natural world was exceptional. That led to her advocacy for the preservation of open spaces and buildings of historic importance. Part of her land on Dodds Lane in Gladwyne was deeded to the National Lands Trust.

Aside from her personal enthusiasms, she led an energetic life of civic and community service. Mrs. Pew died in 1988 at the age of 96. Her obituary reported that two weeks before her death she snagged seven fish at her Pocono Mountain retreat.

1 Skylands, in Gladwyne, given to the Lutheran Deaconesses by Mary Ethel Pew.

3 Joseph N. Pew, Jr.   **4** Alberta Pew

1 *(right)* The T.H. Lukens Dry Goods Groceries and Provisions store was located on Montgomery Avenue near the Mile 7 marker. This 1885 photo shows Thomas Lukens on his delivery wagon, his wife Kate, two sons and daughters-in-law and grandchildren. The second floor was used as Temperance Hall. The section to the right was the Academy Post Office; in 1918, the Women's Club tea room.

BALA CYNWYD

Over the years Bala Cynwyd has been known by a number of names.

Pencoyd. In November 1683, John Roberts, a gentleman farmer, arrived on the sailing ship *Morning Star.* He purchased from Dr. Edward Jones 150 acres in this area and immediately set about clearing the land for farming. He called his new home Pencoyd after his family's ancestral home in Wales.

Academyville. In 1813, the Lower Merion Benevolent School (Lower Merion Academy) opened its doors to *all* the children of Lower Merion. The schoolhouse sits high on a hill overlooking the community which it serves and the area was named Academyville. The community was strictly a rural one. In winter, cut off by snow from Philadelphia, the people had to make their own amusements: sleigh rides, skating parties, barbecues and other types of country pleasures.

Bowman's Bridge. The next change came in 1832 when the Philadelphia & Columbia Railway, the Main Line of Public Works of the State of Pennsylvania, traveled through the area. Where the tracks crossed over Mont-

2 *(right)* The blacksmith and carriage shop of Luther C. Parsons was a necessary fixture at the busy corner of Montgomery and Parsons Avenues. Parsons was a community leader and involved in many civic associations: one such group was The Society for the Detection & Prosecution of Horse Thieves and Recovery of Stolen Horses.

Bala and Cynwyd. In 1884, George B. Roberts, President of the Pennsylvania Railroad, opened the Schuylkill Valley Division of the railroad. Three stations were located in Lower Merion. The first station was named Bala because Mr. Roberts' ancestors came from Bala in the lake region of Wales. Cynwyd and Barmouth were the Welsh names selected for the other two stations.

Land Development. The new rail line forever changed the landscape of this rural community. Until then, it had a small population and consisted of a few mills, farms and estates. Being only six miles from Philadelphia's center, officials of the railroad and real estate developers began to subdivide the farms and estates and build the infrastructure necessary to support their plans for suburban development.

gomery Avenue (near Levering Mill Road) a bridge carried the road traffic over the railway. This intersection, and the community surrounding the bridge, became known as Bowman's Bridge.

Merionville. When this section of the railroad was abandoned and the bridge dismantled, the area was renamed Merionville. The hamlet had a blacksmith shop, a little brick building used as a general store and three or four houses. Twice a year, gypsies would visit the area and set up their camp.

THIRTY MILES AROUND PHILADELPHIA

ON THE LINES OF THE PENNSYLVANIA RAILROAD

In 1913, the Pennsylvania Railroad called Bala and Cynwyd "one of the most rapidly growing and most popular suburbs of Philadelphia." At this time, the railroad offered 22 weekday trains and 15 Sunday trains to the city. To attract middle-class families from the city to the new and upcoming suburbs, the land developers promised "every city convenience and every country comfort. Pure air, Springfield water, gas, electric lights, telephone service and pleasant surroundings."

By 1920, the infrastructure of Bala and Cynwyd was complete. The township provided paved roads, sewers, schools and police. The community equipped a volunteer fire department, a civic association, churches, a library and clubs (such as the Women's Club, Needlework Guild, Garden Club and Community Choral) to make up the town's social networks. Finally, to top it all off, there were wonderful vaudeville performances at the Egyptian Theatre.

BALA'S BUCK ROGERS

Anthony "Buck Rogers," an American icon, was born in August 1928 at 126 Cynwyd Road in Bala Cynwyd. His "father" was the fertile imagination and creativity of 40-year-old Philip Francis Nowlan, the financial editor of rhe *Philadelphia Ledger*. Nowlan and his illustrator, Dick Calkins, created the first science fiction comic strip. Rogers and his female companion, Wilma, first appeared in the August 1928 issue of *Amazing Stories*.

• According to Ray Bradbury, Nowlan and Calkins "introduced rocket guns that shoot explosive bullets; people who fly through the air with jumping belts; hovercrafts which skim over the surface of the earth; disintegrators which destroyed anything they touched; radar-equipped robot armies; television controlled rockets and rocket bombs; invasions from Mar, and the first landing on the Moon."

• In the late 1920s, the head of the National Newspaper Service was searching for a new cartoon strip he could syndicate. Nowlan and Calkins created Buck Rogers which, in its heyday, appeared in over 200 newspapers. Calkins lived and worked in Chicago; Nowlan lived and worked in Bala Cynwyd. And yet, they could collaborate, in the days before fax machines, e-mail and overnight deliveries. • Nolan graduated from Philadelphia's Central High in 1906. He was on the football team, secretary of the chess club and voted one of the three most handsome men in the graduating class. He was in the 1910 class at the University of Pennsylvania.

• Buck Rogers appeared as a syndicated comic strip from 1929 to 1967. In 1939, a Buck Rogers movie starred Buster Crabbe. Buck appeared on TV in the 1950-1951 season, followed by an adaptation of 34 episodes for the 1979-1981 seasons.

• Cream of Wheat sponsored the thrice-weekly Buck Rogers radio show with a secret organization of solar scouts who promised to live healthy, obedient, honest and studious lives. Today, all of the Buck Roger collectibles are highly prized: a disintegrator pistol; "Big Little Books"; lead figures. • Philip Nowlan died in 1940 at 53, leaving behind a young widow, ten children, a legacy of science fiction adventures and a road map for space exploration.

During the housing boom, developers offered modern suburban homes in various styles to please the upwardly mobile middle-class families. Two examples: **2** *(top)* an English Tudor and **3** *(above)* a Colonial Revival style.

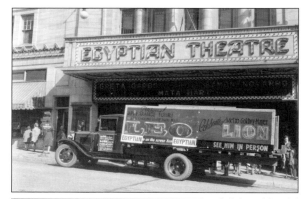

4 *(above)* Patrick J. Lawler spared no expense when he built the Egyptian Theatre in 1927..."Where the Show is Always Good." It was a fine place for Bala Cynwyd residents and their neighbors to see many live attractions.

5 *(left)* Joseph Conway was the theatre manager and also responsible for movie selections and scheduling of other events such as vaudeville acts and the circus.

BELMONT HILLS. The village on the west bank of the Schuyl-kill River was originally called Rocky Hill and is located in the lower section of the township directly across the river from Philadelphia's historic Manayunk. When the Reading Railroad was built in 1838, the village became known as West Manayunk. The first settlers were Welsh, followed by the English, Germans, Irish and Italian-Albanians. The first permanent settler was the wife of John ap Thomas, outstanding Quaker and one of the original purchasers of the Welsh Tract. John died before the family departed for the colonies. On November 16, 1683, Katherine Roberts (who, by custom, had resumed her maiden name) sailed with her children from Chester, England on the ship *Morning Star*. About a month later, she arrived and settled on her 612-acre purchase.

1 *(top)* An old engraving of the first bridge built across the Schuylkill River, linking Philadelphia's historic Manayunk to Belmont Hills in Lower Merion. The bridge was built in 1810, destroyed by a flood in 1850, and never rebuilt.

2 *(above)* The Flat Rock Hotel was popular with farmers from who brought produce from upstate and traveled down Domino Lane (in Manayunk), across the river to Belmont Hills. Canal men enjoyed the inn as a place to relax, enjoy the spirits and play dominoes. The hotel was also called the Tunnel House. It was demolished when the expressway was built in the 1950s.

3 *(left)* The Green Lane Bridge (photo c.1931), looking towards Manayunk. Built in 1833 and rebuilt in 1928, the bridge linked Philadelphia to Lower Merion. The Belmont Avenue ramps to the Schuylkill Expressway are now at this location.

1 *(above)* Belmont Hills as seen from Manayunk, looking west. The church steeple is St. David's Episcopal Church on Dupont Street, Manayunk.

(below) Two paintings by local artist Francis Speight show his romantic, realistic style. *Across the River,* 1926, **2** *(left),* shows Jones Street houses on the west side of the Schuylkill. His 1933 oil *Little Italy* **3** *(right)* looks upriver from atop Jefferson Street in Belmont Hills; Mt. Ararat stands at top left. By 1940, Speight was well-known beyond Philadelphia. Reviews of his exhibitions in New York, Washington, Cleveland, and other cities praised the freshness of his impressionistic style. Unlike his contemporaries in the 1930s and 1940s who made commentaries on social reforms, Francis Speight's spirited brushwork shows the beauty of the working-class neighborhoods of Manayunk.

The deed to Katherine Roberts' property was made out to her in the name of Jones, and her children assumed this name. For the next 14 years, she skillfully managed her large farm parcel.

In the 1880s, immigrants from Italy began to arrive, many descended from Christian Albanians who had fled Moslem Turks to settle in southern Italy. They in turn sent for relatives, and by 1914 the Albanians and Italians constituted a considerable portion of the lower section of the community. The town resembled a Mediterranean hill town with its goats and chickens, garden plots, and women in black, seldom seen on the streets without their menfolk. The upper reaches of the settlement were home to the earlier English, Welsh, Irish, and German immigrants, most of them employed on the area's farms and mills.

1 Mill workers at Rudolph's paper mill rented these row houses *(below)* from Sebastian Rudolph. They were demolished in the 1950s when the Schuylkill Expressway was constructed.

An open area along the river bank between Rudolph's Row and the bridge was a popular site for prize fights, vaudeville performances, carnivals, and gypsy encampments.

Some workers at the Pencoyd Iron Works were housed here when the mill was in operation.
2 The building *(below)*, still standing, had been converted into apartments years ago.

Belmont Hills still has a number of historic homes. Leedom House and the Jones-Smith House are described on the following page. A home located at 100 Lyle Avenue, built around 1787, was sold to Stewart Lyle, master farmer. In 1901, this estate was purchased by Wood, Harmon & Company as a real estate development known as Belmont Heights. Narrow Hills, on 88 acres, was probably named for the strait that separated Jones Island in the Schuylkill from the mainland. The Ashland Heights section was named after the local Ashland Paper Mill.

In the 1950s, the name West Manayunk was changed to Belmont Hills. The diverse community has been an asset to Lower Merion since the days of William Penn.

3 *(lower left)* The first Albanian immigrants to reside in the village were Nicolo Minisci (Myers), wife Maria Domenica, and son George Joseph. Photo c.1910. In 1895, Minisci purchased land on Jefferson Street from William D. Jones for $250 and built their home. They later purchased the house next door for $935. Son George married Alphonsina Scavello, from St. George Albanese in Italy, when she was 16. They had eleven children.

4 *(lower right)* St. George's Day parade,1950. The celebration began around the turn of the century when a handful of Albanians and Italians organized the Mutual Relief Society of San Giorgio, their patron saint. Every May, until recent years, the procession carried the statue of St. George through the steep streets of Belmont Hills.

1 *(right)* Leedom House on Mary Waters Ford Road at Centennial Road. The 15-room stone house was built in 1787 as a manor house of Glanrason Plantation. The land was inherited by Robert Jones, second son of Katherine (Roberts) Jones, in 1689. Gerrard, oldest son of Robert, inherited Glanrason farm in 1746.

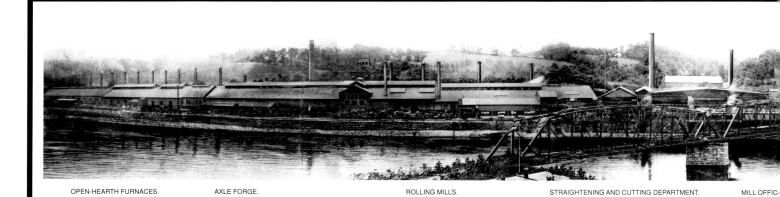

OPEN-HEARTH FURNACES.   AXLE FORGE.   ROLLING MILLS.   STRAIGHTENING AND CUTTING DEPARTMENT.   MILL OFFIC

2 *(above)* A 1900 panoramic view of the vast Pencoyd Iron Works.

3 *(right)* The Pencoyd offices, one of the few remaining buildings in the vast industrial complex.

106

1 *(left)* The 200-year-old building on Mary Waters Ford Road was the home of the late Lewis and Marie Smith for 50 years. Gerrard, grandson of widow Katherine (Thomas) Jones, had built the original stone portion of the farm house in the mid-1700s. Additions were made in the Federal period to accommodate Charles Jones and his 12 children. It was remodeled in the Victorian taste after the house passed out of the Jones family.

In 1969, Marie Smith gave the house, a smaller tenant house, a barn, and grounds to the township for use as a public park. Vacant for five years, the historic Jones-Smith House seemed a sure bet for the wrecker's ball. Thanks to the efforts of members of the Township's Historical Architectural Review Board, a lease agreement was made with a resident who pledged to make renovations. Though structurally sound with a good roof, the plumbing, wiring, and boiler were replaced. The overhaul preserved the home's essential historic character.

.ING MILLS AND MACHINE SHOP.   BRIDGE OFFICE AND SHOPS.   HYDAULIC FORGE.   BOLT AND RIVET SHOP.   STOCK YARD.

THE PENCOYD
IRON WORKS

Remains of a ghost town. The name Pencoyd is Welsh, a corruption of Penn-y-Chlawd, meaning "treetops." Pencoyd was the name of the farm of John Roberts, who came to this country in 1683. The Roberts family (Algernon Roberts and Percival Roberts) founded the iron works along the west bank of the Schuylkill River in 1853.

The plant developed into a vast industry; the village grew and Pencoyd iron became known worldwide. Bridge building was the main manufacture when, around 1895, the plant acquired 40 acres of river front and two miles of rail track.

The Pencoyd works declined after World War I and had a brief revival during World War II. The business was liquidated in 1944. Much of the old site is now occupied by Connelly Containers, Pencoyd's only heavy industry.

The location has lately shown some new signs of life.

2 *(above)* The rear section of the Pencoyd Iron works with a Reading Railroad train delivering supplies to the manufacturing area.

Lancaster Avenue in Ardmore, **1** from the horse and buggy days **2** to the automobile age.

1 North side of Lancaster Avenue in Ardmore, 1910 photo.

ARDMORE began on 410 acres of land bought by Richard Davis in 1686 from five Welshmen for 32 pounds, 16 shillings. One of the few local towns without a Welsh name, the village's original name was Athensville, a nod to the fascination with the Greek revival style movement of the time (1811). William J. Buck reported in his 1884 history, "Athensville is situated on the Lancaster turnpike, seven miles from Philadelphia, and is the largest village in the township. It contains [at the center] 28 houses, three stores and one hotel."

The first roads were but trails, and only horse and foot transportation were available. Conditions were impossible: dusty in hot summer, muddy after rains. The settlement of Lancaster led to a demand for an adequate highway that led there from Philadelphia. In 1796, the Lancaster Turnpike (first one constructed in America) allowed ponderous Conestoga wagons to carry merchandise and interior-bound settlers

That important progress led to a line of inns and taverns along the route to serve drivers and their stage coach passengers. None but the General Wayne remain; the others were replaced by charmless commercial structures.

Early Arrivals. The original settlers of the area were Welshmen who came to work in the neighboring farms and the thriving mill industry along Mill Creek. Then followed a wave of Germans who contributed their industrial skills. Next the Irish added their abilities and found work in the hotels and staffed the lavish estates built in the mid-1800s.

Later Expansion. About the same time, the establishment of railroad systems added to Ardmore's expansion and prosperity. The first Board of Commissioners met in 1900 (at the General Wayne) to establish a local government. The same year, The Autocar Works relocated from Pittsburgh, attracted by good roads, a high grade of labor supply, the closeness to Philadelphia and a location on the main line of the Pennsylvania Railroad. Ardmore is a popular residential area with a lively business center.

ST. GEORGES

St. Georges (**1** *above*) was a large, beautiful, wooded tract near the corner of Montgomery Avenue (then called Old Lancaster Road) and Mill Creek Road, at the end of Anderson Avenue. It is now the site of an apartment house and the Main Line Y. It had a long and interesting history, beginning as a series of inns and ending as the fine estate of the Andersons, a family with a long line of prominent local physicians.

80 Years of Inns. Built sometime before 1730, it began as a stage stop. Richard Hughes built a house there that year and then, as coach travel increased, converted it to an inn called **Three Tuns**. Here the traveler could obtain lodging, food, cider, punch, toddies and stronger liquids. It also served as the post office and unofficial community center. In 1759, Mr. Hughes announced the property for sale. It included a "30 x 20

foot house with cellar, a fine spring of excellent water with an adjoining dwelling house, frame barn and four stables."

It was sold that year to Francis Holton, a Philadelphia tavernkeeper who renamed it **The Prince of Wales**. In 1772, the property was sold to Philip Syng, the noted Philadelphia silversmith. Syng used it as his country residence, enjoying the healthy climate and proximity to a pleasant village. Eleven years later, it was bought by Capt. Robert McAfee who reopened it as a tavern, **The Green Tree**. In 1797, Godfrey Lainhoff was the next owner, who called his inn **St. Georges**.

The Anderson Estate. In 1811, the building (**2** *right*) was purchased by Dr. Joseph Anderson and occupied for five generations by Andersons. It was described in an 1897 book as "a quiet and rustic estate, a pleasant

contrast to the modern life in the suburb of Ardmore. It features koletaria, Irish yew trees, magnolias, a pecan nut tree, a very large persimmon tree, with English canoe-birch trees to brighten the lawn."

It was razed in the 1950s.

ARDMORE'S GINGERBREAD AGE

Ardmore has retained a number of examples of the wooden houses of "The Gingerbread Age." From the mid-1800s through the end of the century, as the suburbs were burgeoning, there was a need for tastefully designed, practical housing at moderate cost. Because Victorians admired the English and American Queen Anne styles of domestic architecture, there was a growing housing market. For those who could not afford an architect (too expensive, too difficult, too time-consuming) one could buy plans books, choose a style and have a local builder put up the house. There were hundreds of designs available; some books

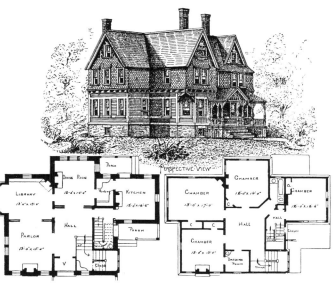

also featured designs for gates, posts, inside doors, hardware and bookcases for the average wood-worker to follow. A medium-quality home could be built, complete, for $2,000 to $5,000. There are no building records, though, for these:

1 Levering House as seen in 1913, later owned by Kate Lesher (Lancaster Pike, opposite South Wyoming Ave.).
2 Josiah S. Pearce Home, built in 1868 (northeast corner of Lancaster Pike and Station Road).
3 Charles Kugler Home, built about 1875 (southeast side of Lancaster Pike, west of Church Road).
4 Dr. Smith's House, 1911 photo, after removal to Cricket Avenue.

BUSINESSES, along a short commercial stretch of "The Pike" in Ardmore, are shown in approximately their original locations. A few of the establishments are in business today.

<2

3>

4>

1 A. Talone Cleaners, photo c.1900s, still continues to serve the public.

2 Photo c.1915, of corner site of the Andrew P. Rolli Insurance Agency.

3 Odd Fellows Hall, built in 1846, seen in a c.1923 photograph.

4 1915 photo of building, next to the Autocar plant, that housed W.E. Morris Lunch Room; Nick Talone Barber Shop; W.W. Francis Stationery, Candy, Cigars; A.A. Francis Jewelry.

NORTH>

WOODSIDE AVE.

<WEST   LANCASTER AVE.

HOLLAND AVE.

GREENFIELD AVE.

1   2   3   4

<5

6>

<7

8>

<9

5 Y.M.C.A. Building, 1910 photo, housed a barber shop and the Township's first free library on the first floor.

6 Commercial blocks at corner, seen in 1940s photograph.

7 Dirigo Club House, built 1890; Republican Club; James S. Lyons & Bros. Plumbing Supplies; Eddy McKenty's Restaurant; Bill Werner's Poolroom. Franklin Azpell, harness maker, was in building on the left.

8 Early photograph of William Lesher's General Store, built in 1880.

9 Williamson Store, 1911 photo.

7

5

9 6

ARDMORE AVE.

LANCASTER AVE.   EAST>

8

<10

11>

<12

13>

10 N. Harrison Store, 1911 photo, formerly the Baker Store.
11 Commercial block, early 1940s.
12 Palace Movie Theatre, c.1910.
13 Ardmore Post Office building.

14 *(left)* Looking east on Lancaster Pike from Ardmore Avenue, c.1940.

NORTH>

<WEST

LANCASTER AVE.

ANDERSON AVE.

10

12

11

<14

15>

16>

<17

14 Merion Title and Trust Company
building and *(below)* President
Josiah Pearce (1841-1915).
Built in 1892, the building was
severely damaged by fire in 1977.

15 1917 photo of retail row.

16 Ardmore Trolley Station, c.1910,
and Llanerch Railway Station.

17 Ardmore National Bank.

STATION RD.

17 | 13 14

15   **16**

CRICKET AVE.

RITTENHOUSE PL.

LANCASTER AVE.

EAST>

1 Overview of Edward R. Price farm, looking north to Montgomery Avenue at Old Gulph Road, which stretches down at right (not yet renamed Narberth Avenue at this time, 1883). Fenced cowpath in foreground soon became Price Avenue. The nucleus of Price's town of Elm is under construction in the foreground here, at a site which has since become Montgomery Court Apartments. The Philadelphia & Columbia Railroad passed over about where the cowpath is.

"NARBERTH, the hole in the donut," "Narberth, the heart of the Main Line." Such sayings hardly convey the true spirit of Narberth...the "hole" referring straightforwardly go the borough's agreeably "landlocked" position totally surrounded by Lower Merion Township, and the "heart" quoted from a familiar boosterish mid-1994 bumper sticker seemingly offering a riposte to the persistent snobbish remark that Narberth is just too egalitarian to be considered a *typical* Main Line town. Or the version that gets more quickly to the point, insisting simply that Narberth is *not on* the Main Line. Yet the question that more regularly rivets public attention now that Narberth has become a trendy address in the 1980s and '90s is that several other Lower Merion communities also *considered* adopting independent rule. So how come Narberth actually went ahead and *did* it, and what has this meant overall?

2 Ancient stone smithy owned by the General Wayne Inn opposite it, said to be where General Cornwallis' horses were shod. Replaced by gas station in the 1920s.

3 *(above)* Rees Price House built 1803 by Joseph Price. Edward R. Price, grandson of Rees Price, who founded the town of Elm, was born, lived all his life and died in this house.

4 *(below)* The General Wayne Inn appeared on a 1930s postcard.

Creation here of a town in 1881 was as much tension as energy...a move intended at the outset to bring neighborhood order out of chaos during the area's disruptive race track era. Although introduction of Narberth's borough government in 1895 (to replace more conventional, broader-based township rule) appears in principle a dramatic change of approach, it was a natural extension of preoccupations developed within a couple of new community-minded residents' organizations and coming to a head in the early 1890s.

For this period had been preceded by a decade of speculative starts and stops at constructing different kinds of housing for a new town. Once this bridge to independent rule had been crossed and the borough, occupying 0.52 square miles, existed, Edward R. Price's original goal of starting a town on his farm might have seemed like a mission accomplished. Actually, *much* still remained to be done to make the new municipality fully operational. And those were the tasks of the first fifty years.

Narberth's proverbial small-town feel is dependent on many factors....especially the closely knit character of its neighborhoods where siblings and cousins often settled near one another during that first half-century. Also the rare super-abundance of community organizations, then and now, that people may join here compared with fewer if larger such groups in the Township's neighborhoods.

Another enhancement of Narberth's cohesiveness: this is virtually the only Main Line community with its town center along the same main street on which its rail station is directly located.

The period before World War I saw the build-up of that town center, and also construction of the first and biggest wave of hundreds of small and semi-detached houses on the north side of town. Development of the south side continued at a slower pace.

1 Libertyville House, 1226 Montgomery Avenue. Cellar under front door contains the huge base of chimney of ancient log cabin formerly linked to two-bay Federal era stone wing at left; wooden Victorian unit replaced cabin; mid-19th century justice of peace's lockup is in the cellar; Liberty Pole believed raised here in "quasi war" with France.

2 Elm Station, three-level stone building north of the tracks, 1870, with ticket office, waiting room on platform level, living quarters for station master's family above, and business offices on street level. Joseph M. Wilson, architect. Razed.

117

1 *(above)* Small wooden house of reputed "witch" Betty Conrad; late 18th century with Victorian additions; razed 1980.

2 *(right)* 19th century slaughterhouse at Libertyville; many later reuses, but eventually demolished for a housing subdivision.

Libertyville. The earliest-settled part of Narberth, believed to be where Swedes traded at the "ancient Indian spring" with the Susquehannock Indians (a breakaway tribe of the Iroquois). Libertyville at its center still has one of its two known early log cabins, this one plastered over. Also traditionally thought to be the site of the raising of a patriotic Liberty Pole denoting a Federal era international incident on the high seas that may have given the surrounding area its first name, Libertyville. • The heart of this old district had been along Montgomery Avenue in the vicinity of the present Hansen-tract houses.

In this vicinity was the tiny wooden house of the reputed "witch" Betty Conrad, mentioned in Joseph Price's *Diary*. • A small densely settled area with a separate identity since colonial times when a good water supply made it habitable, and sandwiched between exceptionally large farms, that Libertyville nucleus long functioned as a service area for its agricultural neighborhood. By the mid-19th century, it featured a slaughterhouse widely used by the region's farmers. That relic survived long afterward as a shop for high-quality Arts & Crafts objects and garden accessories.

The next generation after the borough's founders to take leadership began with a flourish in 1914. New ideas proposed focusing on problem-solving and civic beautification so that the municipality and a new civic association should shoulder such responsibilites cooperatively. This second-generation momentum soon launched a rare Progressive Era initiative. A Garden Cities model community (Narbrook Park) was established on a partly swampy tract of land...a project lately referred to as Pennsylvania's first conservation subdivision. Also in 1914, the cherry blossom was chosen as Narberth's town tree and planted plentifully at key locations in full public view...our front street, Montgomery Avenue and along Penn Valley's Braeburn Lane in the Township. Thus a tradition was launched of city folk coming out to Lower Merion and Narberth to view cherry blossoms and crabapples blooming in April.

The borough's population having tripled by the end of the first decade, the numbers kept climbing steadily, reaching their peak of just under six thousand residents around 1950. Construction of the main playground had been authorized by the townspeople in the mid-1920s, which is considered early. And a community building complex housing the library, a women's club and the American Legion post was constructed adjacent to the playground around the same time. A popular fireworks tradition dates back to 1922 and the Memorial Day parade is another regular event, sponsored by the Narberth Civic Association.

The suburbanization trend following World War II left Narberth edgy and wanting to catch up. Here was a community with scarcely any open land suitable for new construction. So the town fathers welcomed developers who started demolishing big corner Late Victorian houses and replacing them with apartment blocks and, closer to downtown, with low-rise commercial buildings.

1 View to northwest from Narberth Station. Signal tower at left; dormer window of new business block visible behind telegraph pole; rear of new general stores at center on the main street houses. Photo c.1898; sign of John B. Clothier, Goodman & Clothier, developers.

2 Narberth Presbyterian Church, (*left*) built of Holmsburg granite, 1897. J. Cather Newsom, Architect.

3 Elm Hall *(below),* completed 1899. Built by members of Narberth Fire Company, mostly with donated funds; upstairs rented for municipal offices; used, with modifications, to 1960.

1 (above) Oldest house in Narberth, now called #610 Shady Lane, is in the heart of the old Libertyville district. It includes a log cabin at right. John Kernan, his wife, three daughters and a friend pose for this 1911 photograph. Kernan bred trotting horses here on his farm.

2 (left) Vauclain-Barrie House on Price Avenue, 1883; only surviving house that Edward R. Price personally built for his town of Elm; currently a Methodist parsonage.

Town of Elm. Edward R. Price founded the Quaker-friendly town of Elm on his hundred-acre farm near Elm Station in 1881, commissioning large mansions (designed by Isaac H. Hobbs) to be constructed there for a start ...and inviting an experienced town-builder Samuel Richards (a grandson of naturalist John Bartram), to settle there with his family and keep a close eye on things. Even so, development was initially sporadic, but picked up toward the end of the decade with a flood of somewhat smaller Late Victorian houses on narrow lots. Eventually Richards had

the satisfaction to place his "John Hancock" on the successful petition to sever connection with Lower Merion Township and declare Narberth's status as an independent borough in 1895. • Although other towns *considered* independence, Narberth went the distance because it had a structure already in place to enable it to reach that goal. It was largely due to Price's earlier initiatives as a town-builder and the involvement of his proactive developer, Samuel Richards and his associates, most of the major players being Quaker.

3 (above right) August H. Mueller House, "Romar-Florem," 1891, residence of Narberth's first elected burgess (mayor) in 1895. He bought the house new. Razed.

4 (right) Edward Forsythe House, designed by Charles W. Bolton, architect, 1888. Built for the town of Elm, it stands, much remodeled, between Price and Wayne Avenues.

1 May Day, c.1927, in Narbrook Park.

2 Promotional postcard, c.1920, for Narbrook Park, created and developed by Narberth Civic Association.

Narbrook Park. A model community built by a civic association, it is an uncommon concept in the suburbs. Yet Narberth Civic Association undertook such a project in 1914, breaking ground in 1915 for what was to feature preserved open space surrounded by well-designed small houses...35 of them, as it turned out...on 14 acres. • As befits an effort sponsored by the whole community, the citizens were involved in every stage of the process. They met and talked with urban planners brought in from New York and Philadelphia. The architects lectured on the importance of placing voluntary restrictions on the design of the houses. There was a contest to name the project, at first tentatively called Narberth Garden. • Served by its own residents' association almost from the start, this community has been unusually successful in maintaining itself over the years by looking after its own road repair, tree planting, shared work projects and fostering a spirit of cooperation that includes seasonal get-togethers both outdoors and in.

There has to be something encouraging in the fact that families with young children are pouring into this old-fashioned town which, besides its long history of strong civic life and civic betterment, happens to be the third most densely settled residential community in the state. For it means that lots of independent-minded young people, by coming here, are willing to swim upstream against a swift current now sweeping so many Americans into new tract houses on ravaged farm landscape.

3 Haverford Avenue, Narberth business district's main street, c.1950s, looking east.

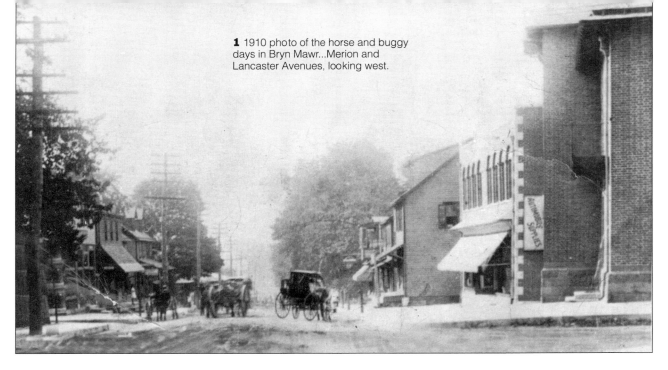

1 1910 photo of the horse and buggy days in Bryn Mawr...Merion and Lancaster Avenues, looking west.

BRYN MAWR is a community of approximately six thousand people located nine miles west of Philadelphia on the Main Line. Although it has no formal boundaries, portions of it are contained in Radnor and Haverford Townships with the largest portion being in Lower Merion Township. It has evolved from a colonial farming society into a cosmopolitan suburb.

The land Bryn Mawr occupies was originally part of the charter given to William Penn by King Charles II in 1681. Even though he had legitimate British title to the land, Penn believed that the Lenape Indians, "the original people" and true owners of the land, should be compensated.

In July 1683, Penn bought the land from the Indians, an action which gained the Indians' great respect and established peaceful relations between the European and indigenous communities. The following February, Penn subdivided the land and sold it as part of the 62 square mile Welsh Tract to primarily middle-class Quaker farmers.

First Stage of Settlement. The original families and their immediate descendants who occupied this land confronted a vast forest of rolling hills, fertile soils, abundant water and a moderate climate. They included Rowland Ellis from Wales who settled here in 1704, naming his farm Bryn Mawr (from the Welsh "great hill"). In 1719, it was renamed Harriton by Richard Harrison and his wife Hannah Norris.

South of the Ellis tract was land owned by the Humphrey family. Purchased by Benjamin and John Humphrey in 1683, it included land upon which Bryn Mawr College and The Baldwin School are located.

West of the Humphrey tract was land bought in 1708 by William and Reese Thomas, which eventually became the Ashbridge estate. Of note is the Cornog log cabin, on the northwest corner of County Line Road and Mondela Avenue, built around the beginning of the 18th century.

2 *(above)* Photograph c.1877 of the side view of the Humphreys homestead, The Lindens, at 845 Lancaster Avenue.

1 (below) Lancaster Avenue early in this century...at Merion Avenue, looking east.

2 (below) A typical town residence (still standing) on Old Lancaster Road.

Agricultural Development. During the early period, the community supplied food and tobacco to the growing Philadelphia market. It was a crossroads, providing access to local producers for commerce and communication.

The Revolution. The community provided leadership in our struggle with Great Britain. Charles Thompson, owner of Harriton, was Secretary of the Continental Congress. The Continental Army retreated through the area on September 12, 1777 from the Battle of Brandywine; General Washington stopped at Buck Tavern three days later. In the winter of that year there was a battle here between the American Generals Potter and Sullivan and British Lord Cornwallis.

Humphreysville was the name of the community at the turn of the 19th century, honoring the Humphrey family who had amassed a large amount of property.

In 1831, Milestone House was built by a member of that family at 845 Lancaster Avenue, in front of the 9th milestone on the original Lancaster Pike. This marker is now located in front of the Ludington Information Center. The home was demolished in 1955.

In 1834, the State Legislature enacted the first common school law and Lower Merion, as the only supporter of the act in the County, opened its first public school in 1835.

By 1858, the town consisted of 21 houses, a two-story school-

house and many private estates. The town was growing, but it was still a rural community. It was about to undergo profound transformation as it entered a new technological age.

Railroad Expansion. In 1832, the Philadelphia & Columbia Railway constructed its "Main Line" between Philadelphia and Lancaster. In 1859, a station and telegraph office was built at Whitehall (the intersection of Bryn Mawr Avenue and County Line Road). The building remains, now occupied by the Bryn Mawr Hospital Thrift Shop.

3 (above) The office of the Bryn Mawr News on Lancaster Avenue in the 1940s.

4 (left) William Ramsey's General Store "Feed, Flour, Groceries, Dry-Goods, Paints, Oils, &c.", built about 1870. It also served as Bryn Mawr's post office. Present site of the Bryn Mawr Trust Company.

123

1 *(top)* Bryn Mawr National Bank, early 1900s, at 800 Lancaster Avenue.

2 *(center)* Built in 1887, the building housed the Bryn Mawr National Bank on the left and the Bryn Mawr Trust on the right, 1895 photo. Site of present post office.

3 *(bottom)* 1950 photo of Penn House at Lancaster and Penn Avenues.

In 1857, the Pennsylvania Railroad Corporation acquired the Philadelphia & Columbia. It also purchased all the land bounded by the rail line and named this new development Bryn Mawr. By 1869, this name replaced Humphreysville.

Victorian Summer Resort. With the coming of the railroads, Bryn Mawr became a fashionable summer destination. The White Hall Hotel opened in the 1830s; the Bryn Mawr Hotel in 1871. A number of inns and boarding houses were established to meet the tourist demand during the Centennial Exposition: Summit Grove House, the Humphrey Board House, The Penn Inn, The Pines, The Farmhouse and The Castnor House.

The Real Estate Boom. The Pennsylvania Railroad aggressively promoted the town, creating a demand for elegant country residences. Many of the new owners commuted regularly to Philadelphia, preferring quiet country living to the hustle of city life. Thus, Bryn Mawr became one of the first commuter suburbs.

With this influx of population, the institutions which provide support and service for the physical, mental and spiritual well-being of a community were created. By 1900, six churches were established; a post office, hospital, two private schools, a college, the water company and two banks were founded. By 1884, Bryn Mawr was the most populous town in Lower Merion Township with over 300 homes and many small businesses.

1 (right) Early photo shows John Fish, at right, with his son Walter in their Lancaster Avenue shop.

JOHN FISH & SON

John Fish & Son lays claim to be the oldest retail store on the Main Line. John Fish left Plymouth, England in the spring of 1888, arrived in New York and soon after opened a watch repair shop in Bryn Mawr. Three years later, he returned to England where he took a bride. Upon their return, they started construction of their store and home at 1018 Lancaster Avenue. • In continuous operation since 1888, this firm of family jewelers is also widely known for its repair and service of antique clocks. Their work is so extensive that they now have a reservation list for clock repairs. As

more and more craftsmen die or retire, fewer young people are interested in this specialty. • John's two sons managed satellite stores in Ardmore and Media. After a business career of 42 years, John Fish sold his Bryn Mawr establishment to his son Walter who, in 1968, accepted into partnership *his*

son, George David Fish. • The family continues to maintain a jewelry and clock store for four generations of Main Line customers ...with the help of their wives, silversmiths, diamond setters, bead stringers, jewelry designers and goldsmiths. Quality work, still done by hand!

The Automobile Suburb. By 1904, most of the roads which exist today had been completed, under the supervision of the Pennsylvania Railroad's A. J. Cassatt. The presence of the automobile began to be felt; gas stations were erected; Lancaster Avenue was widened in 1936 to accommodate increased traffic and parking spaces for autos.

　　During this period, developments of smaller homes were con-

structed along Lancaster Avenue to provide housing for the working people of the community. They were neighborhoods for the professional class, for small shopkeepers, for the black population and for the Irish and Italian immigrants who came to Bryn Mawr around the turn of the century.

Bryn Mawr Today. A mature, postwar suburb, Bryn Mawr begins a new century with a distinguished history and exciting future. The town has shaken

off its sleepy beginnings and now encompasses a vibrant commercial center with the finest small specialty shops in the region. It boasts one of the most beautiful residential areas in the country. However, its greatest asset are the people: captains of industry, doctors, lawyers, business people, artists, teachers, architects, professors, tradespeople with all the skills and resources that are necessary to preserve and expand Bryn Mawr's impressive quality of life.

---

2 (below) Bryn Mawr Hardware, at 903 Lancaster Avenue.

BRYN MAWR'S WHITE HORSE

Children love the horse, pose for pictures with him, "ride" him and make their mothers drive out of their way to see what outlandish costume he's wearing for the season. And he's old, left over from the days of saddles, bridles and harnesses. He's trundled out every morning at 8:30 to stand watch at the entrance. • There used to be a saddle shop where Bryn Mawr Hardware Company now stands, and there were *four* white horses, of different heights, to help fit riders to saddles, and saddles to horses. Three plaster horses disappeared, no one knows where. • Betty McClenahan Hamill and husband Adam founded

the present store in 1926. For years they ran a sort of employment agency in the back of the store where householders could hire chauffeurs and maids. It's still a community gathering place. When Betty died, she left the property to her siblings; brothers William and Samuel joined Betty's sister Lillian and staff and in 1999 *their* offspring run the store. • Samuel's daughter makes seasonal costumes for the horse. Our steed has been seen in Easter bonnets and rabbit ears, at Hallowe'en a headless horseman sits astride carrying a pumpkin for his head and at Christmas, Santa Claus rides!

1 In 1881, a mansion was built on six acres on Montgomery Avenue in Ardmore for a Mr. Blummer. Two owners later, it was sold to Alan B. Rorke, a prominent Philadelphia builder. He named his summer home, Thorncroft.

An 1897 history reports, "George Hewitt was the architect of the grey stone edifice of ample dimensions, surrounded by a piazza. Mr. Rorke added various embellishments and improvements...a porte cochère..and erected an artistic stable with a red tile roof."

The next owner, Edward S. Dixon, Sr., upon his death in 1920, left the estate to his son. Six years later, the son sold the house and land to the Suburban Company.

SURURBAN SQUARE was developed by James K. Stone in 1926. He purchased the property from the Suburban Company in that year for $365,000 and commissioned an architectural firm, Dreher and Churchman, to design a shopping center on the site of Thorncroft. The original plan was to have a bank, post office, food market, small stores, a department store, an office building and a movie theatre. The same building material was to be used for all the structures. There were to be only two tall buildings: a department store and the Times-Medical Building. Parking spaces for cars were to be in the center and around the perimeter and on two wide streets with diagonal parking.

When construction began in 1927, a furor ensued. Local residents were concerned about the traffic and the decline of property values. Ardmore business owners feared a drop in revenues, but building moved forward,

In 1931, the center was named Hestobeen Square for three of its developers. Five years later, a contest was held to find a new name and Suburban Square was chosen.

In the 1970s, a street was replaced by an attractive pedestrian courtyard and walkway **2** *(below)*. At the left is Strawbridge's; on the right, the Times-Medical Building.

1 *(above)* Suburban Square in the late 1920s. Note the early Sunoco station.

Suburban Square was not the first outdoor shopping mall in the United States, but Strawbridge & Clothier was the first major department store that opened a suburban branch... to be followed by Wanamaker (in Wynnewood) and Saks Fifth Avenue and Lord & Taylor (along City Line Avenue). In 1937, Strawbridge's added a separate Men's Store, across the way, on the ground floor of the Times-Medical building **2** *(right).* There are seven floors of medical offices. The *Main Line Times* was an original occupant. Recent improvements include additional shops and landscaping **3** *(below)* that have added a certain European charm.

MEMORIES

"We left Delaware when I was about four because our house burned down! We came up to Ardmore and lived with my grandmother at 329 West Spring Avenue. • Across the street from us were Italian people, four or five families of them, and they had goats. There was a creek behind there and that was the goats' grazing ground. At the south end of Holland Avenue there was a big grazing ground and Mr. Duncan used to take 25 to 30 cows to graze there every day. • The Italians kept goats for the milk. They sold it and their kids drank it. I know they used to make cheese and stuff from it. Mr. Duncan had a general store on Spring (between Ardmore and Greenfield). Everybody went there, the Italians, the blacks. • Italian families lived on both side of us, we were all mixed in. When a lady would go the the hospital to have a baby, my grandmother would take her children in. My brothers would sleep on the floor while her children would sleep in the bed. • One time, when we were kids, the Ku Klux Klan was in our neighborhood. It was near Eastertime and my mother and aunt had gone to Philadelphia to shop for clothes. About ten o'clock we heard this shootin.' My mother and them never got home and we were wild. My brothers called the neighbors and walked to the trolley line to look for our folks. They were afraid they'd get shot and killed. They finally got home after the Klan had burnt the cross and two people were killed over there on Holland Avenue. • I never had roller skates, but when you came home from school, you did your chores in the house. Then we played jacks on the porch and jumped rope...tore up more shoes than jumped! At nine o'clock the bell was rung. You came in for lesson time. Then bath time. Then off to bed."

Loretta Long Loudermilt

1 *(above)* A typical double house on Arthur's Round Table. Each house follows a simple ell-shaped plan. Pairs are connected at the base of the ell to create a central courtyard. Every pair differs slightly. Many have been modified since their original construction. Photos show typical Arts and Crafts techniques: **2** *(top left)* Lead came windows with small panes and exterior stone chimneys with decorative brickwork are typical features; **3** *(top right)*, **4** *(bottom left)* Various brick patterns are used between the half timbers; **5** *(bottom right)* A steeply pitched projecting gable with intricate timber work, stucco infill and diamond-patterned casement windows.

ENGLISH VILLAGE

During the 1920s the population in Lower Merion Township grew faster than in any other decade. Housing shortage after the First World War, an interest in "garden suburbs" and improved railroad transportation were some of the causes of outward city migration. A need for new housing, and a builder's fascination with the architecture of Shropshire, after a stay in England for military duty, resulted in the construction of an English village in Wynnewood during 1925.

A Picturesque Village. The builder, Donald M. Love, collaborated with his brother S. Arnold Love, a practicing Philadelphia-area architect. Together they created a Tudor village, using street patterns, architectural designs, construction technologies and building materials that evoked "old England." On a five-acre rectangular tract between Cherry and Wister Roads, west of Montgomery Avenue, they laid out narrow winding lanes in the shape of an oval (Arthur's Round Table) with a snake-like tail (Love's Lane) that ran between the

two parallel roads. By 1928 the planned development was completed with ten double and nine single houses. Real estate value of the time has been quoted as $9,000 per home.

The quaint charm of this small development arises from a compact design that avoids sidewalks and sets the buildings close to the street, but often irregularly. Stone or brick walls, hedges, fences and well-positioned plantings create protection and add to the character of each unit.

The houses are all two or two-and-a-half stories tall and roofed in wood or composition shingles. The shapes are basically rectangular or ell-shaped with asymmetrical configurations of gables, chimneys, porches and garages. The principal building material is local stone, cut thin and neatly coursed.

Tudor Details. The English character derives from the use of exposed half timbers in both upper gables and full walls. A look of age and the Arts and Crafts tradition of the time were emphasized by use of irregular or bent timbers, natural crooks and sawn brackets. The use of old barn wood and railroad ties helped cultivate the sense of antiquity.

Stucco or used bricks, laid in various patterns, provide infill between the timbers. Massive end chimneys of stone and decorative brick contrast with delicate leaded and small-paned windows used throughout the facades. Historicizing details such as casement windows, rain barrels, bird houses and statuary niches add special flavor.

Throughout the complex of 29 homes the uniform scale, building materials and color palette of natural earth tones integrate the development. Building interiors feature the use of Arts and Crafts detailing such as Mercer tile, exposed roof trusses, wide oak floor boards, window seats and large stone fireplaces.

Artistic Charm. During a period of interest in revival architecture and craftsman finishes, English Village was an instant success. Rapidly the residences became known as an enclave for artists and writers who sought quiet, intimate surroundings. Many created studios and artist's spaces within their homes.

Arthur Love himself lived in a single until for many years. Another brother, who painted but never cooked, lived in a home designed without a kitchen. Today, English Village remains an outstanding and unique architectural development of the early 20th century.

1 *(above)* A picturesque home.

2 *(center)* This single house shows the asymmetry and irregularity of many houses in the village. Note the extensive wall of half timber and brick patterning plus gable peaks, projections and various window sizes.

3 *(below)* Another single home on Love's Lane shows the use of clapboard at one gable end and an artistic projecting gable in the otherwise half-timber and stucco facade

Be it Remembered That I Jacob Jones of Lower Merion Township in the County of Montgomery in the State of Pennsylvania being of sound Mind Memory and Understanding thanks be to Almighty God for the same and all other his Mercies! Do make and publish this my Will and Testament in manner & form following viz.

First. I will that all my just debts and funeral Expences be fully paid by my Executors herein after named.—

Item. I give and bequeath unto my beloved Wife Mary Jones the sum of One hundred Pounds to be paid her out of my personal Estate. I also give unto my said Wife Mary Jones all and singular my Household and Kitchen furniture

LOWER MERION ACADEMY. Jacob Jones, a devout Quaker, seemed to believe in education for all children whether they could afford it or not. Since he had no children of his own, he left an enduring educational legacy to the entire community. Jacob provided a trust and appointed Trustees to make his dream become a reality. The Trustees fulfilled Jacob's wishes by constructing a building, hiring teachers, governing the free school and admitting as many poor and orphan children from the Township as the proceeds of the trust would dictate. After the Township became part of the "general system of education," the Lower Merion Academy became one of the first centers of learning. While the Academy has passed through as many changes as society has, the Academy always remained a constant symbol of education and benevolence.

1 *(top)* First page of the will of Jacob Jones, dated 1803, in which he established a trust and gave land to build the first free school in this Township.

2 *(center)* Pages from spelling books and primers from the 19th-century.

3 *(right)* View of the Academy in the 1950s, seen from the playing fields, situated between Bala Cynwyd Middle School and Cynwyd Elementary School.

Three wills provided funds for the Academy building: John Roberts left 50 pounds in his 1803 will; Elizabeth George, in a will proved three years later, directed the residue of her estate be given to the estate of Jacob Jones, her brother. It is, however, the will of Jacob Jones which was the most generous in funding of the Academy. In his September 1803 will, he gave not only 800 pounds to erect the school building, but another 500 pounds in trust on landed security to employ teachers.

The interest from the monies was to employ teachers and to instruct free of expense "...as many Poor and Orphan children of both sexes living in the Township...without regard to their religious Profession or Education." He included a parcel of land (approximately 10 acres) "...at the West end of my Plantation..." Although the will was proved in April 1810, the trust was not established until the death of his wife, Mary, the following year.

Jacob based his will on several Quaker principles set forth in the Yearly Meeting directive of September 1778. It offered constructive advice on how to establish Quaker schools; for example, land to be provided for raising food and to erect a house so the teacher would not have to board with families of students, which was the custom.

The directive also encouraged Friends to provide a fund so the teacher could be paid and "poorer Friend's children" could attend. Jacob, however, went one step further and included all the children in the Township regardless of their religion.

The Trust and the Trustees. Jacob appointed five men and their heirs and assignees to oversee the trust. In the beginning, they had to decide who would build the school, how it should be constructed, how the school would be governed, who would qualify for the "free of all expenses" schooling, and who would teach.

1 *(top)* The Academy and Union. Sunday School (building at right) as seen in 1886 photo. Israel Irwin, on horseback, with wife and three daughters, Laura, Cora and Della.

2 *(center)* Vintage 1903 photo of the 4th, 5th and 6th grades at the Academy. Total enrollment: 78.

Early photos of Israel Irwin, **3** *(left)*, and Clifford Levering, **4** *(right)*, Headmasters of the Academy and Superintendents of the Union Sunday School.

The Building.

In 1812, the Trustees selected Joseph Price and Nathan Lewis contractors "for Building Lower Merion Benevolent School house." The memo stated that the Trustees would pay $5,700 which the builders would use to pay for the materials and wages of the workmen. The "architects" were to find the materials for building "...a good and substantial stone house for a school and the accommodation of a Family 55 feet front and 36 deep three stories in the front and two stories and a Cellar back."

The Plan.

The ground floor consisted of a dining room, cellar, and kitchen with a bake-oven fireplace, sink, and flues for "boilers." The second floor was divided into three rooms: one for a large schoolroom, another for a small schoolroom, and the third room was for the "accommodation of a Family."

An entry and staircase was to separate the large room from the smaller rooms. The large schoolroom had a master's seat and desk with enough seats and tables for forty "scholars."

The building was to be finished and painted on May 1, 1813. An insurance survery done for the Green Tree Mutual Assurance Company the following year, placed an evaluation of $4,600 (1814 dollars) on the schoolhouse. The schoolhouse with so many rooms and levels was an unique example of public architecture for its time.

The Teachers.

The building also served as a residence for the Headmaster and his family, and other teachers as well. Trustees agreed to hire teachers who "unequevocally profess to be a believer of the Purity and Divinity of the Christian religion...and best Qualified by theire Moral conduct and Scientific abilities."

An early teacher's contract with Joshua Hoopes, the first Headmaster, was for three years and five months. Joshua was expected to farm the ground, keep the buildings in good repair and teach the "scholars." He had to pay 50

1 *(above)* Early engraving of the Academy as it appeared on John Levering's 1851 map.

2 *(below)* A photo taken during World War I when the area in front of the Academy was used as a parade ground. Despite a few alterations overs the years, the building's architectural integrity remains.

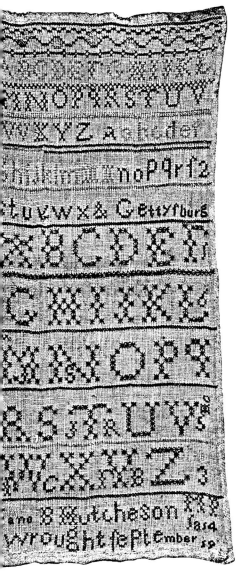

1 *(left)* Cross-stitch (1814) by 11 year old Jane B. Hutcheson. School girls were required to learn needlework and practice the art of making samplers.

2 *(below, left)* Philadelphia flourished as the center of an ambitious publishing trade in the 18th and 19th centuries. Printers specialized in schoolbooks, Bibles, technical texts and magazines.

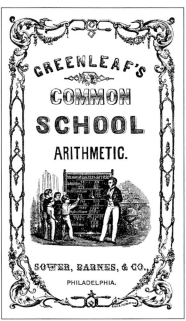

cents for each student he taught for each quarter, as rent for occupying the schoolhouse and using the acreage and the farm buildings. Joshua also needed the approval of the Trustees to hire other teachers.

Those who succeeded Hoopes lasted for one to three year terms, except for Israel Irwin who served for 23 years. Teaching was not as secure a profession as it is today.

The Opening. The Lower Merion Benevolent School opened its doors to students of both sexes on November 1, 1813. Girls were taught reading, writing, arithmetic, English grammar and plain needlework. The boys were taught reading, writing, English grammar, Vulgar and Decimal Arithmetic. Tutition was three dollars per quarter "with reasonable compensation for firewood and stationary..." The Trustees held quarterly examinations of the students with their parents, guardians, or masters present. Attendance was often poor.

The System. In 1834, Pennsylvania enacted a law to "establish a general system of education by common schools." Until that time, several types of schools were operating within the Township: schools run by churches; by trustees who held the school as real estate for the benefit of the neighborhood; by a teacher for profit and by bequest.

By November 1835, six schools (including the Academy) formally joined as "common schools." For the year 1836, the directors of the Lower Merion School District agreed to pay $150 to use the Academy. This joint administration of the School Directors and the Trustees governed the school until 1914, when the Academy closed. The larger Cynwyd Elementary School was built on Academy grounds, due to an increase in the stable school population.

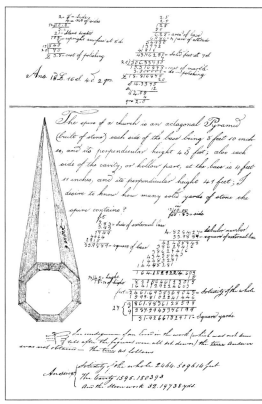

Different details of the Academy students' copy book: **3** *(above)*, Luther Parson's colorful letters from the 1890s and **4** *(below)*, the problems and solutions of trigonometry from the 1830s.

1 *(above)* 1880s photo of the Academy and the Union Sunday School (at right).

2 *(below)* Song book published by Lippincott in 1873, used at the Union Sunday School.

3 *(below, center)* Cover from an 1893 anniversary program.

4, 5 *(below, right)* Epigrams from the copy book of Susanna Evans done in 1829.

Union Sunday School. While the Academy took care of the educational needs of the community, the Union Sunday School provided the spiritual needs. Before there were enough people to support separate congregations, the Union Sunday School filled the void. At first, the Trustees allowed the Sunday School to meet at the Academy. Clifford Levering and Israel Irwin, two Headmasters of the Academy, became the Superintendents of the Sunday School. From 1861 to 1915, the Sunday School provided a place for non-sectarian worship and was the center of social acitivity in the community: strawberry festivals, oyster suppers, picnics, a speaker on Anniversary Sunday.

134

GEORGE FOX,
THE FRIENDS,
AND
THE EARLY BAPTISTS.

BY
WILLIAM TALLACK,

LONDON:
S. W. PARTRIDGE & CO., 9, PATERNOSTER ROW.
1868.

1 *(above)* Headmaster Irwin supported the library by purchasing a share at $5. The Lower Merion Library Company was housed in the Academy building.

The library's collection was as varied as its readers. Lower Merion was a mill and farming community which needed "how-to" books. **2** *(below),* an 1842 guide to constructing and operating mills; an 1832 reference book of a farrier. Comparative religion was encouraged with treatises on a wide range of beliefs from an 1868 book, **3** *(right)* on the Quakers to the 1840 edition about Jewish history. Appreciating one's surroundings was important: 1840s books on American birds and native flowers. A.J. Downing's 1854 volume on house construction was used by Township builders and some of these styles can still be seen today.

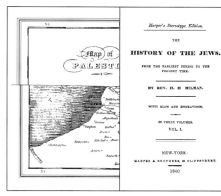

THE
HISTORY OF THE JEWS.
FROM THE EARLIEST PERIOD TO THE PRESENT TIME.

BY REV. H. H. MILMAN.

WITH MAPS AND ENGRAVINGS.

IN THREE VOLUMES.
VOL. I.

NEW-YORK:
HARPER & BROTHERS, 82 CLIFF-STREET.
1840.

The Library.

Education expanded beyond the walls of the Academy into the community when, in 1842, the Trustees established the Lower Merion Literary Company on the third floor.

The library was established by people who donated their own books. Supplemental funds were raised by selling stock shares which purchased the "Harpers' Family Library" and the "Harpers' Classical Library" of 434 books, at a cost of 50 cents a volume.

To this core Quaker collection, other titles were selected to give the library an uncensored window on the world. Such thought-provoking authors as de Tocqueville, Dickens, Darwin and Harriet Beecher Stowe were liberal additions.

By 1874, the collection had grown to over 1,400 volumes and the Academy was overcrowded. After the Union Sunday School was relocated to its own building in 1876, the entire library went to the new facility. With the construction of the Cynwyd Elemenatry School in 1914, the Union Sunday School was removed, and the library was left without a home.

In 1915, the Bala Cynwyd Library Association was founded (with the help of the Bala Cynwyd Women's Club) to preserve the library for the community.

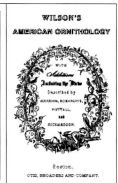

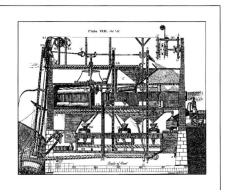

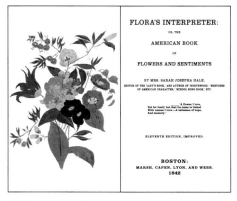

FLORA'S INTERPRETER:
OR, THE
AMERICAN BOOK
OF
FLOWERS AND SENTIMENTS

BY MRS. SARAH JOSEPHA HALE,
EDITOR OF THE "LADY'S BOOK," AND AUTHOR OF NORTHWOOD, "SKETCHES OF AMERICAN CHARACTER, "SCHOOL SONG BOOK," ETC.

ELEVENTH EDITION, IMPROVED.

BOSTON:
MARSH, CAPEN, LYON, AND WEBB.
1842

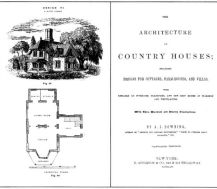

THE
ARCHITECTURE
OF
COUNTRY HOUSES;
INCLUDING
DESIGNS FOR COTTAGES, FARM-HOUSES, AND VILLAS,
WITH
REMARKS ON INTERIORS, FURNITURE, AND THE BEST MODES OF WARMING AND VENTILATING.

BY A. J. DOWNING,

NEW-YORK:
D. APPLETON & CO., 346 & 348 BROADWAY.
1854.

EARLY SCHOOLS. Before the Township school system started in 1835, schools were administered by religious organizations (for example, Merion Friends, 1769; St. Paul's Lutheran, 1787) by trustees who held the school as real estate to benefit the neighborhood...by a teacher for profit...or by bequest (Lower Merion Academy). After 1835, six schools joined as "common schools" to form the early school system: Fairview, Mt. Pleasant, Merion Square, Lower Merion Academy, Pennsville School (Blockley) and Union. The school directors built their first schoolhouse, "Wynne Wood," by 1836. With a growing stable school population, the 1870s saw the School Directors build and enlarge the schools that we remember today.

1 (*below left*) St. Paul's Old Dutch Schoolhouse, built in 1787, seen in 1911 photograph.

2 (*below right*) The school house today, after a recent rehab by local Boy Scouts.

3 (*bottom left*) Fairview School class photo, c.1900.

4 (*bottom right*) Painting of the Fairview School by Margaret Doran, based on a photo by Marian Ewing, who attended Fairview many years ago.

1 *(top left)* Photo of the second Wynnewood School, (the 1836 two-storied building burned in the 1860s). Built during the 1870s, it was located near the corner of Lancaster Avenue and Wynnewood Road.

2 *(top right)* Wynnewood class photo, c.1900.

3 *(center left)* Pencoyd and **4** *(center right)* Mt. Pleasant, like Wynnewood, are now gone.

5 *(below left)* Only the Merion Square School survives today as Gladwyne Montessori.

1 *(right)* Ruins of stone **Ardmore Public School,** built c.1876. When the photo was taken, in October 1900, (after devastating fire) it had served as both an elementary and Lower Merion's first high school from 1894 to 1910. (Rebuilt of stone in 1901.) Located on south side of Ardmore Avenue and West Athens Avenue. Demolished c.1963. Site now has subsidized housing facility.

2 *(below)* **Ardmore Avenue School,** rebuilt of native stone in 1901 after fire. Served as both elementary and high school until 1910 when new high school was built on Montgomery Avenue at School House Lane.

Bala School, 3 *(left)* constructed of stone in 1888. Located on the southeastern corner of Union and Bala Avenues. Demolished c.1974 when the new Bala School was built at Highland Avenue and Old Lancaster Road, adjoining the Bala Cynwyd Public Library. Site now owned by Township and has a gym and park.

1 *(right)* **Bryn Mawr School** on the north side of Lancaster Avenue, opposite Prospect Street. Levering's 1851 map showed a Union School House at about the same location. Two and a half story native stone building appears on 1871 map. Served until c.1915 when new brick school was built on the southeast corner of Bryn Mawr Avenue and Old Lancaster Road. Used again briefly in 1923-24 when there was a delay in opening Ardmore Junior High. On the 1926 map, school is shown as Moose Home and later Moose Hall. Demolition occurred after 1936. Now a parking lot.

2 Class at Bryn Mawr School, c.1890s.

3 *(left)* **Cynwyd Elementary School,** Bryn Mawr Avenue, Manayunk and Levering Mill Roads. Photo c.1930s, looking northwest. Brick building designed by Savery, Scheetz and Savery (architects for Ardmore Junior High, 1923-24 and the Administration Building, 1931-32, in Ardmore.) It was built in 1914 at a cost of $57,010 on land owned since 1812 by the Trustees of the Lower Merion Academy.

1 Merion Elementary School. Native gray stone, built 1925. North side of Bowman Avenue between Baird Road and South Narberth Avenue. Still in use.

2 Narberth Public School, photo c.1940. Native gray stone building designed by D. Judge DeNean, c.1892, for the Lower Merion School District at the northeast corner of Sabine and North Essex Avenues. Bought in 1895 by the Borough of Narberth. Used for all grades through high school until 1923, after which the borough paid tuition to the Lower Merion School District for each of its students after 8th grade to attend Lower Merion Junior and Senior High Schools. Demolished in 1961, the site is now being used for daycare.

3 Ardmore Junior High decorated with winter scenes in the windows and a holiday star over the Indiana limestone motto: "Enter to Learn / Go Forth to Serve." Photo taken in 1948 when Edward Holyoke Snow was principal. Demolished in 1992, the site now a parking lot and storage facility.

1 Lower Merion Junior High's first faculty, 1923-24. Principal Edward H. Snow, a New Englander, is in back row, center.

2 Audience in the auditorium watching Ardmore Junior High students, early 1930s. Demolished 1992. The stage portion is now a storage facility.

3 Shop class for boys, c.1930s, at Ashland Elementary School. Traditionally, girls had classes in cooking and sewing when the boys had wood and metal shop. The Belmont Hills School reopened in 1998 after extensive renovations.

1 Boys' shop class, Lower Merion Junior High School, c.1930. The print shop teacher was Bernard McManus.

2 Girls' domestic science class, c.1930. Ashland School had a suite of rooms, including a kitchen, living room, bedroom and bathroom. The girls learned how to care for all the rooms in their future homes/apartments.

3 Silence and order reign in the library at Lower Merion Senior High, c.1930s.

1 Lower Merion High School football team, 1919.

2 Aerial view, c.1950, of **Lower Merion High School complex.** *(from top)* bus garage; Clarke House; Pennypacker Field. *(left to right)* Technical Building, c.1938; cafeteria wing, 1950; Lower Merion Senior High School, built 1910, demolished 1963; Administration Building; Ardmore Junior High, built 1922-23, demolished 1992. *(foreground)* General H.H. Arnold Athletic Field, stable demolished c.1960s.

3 Students in front of Lower Merion Senior High, c.1950s, waiting for one of the ten school buses. The building was demolished in 1963 and replaced by the present high school.

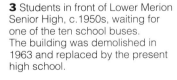

THE EPISCOPAL ACADEMY was founded in 1785 by the Right Reverend William White, the first Episcopal Bishop of Pennsylvania. Among its charter trustees were leading citizens of Philadelphia and signers of the Declaration of Independence and the U.S. Constitution. The school stressed both a classical education (Latin and Greek) and more practical study (business mathematics). The original campuses were in the city of Philadelphia and, after World War I, their quarters seemed more suitable for a hotel or an office building. Should they merge with another school? Should they move? The decision was made in 1921 to purchase John O. Gilmore's 19 acre estate Yorklynnne along City Avenue, then an unpaved country lane. The academy has, over the years, expanded to 32 acres and features a number of classroom buildings; athletic fields; a library-learning center; theatre, music and art facilities; a high-tech computer facility and two gymnasiums. Episcopal offers college preparatory education for more than 1,000 girls and boys from junior kindergarten through the twelfth grade.

1 *(left, from top)* The Episcopal Academy's 1887 location on Fourth Street, between Market and Chestnut, in Philadelphia; **2** Fall of 1882, the academy's football team practice on the University of Pennsylvania field; **3** Sketch class, 1921, theater and cafeteria in background;

4 *(right, top)* Late 1890s view of Gilmore's Yorklynne estate, before the academy's relocation; **5** The Forestry Club poses in the rear of Yorklynne, 1951.

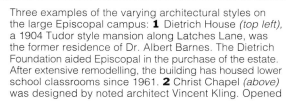

Three examples of the varying architectural styles on the large Episcopal campus: **1** Dietrich House *(top left),* a 1904 Tudor style mansion along Latches Lane, was the former residence of Dr. Albert Barnes. The Dietrich Foundation aided Episcopal in the purchase of the estate. After extensive remodelling, the building has housed lower school classrooms since 1961. **2** Christ Chapel *(above)* was designed by noted architect Vincent Kling. Opened in 1962, Academy students attend service three times a week and a special lower school service is held once a week. **3** The Roger Annenberg Memorial Library Learning Center *(above),* designed by Mirick, Pearson, Batchelor in 1972, is the central core of Episcopal's Main Building which houses its middle and upper schools. **4** Upper school students *(below)* are "Big Brothers" and "Big Sisters" to lower schoolers, a project of the nationally recognized Community Service program.

FRIENDS' CENTRAL SCHOOL was founded in 1845 by a joint committee of three Philadelphia Hicksite Meetings. All children of Quaker families were welcome to attend as were children of non-Friends families. On opening day in September 1845, there were 98 boys and 102 girls in the five classes ...a 15 dollar tuition for each term. There were many difficulties in the first few years. However the desire of the education committee to have a school and maintain its program of education never wavered despite the competition of free public education in Philadelphia and earlier Quaker schools. During the next 68 years, the school's enrollment dramatically increased. Despite several relocations of the schoolhouse, the need for more classroom space increased and there began a search to expand their city school facilities. The spot was found on City Line Avenue, near 66th Street, the Wistar Morris Estate. Here were 15-1/2 acres surrounding the mansion house.

(from top): **1** Friends' Central at 15th and Race Streets, Philadelphia, in 1880; **2** 1930s aerial view of the campus off City Line Avenue; **3** The school's relocation to Wistar Morris' Green Hill Farm; **4** Reception room in the estate, pre-1925.

1 *(top, left):* Mr. Crouch's chemistry lab, 1926; **2** *(right):* Library, early 1940s; **3** *(below)* Recent campus scene.

The Morris residence, modeled after a Scottish castle, became the main school building. The surrounding cottages were used as a science laboratory and residence for the headmaster; the barn for art classes, locker rooms and maintenance. The site also had spacious land for playing fields. A gymnasium was soon built.

Here the school has remained since 1925, surrounded by the beautiful campus which is part of the land grant to William Penn by King Charles II of England. New buildings have been added: science labs replaced the old gardener's cottage behind the residence; two buildings were added nearby to increase classroom space. The Linton gymnasium enlarged the playing courts

for the Rex gym. A swimming pool was an important addition for the summer day camp and neighbors.

In 1986 the barn was gutted and transformed within the original stone walls into the Blackburn Library.

With the school's purchase of the Montgomery Country Day School in nearby Wynnewood, it was able to greatly expand the Lower School facilities.

Over the years, the educational process and programs have developed a unique process for preparing the students for life. The school's strong mission and commitment to the principles of the Society of Friends have continued since 1845.

ANOTHER PENN COTTAGE?

In the 1970s, Friends' Central purchased the Montgomery Country Day School on a 15 acre tract on Old Gulph Road in Wynnewood for its Lower School facility. Late in the 1800s, the estate was called Pennshurst, **4** *(above)*. It was built by an Englishman, Hugh Burgess, and had replaced a home called Penn Cottage, formerly occupied by Peter Penn-Gaskell, a great grandson of William Penn. The Gaskell family was proud of the Penn association. In 1785, Peter Gaskell began hyphenating their name. Mary Penn-Gaskell, the mistress of Penn Cottage, was a daughter of George McClenachan who bought 378 acres of confiscated property of John Roberts, the miller who was hanged during the Revolution. A notable event occurred there in 1852 when Granville John Penn, last scion of William Penn to visit America, was lavishly entertained. 16 descendants of William Penn are buried in the Lower Merion Baptist Cemetery in Bryn Mawr.

THE HAVERFORD SCHOOL. In 1882, several prominent Main Line families, including as the prime mover, Mrs. Alexander J. Cassatt (wife of the president of the Pennsylvania Railroad) felt the need to establish a fine boys school in the area. The following year, Mrs. Cassatt and her followers offered to build a schoolhouse on the grounds of Haverford College. It was then agreed upon that the school would be directed by the college managers and used as a feeder school to the college. The new boys preparatory boarding school was opened on September 13, 1884 as The Haverford College Grammar School. Mr. Dean Sharpless was appointed as the Manager and later that year Charles Summer Crossman was named the Headmaster. By 1903, the school withdrew from the college and became an independent non-profit school still known as The Haverford School.

1 *(top)* Early photo, c.1916-1917, shows the new gym at left and The Oaks on the right.

2 *(above)* Aerial view, c.1930. Haverford College at upper left with Haverford School in the foreground, including Wilson Hall (bottom left), the new Junior School and the Gym (at right).

3 *(right)* The Haverford School Class of 1902, c.1899 photo.

1 *(from top)* 1906 school play, *Bill B.*, a one act entertainment, and an opera, *Laya Krachina.* Performances were at the Merion Cricket Club in March.

2 The Omega Club, 1931.

3,4 1990s photos featuring various fine arts and sports activities around campus.

5 Taking a spring break with buddies, c.1995.

1 Formerly the Bryn Mawr Hotel, The Residence of The Baldwin School was designed by the distinguished architect Frank Furness and constructed in 1892. It was placed on the National Register of Historic Places in 1979.

2 Florence Baldwin was born in 1858 in Wisconsin. After graduating from the Howland School in upstate New York, she earned a bachelor's degree in philosophy from Illinois Wesleyan College and studied at Cornell University. She founded Baldwin as a prep school upon the request of Dr. James E. Rhodes, president of Bryn Mawr College. After its first year, Miss Baldwin's School sent four of its five graduates to Bryn Mawr. **3** By 1896, the school had grown to over 100 day and boarding students (at right). Florence left the school in 1906 and married James Nugent. She died in 1926.

THE BALDWIN SCHOOL, an independent school for girls in Pre-Kindergarten through 12th grade, was founded in 1888 by Florence Baldwin as a preparatory school for young women planning to enter nearby Bryn Mawr College. Assisted by her sisters, Anna and Helen, Florence conducted classes in their mother's house on the corner of Morris and Montgomery Avenues. In 1896, the school leased the Bryn Mawr Hotel, located across from the Baldwin home, for the winter months. In 1922, the school purchased the hotel and its grounds and within three years added the Schoolhouse which now houses the Middle and Upper Schools. The last boarders graduated in 1974, and the Residence, or main building of the former hotel, was converted into offices and faculty apartments as well as art and music studios.

1,2,3 *(left and center)*
Baldwin campus scenes.

In 1975, the Lower School was added to the Baldwin campus, and in 1998 a new Early Childhood Education Center was opened especially for Pre-Kindergarten and Kindergarten girls.

Today, there are more than 4,000 Baldwin alumni, and they live in nearly every state of the United States and in many foreign countries. Many of them return every spring for reunions.

In 1998-99, 604 girls entered the familiar wrought iron gates to study at Baldwin. Of those, 22 percent receive financial aid, including full scholarships. As a college preparatory school, Baldwin sends all of its graduates on to higher education. Seniors choose such colleges and universities as Harvard, Princeton, Yale, Brown, Stanford, Williams, Wellesley and the University of Pennsylvania. In 1998-99, 38 percent of the senior class achieved recognition as both National Merit Scholars and Commended Students.

Baldwin still honors the aims set by Miss Baldwin, adapting them to the needs of today. The school's commitment to remaining a single-sex institution assures young women the opportunity to develop competence, confidence and responsibility in a diverse and caring community.

4 The Residence *(below right)* may be Baldwin's most famous building, but it is not the only one on the 25-acre campus. A three-story science building was opened in 1961 and enlarged in 1995 to accommodate the growing number of girls interested in studying the sciences. **5** The four-story Schoolhouse was completely modernized to provide for technological capabilities in 1998, but the elegance and warmth of its architecture were maintained *(below left)*. Today's campus also includes a gymnasium, indoor pool and outdoor pools, tennis courts and several playing fields.

THE SHIPLEY SCHOOL, now a coeducational day school in Bryn Mawr, was founded in 1894 by the three Shipley sisters, Hannah, Elizabeth and Katharine (**1** *left*), to prepare young women for Bryn Mawr College. The children of a Quaker father who encouraged his daughters in intellectual pursuits, the sisters themselves were well educated and well traveled. All had studied abroad and Katharine graduated in the first class at Bryn Mawr. Theirs was not to be a mere finishing school. The Shipleys' aim was: "to fit [the student] to enter college with a mind trained to habits of scientific study." They also emphasized "character building."

By 1913, the School had 75 boarding students and 39 teachers. The early brochures describe Shipley as a "home school," not a "school away from home." Students lived in three residences and studied in the "schoolhouse" **2** *(above)*, purchased in 1895, faced in brick in 1906, and still standing as the main School building. Students were expected to participate in the life of the community in addition to pursuing their academic studies. And while they look quite demure in their Commencement dresses **3** *(below left)* and went regularly to concerts and the theater, they played basketball and baseball and rode bicycles and horses. They also earned scholarships **4** to Bryn Mawr. "Fortiter in re, leniter in modo" ("Courage for the deed, grace for the doing") was and is the School motto. From the beginnings there was an emphasis on each individual developing her own abilities and talents. There never was a "Shipley mold."

In 1998, with 795 students in Pre-kindergarten through twelfth grade, Shipley on the surface is a very different place from what it was in 1894. It no longer has boarders; it has been coeducational for 25 years. Boys and girls go on to a wide variety of colleges. The genius of the Shipley sisters was to establish a mission which allowed for flexibility in changing times. **1,2,3** Their emphasis on academic excellence and on concern for the body and spirit as well as the mind of each individual child is still the basis of Shipley's mission and philosophy.

A MORAL COMPASS

Margaret Bailey Speer (1900-1997), **4** the fourth Headmistress of The Shipley School, arrived in 1944 after a distinguished career at Yenching University in Beijing, China. A graduate of Bryn Mawr College, she went to China to teach English. By 1934 she was Dean of the Yenching College for Women, a position she held until December 1941, when the Japanese occupation forces in China closed down the university. After a period of house arrest and then internment by the Japanese, Miss Speer returned to the United States in 1943.

• For 21 years until her retirement in 1965, Margaret Bailey Speer carried out and reinforced Shipley's original mission. Her intellectual standards were high. Her understanding of people was deep. Her global vision, her genuine concern for humanity, and particularly her sense of justice profoundly influenced an entire generation of Shipley students. Teaching by example and by parable, she had a light and often humorous, but nevertheless firm touch. She worked tirelessly not only to educate and broaden the minds of Shipley students, but those of others as well. She ensured that African-American students would be welcome at Shipley and was a founder in 1966 of the Bryn Mawr Presbyterian Church Tutoring Program, in which students of Main Line independent schools still tutor children from the inner city. • Respected by her peers as well as her students, Margaret Bailey Speer was a president of and also served on the boards of the major associations of independent schools and a number of other organizations concerned with education and justice. Miss Speer was one of the first women elected as a Member of Session, the governing body of the Bryn Mawr Presbyterian Church.

1 *(above)* A 1932 aerial survey of the Sisters of Mercy Convent and Schools. Waldron Academy for Boys is shown in the right forefront.

2 *(above)* Sister Mary Walburga, principal at Waldron Academy for Boys from 1929 to 1957, interacts with her "gentlemen in gray."

3 *(right)* A view of Waldron Mercy Academy as seen from along Montgomery Avenue.

WALDRON MERCY ACADEMY. The vision of two Sisters of Mercy, Mother Catherine McAuley and Mother Mary Patricia Waldron, enabled the establishment of Waldron Mercy Academy and its sister high school, Merion Mercy Academy. Mother Catherine McAuley, an Irish heiress who dedicated her entire fortune to helping the poor in Dublin, founded the Sisters of Mercy in Ireland in 1831. In 1861, under the leadership of 26-year-old Mother Mary Patricia Waldron, the first ten Sisters of Mercy arrived in Philadelphia from Manchester, New Hampshire, to serve the poor, the sick and the uneducated.

1 *(below)* The 1930 graduating class of Waldron Academy for Boys.

2 *(right)* The Waldron Academy for Boys Band.

The Move to Merion. In 1884, Mother Mary Patricia Waldron purchased the eight-acre Baner property in Merion as a country retreat for sisters who became ill while ministering in the city. In 1885, the Sisters of Mercy acquired the adjoining Morgan estate, a 13-room stone homestead that served as St. Anne's Convent, and a farmhouse which accommodated the Village School for poor, local farm children.

Separate Schools Established. In 1885, in this same convent, the Sisters of Mercy started Mater Misericordiae, an academy for young ladies and little boys under 12 years of age.

By 1892, the academy facility was inadequate and a new building named Mater Misericordiae Academy was begun. The building had classrooms, accommodations for female boarding students and living quarters for the sisters. The male boarding students remained at St. Anne's until 1923 when Waldron Academy for Boys was built on its site.

Further Developments. To meet the ever-evolving needs of students, significant growth and changes have taken place within the historic walls of Waldron Mercy Academy throughout the years. In 1946, the practice of boarding students ended. During the 1950s, in addition to the sisters, others joined the Waldron faculty in increasing numbers. A pre-school and a Montessori program followed, enrolling both boys and girls.

In September 1987, Waldron Academy for Boys and Merion Mercy Academy for Girls (Lower School) officially merged and reopened as Waldron Mercy Academy in a newly renovated facility. Today students from pre-school to eighth grade attend Waldron Mercy Academy, an educational ministry of the Sisters of Mercy, where academic excellence is achieved in the spirit of openness, trust, hospitality and outreach.

3 *(below)* May Day activities at Mater Misericordiae Academy c.1930s.

4 *(right)* Academy students continue to serve the poor through the school's community outreach program.

1 Founders Hall *(top)*, the first building built for the Haverford School, was completed in 1833. Students and faculty lived, ate and held classes there until 1877. Although the inside of Founders Hall has changed, (it now contains administrative and academic offices), the outside has remained architecturally simple, and had only two additions: Gest Hall in 1853, and Founders Great Hall in 1905. John Sartain's engraving of Founders Hall shows how the building and grounds looked in 1845. **2** A plaque *(above)* commemorates the 16 incorporators of the Haverford School Asssociation; **3** the original plan of Founders Hall; **4** the stylized logo which is found on recent Haverford materials.

HAVERFORD COLLEGE. In the late 1820s, a few Orthodox Quakers decided "to take into consideration the propriety of establishing a central school for the instruction of the children of Friends in the advance branches of learning," because many Quaker children were attending non-Quaker colleges such as Yale and Brown. They felt that their school should "turn out well instructed, serious, reflecting and useful men." Haverford College, founded 1833, was known for many years as The Haverford School, since the minimum age of entry for students was 12 years old. Although many Friends around the Northeast gave money for the original funding of the school, (in the first month of fundraising, $43,500 was raised), Haverford was in severe financial trouble by the 1840s, and in 1846, the school was forced to close. However, Haverford's loyal alumni raised more than $70,000 to reopen their beloved school, and in 1848, Haverford reopened to admit non-Quaker students. **5** *(below)* Haverford became a college in 1856, when the Legislature granted it a charter to award degrees.

1 Until 1882, the Haverford College Dining Hall *(top)* was in the basement of Founders Hall. It was moved to the first floor; then in 1907 it was moved once again, this time to the newly completed Great Hall, a large room in the back of Founders Hall. While it was utilized as a dining hall, it had "portraits of honored worthies of the past on the walls," which are now in the Sharpless Gallery in the Magill Library. Founders Great Hall was used for dining until 1969, when the current Dining Center was built. **2** The Great Hall *(right)* is still used for a wide range of events, including banquets, concerts and dances.

3 The photograph *(below)* is of the Haverford College community in 1898. In January 1897, the freshman class asked President Isaac Sharpless, seated 9th from the right in the 2nd row, for the chance to have an honor system. Sharpless obtained the faculty's agreement to allow "honor examinations" ...exams without proctors. Although the class of 1901 voted against the Honor System, the class of 1902 chose to implement it again, and since 1898, every incoming class has had the Honor System. It is an integral part of life at Haverford, and every year at Spring Plenary, the student body decides whether or not to retain the Code for the next academic year. At first, the Honor System only covered midterms and finals, but it was eventually expanded to include all aspects of academic and social life; relationships between members of the community are based on a foundation of mutual respect and concern for each other. The Honor Code continues to bring the Quaker values of honesty and respect to Haverford.

Before any Haverford School buildings were constructed, **1** Woodside Cottage *(above)* was a farmhouse on the land. It was named Chase Cottage in 1860 when President Chase moved into it, but was later re-named Woodside Cottage. After housing other presidents and faculty, Woodside now houses the English Department. **2** John Collins' 1833 drawing of a student room in Founders Hall *(right)* illustrates how easy it was for "some of the larger boys...[to] readily reach to the other side [of their rooms] with out-stretched arms."

3 In 1877, Barclay Hall *(left)* was built to allow for expansion of the College. The Victorian Gothic dorm was designed by Quaker architect, Addison Hutton. A fire claimed the dorm's tower in 1946. Although most of the bedrooms in Barclay were miniscule, they had studies attached to them.

4 Soccer *(above)* has long been a favorite sport at Haverford. In 1905, Haverford defeated Harvard in the "first modern intercollegiate match," and organized the "Intercollegiate Association Football League of Columbia, Cornell, Harvard, Haverford and Penn." Haverford has won many league and division titles, and has had All-American recognized players.

Though the Society of Friends had meetinghouses in Merion, Haverford (near Oakmont), and Radnor (at Ithan), a local group of seventy Friends began to meet (in 1827) at a tenant house on the farm of Samuel Garrigues. But that soon proved to be too small after the 1833 opening of Haverford College. **5** The present house *(bottom, left)* on Buck Lane was built in 1834 at a total cost of $2,200 for the land and the building. The meetinghouse was enlarged in 1894. Haverford faculty and students members have been meeting there since then.

Between the 1860s and 1887, the sophomore class burned their least favorite course book at the end of the year in a ceremony referred to as Cremation. At first, Paley's "Evidences of Christianity" was chosen, but it was difficult to defend a Quaker College burning, "the book which was supposed to safeguard the faith"; so math books written by Wheeler and Wentworth became the preferred choice. Although Cremation originally took place in the woods behind the gym, it became so popular that it was eventually performed in front of Barclay. **1,2** The class printed invitations *(right)* and dressed in wild costumes such as those donned by the class of 1888 *(below)*.

3 Haverford's first observatory was built in 1834. In June 1852, plans for the current observatory *(below)* were begun. By 1854, the observatory was fitted with its equatorial telescope, transit instrument and Bond's magnetic register. **4** The Duck Pond *(bottom)* has long been used for ice skating by Haverford students, and in the1950s it was also used for punishing "naughty" freshman...they were thrown into it, fully clothed. The pond was apparently only a winter novelty (it was a pasture in the summer) until the 1930s when a student created plans to make it a permanent fixture.

GIFTED GRAD

Rufus M. Jones (class of 1885) was born in 1863 in South China, Maine. Rufus entered Haverford on a full scholarship in the fall of 1882 as a sophomore. While at Haverford, he took advantage of everything offered to him. In addition to holding many leadership positions at Haverford, he had almost enough credits to graduate by the end of his junior year. Rufus did work for a Master's degree in History during his senior year, even though he was majoring in Philosophy. After graduation, Rufus taught at Oakwood Seminary in New York State, where he met his first wife, Sarah Coutant. He accepted a position at Haverford in 1893, as a part-time philosophy professor. During his 41 years as professor, Jones wrote over 50 books on topics such as philosophy, mysticism, religion and history. Rufus married Elizabeth B. Cadbury in 1902, three years after Sarah died. In 1917, he helped found the American Friends Service Committee (AFSC), a group committed to peace through non-political service. As well as being a beloved professor and scholar, Jones served for 50 years on the Bryn Mawr College Board of Trustees and was one of the founders of the Quaker Five Years Meeting in 1902. During his lifetime, he gave Haverford College his personal collection of nearly 1000 books on mysticism and left a fund to care for this collection. It now includes 1400 books from the Renaissance period to the present. Rufus Jones died on the Haverford campus in 1949.

5 Rufus M. Jones

There is a wide range of architectural styles. on campus The Victorian houses **3,4** *(below)* were built in the 1880s for faculty. **5** The Fine Arts building *(center, right)*, built in 1987 is one of the more modern looking buildings on campus. Quaker-affiliated architects Cope, Lippincott and Slifer designed the building with large windows so that as much indirect light could get into the studios as possible.

During World War II, women came to Haverford to train for American Friends Service Committee reconstruction projects. **1** They also took classes *(above, center)* and lived on campus during the year. Their presence re-opened the discussion over coeducation. David Long (class of 1948) stated, "at the heart of Quakerism is equality, both of race and sex...Haverford is assuredly out of line with the essence of (Quaker) tradition."

2 Serendipity Day Camp *(above, right)* was born in the 1960s out of some young Ardmore men's desire for a good relationship between the college and the community. Staffed by Haverford College students and community members, Serendipity is run

by 8th Dimension, Haverford's Community Service organization. It is a camp for children between the ages of 6 and 13, and has racially and economically diverse campers from surrounding areas as well as from Philadelphia and New Jersey.

6 During the McCarthy era (the 1950s), Haverford's first black professor, sociologist Dr. Ira de A. Reid, *(right)* was accused of being a communist and his passport was revoked. However, the college stood by him during the months it took to clear his name.
• Although first year women were not admitted to Haverford until 1980, there were women on campus before then. In the early 20th century, women were graduate students at Haverford's T. Wistar Brown Graduate School. In 1918, Eleanor May Gifford was the first of a few Haverford women to receive her MA. • In 1864, the college hosted and won the first intercollegiate cricket match in America against the University of Pennsylvania. Haverford has continued to be one of

the few undergraduate institutions that is "regularly instructing Americans in cricket." Until the 1970s, the college also had a football team, and games against rival Swarthmore College brought community spirit to an extremely high level. In the early 1930s, women's sports were joint with Bryn Mawr College. Today, Haverford has its own women's teams. • At the turn of the century, Asians were the first minority students to be admitted to Haverford. In 1907 and 1926, the first Puerto Rican student and the first black Jamaican student respectively, graduated. In 1968, the minority population at the college grew, both in the faculty and the student body. However, Haverford has striven to "institutionalize its commitment to diversity."

1 Haverford's first seven library books, *(right)* including Sewell's *History of the Quakers* and George Fox's *Journal*, were donated in 1833. **2** Later, these books, along with about 1000 others, were moved from Founders Hall to the new Alumni Hall, the original wing of Magill Library *(center)*. They are now located in the Quaker and Special Collections. **3** All rare books were removed from the regular stacks *(below)* to the Quaker Alcove when it was created in 1942. Quaker and Special Collections, which is now one of the major Quaker collections in the world, also contains manuscripts, archives and graphic materials.

GIFTED HAVERFORDIAN

Before he was a famous artist, **Maxfield Parrish** was a Haverford College student. He matriculated at the college in 1888, but dropped out in 1891 in order to pursue a life in art. While at Haverford, Maxfield (known then as Frederick) studied architecture in the "Classical Section" of study. Maxfield's amazing artwork did make a large impression while he was still at Haverford. His room in Barclay Hall gained campus-wide fame for its elaborate wall decorations executed in chalk and crayon. His physics and chemistry notebooks were also known for their incredible illustrations. Among his other artistic creations while at Haverford were place cards, program covers and college publication illustrations. After Haverford, Maxfield produced murals, posters and advertisements for products such as Jell-O and Hires Root Beer, and illustrations for books and magazines. Maxfield Parrish was born in Philadelphia to well-to-do Quaker parents in 1870, and was greatly influenced by artwork he saw on trips with his family to Italy and other western European countries.
In 1897, Parrish was inducted into the Society of American Artists, and by 1925, he was considered by some to be one of the three best artists of all time.

4 1905 portrait of Parrish by Kenyon Cox.

BRYN MAWR COLLEGE (1885) was founded upon an endowment from Dr. Joseph Wright Taylor, a Quaker businessman and physician. Dr. Taylor had observed the frustration of a daughter of a Baltimore friend who was unable to study at the graduate level. That young woman, Martha Carey Thomas, enrolled at the University of Zurich, graduating summa cum laude with a PhD. Taylor, a devoted member of the Society of Friends, died in 1880. He bequeathed the bulk of his estate to fund an institution "for the advanced education of females" providing "all the advantages of a College education which are so freely offered to young men." (Nearby Haverford College, another Quaker institution, had begun in 1833). Bryn Mawr's first president was Dr. James E. Rhoads, also a Quaker with close ties to Haverford College; the first dean was M. Carey Thomas. After Dr. Rhoads' resignation, Ms. Thomas began a lengthy tenure (1894-1922). It was she who gave Bryn Mawr its special identity as a college determined to prove that women could successfully complete a curriculum as rigorous as any offered to men in the best universities.

1 Aerial view of the campus,1958. The "Collegiate Gothic" buildings were set along the perimeter of a central green space.The grounds were planned by Calvert Vaux, then by Frederick Law Olmsted.
2 *(below)* Cornelia Otis Skinner as Queen Elizabeth on May Day 1932.

1 Taylor Hall (*below*), designed by Addison Hutton, featured the high Victorian Gothic style of the times. The original campus building, it featured an asymmetrical tower, rich silhouetting, original detailing.

Hutton chose monochromatic cut grey stone in keeping with the college's heritage, reminiscent of "a certain style of Quaker lady dress." It now contains some administrative offices and classrooms.

2 Wyndham House (*below*, c.1876) is the oldest house on campus. Built in 1796 by Quaker widow, Patience Morgan, who added a handsome stone building to an old farm she inherited. When the family went into debt, it was sold to Thomas

Humphreys (Bryn Mawr was first called Humphreysville) in the 1800s for $8,682. Thomas Ely became the owner in 1893. The college purchased it in 1926 for a residence hall. It now provides guest quarters, office space and a dining facility.

GIFTED GRAD

Katharine Hepburn (Class of 1928), remembers her Bryn Mawr days in her autobiography, *Me: Stories of My Life* (Alfred A. Knopf, 1991). She furthered a Connecticut family tradition: her mother, also named Katharine Houghton Hepburn, was a Bryn Mawr graduate...and so were her mother's sisters. Before college, her aunts also attended the Baldwin school next door.

"My first year, I lived in a suite in Pembroke West...room and bedroom, ground floor, first door on the right. Having not been in school for several years, I really was not at home or at ease with a lot of strange girls. I used to go to bed early. Then I'd get up at four thirty and go down the hall to the bathroom and have solitude in the hot and cold showers in the john. I used to eat fruit and cereal and milk for breakfast, so I could have that alone in my room, and avoid too many girls. I certainly did not consider myself beautiful. I was just painfully self-conscious. My second year, I'd gotten used to all the girls and I supposed they got used to me. I belonged to a particular group. Easier to function with protection of a few others. These have more or less remained my friends, especially the ones living in New York and Connecticut • My last three years at Bryn Mawr were nowhere near traumatic. I wasn't a member of any club but I acted in several plays, which was fun...and fooled around with my pals and laughed a lot. In my last year I played Pandora in *The Woman in the Moon*. This was part of a big May Day production." Through a friend who lived next door to the campus, Hepburn met a wealthy young man from Strafford named Ludlow Ogden Smith. He courted Katherine and they were married after her graduation in 1928. Hepburn has remained a devoted Bryn Mawr alumna, making return campus visits over the decades.

3 Bryn Mawr Yearbook photo, 1928.

163

"They carry the distinguished mark..
the credible vigor, the subtlety of
mind, the warmth of spirit, the aspiration,
the fidelity to past and present."
E. B. White

1 *(above)* The first class, 1886 photo, and the faculty. M. Carey Thomas was determined to establish a college for women that blended the best of Smith, Vassar and Wellesley with the rigorous scholarship standards of Johns Hopkins. She recruited a young, largely male, faculty newly trained in German universities. She limited their teaching time to encourage study and research. Bryn Mawr became the first women's college to develop graduate instruction leading to a doctorate for women.

2 The annual May Day festival started in 1900 *(below)*. It probably grew out of M. Carey Thomas' love of the theater and the romance of earlier times. It was an Elizabethan extravaganza featuring Maypole dances and elaborately costumed plays, all staged as a way to raise funds. The May Day tradition continues, to the delight of students, parents and the community. The generosity of an alumna's family later led to Goodhart Hall *(opposite page)*.

wo early dormitories, **1** Pembroke Hall West, 394, and Rockefeller Hall, 1904, **2** (center), e seen in old photos. Both designed by ope & Stewardson, they reflect M. Carey homas' desire to emulate the architecture famous English universities.

3 Goodhart Hall, 1928, (bottom), designed by Arthur Meigs, filled the college's need for an auditorium. It is embellished with ironwork by Samuel Yellin. It is named for Marjorie Walter Goodhart of the Bryn Mawr class of 1912.

GIFTED GRAD

Marianne Moore (Class of 1909), born in 1887, grew up in Carlisle, Pennsylvania. She never knew her father; her tight family was dominated by a mother who, early on, instilled high ideals and diligent work habits in her. Family friends had gone to Bryn Mawr and this stimulated the Moores' interest. Soon this spirited young woman was surrounded by a circle of affluent friends with a broad range of interests. Marianne kept up a lively correspondence with her mother, revealing her unhappy and homesick freshman year. Mrs. Moore constantly implored her to persevere through discipline and self-control. • Marianne enjoyed shopping in Philadelphia. She sent home sketches of dresses she couldn't afford; whereupon mother sewed a wardrobe that matched Marianne's classmates. It was on a Philadelphia trip that she first saw a black tricorn that eventually became her trademark. Moore now had a circle of interesting friends who enjoyed parties, plays, concerts, pageants, lectures and sports activities. Marianne ignored a teacher's advice *not* to become an English major in her sophmore year and began submitting stories to Bryn Mawr's literary magazine, *Tipyn O'Bob* (Welsh, meaning "a little bit of everyone").
In the next years she submitted both fiction and poetry. • Moore read widely; admired the advanced social attitudes of G. B. Shaw, the feminist themes of Ibsen, the suffragist beliefs of Jane Addams. Now acclimated to Bryn Mawr life, she began her lifelong devotion to both social awareness and artistic excellence. • Long before her death in 1972, Marianne Moore ranked with Emily Dickinson among America's finest women poets. As editor of *The Dial* magazine (1925 to 1929) she played an important part in encouraging young writers and publishing their work. Her *Collected Poem*s won the 1952 Pulitzer Prize for poetry. **4** (below) Miss Moore at Bryn Mawr.

[Adapted from *Marianne Moore: A Literary Life*, Charles Molesworth, Atheneum, New York, 1990]

MEMORIES

"In 1960, architect **Louis I. Kahn** and Bryn Mawr College president, Katharine McBride, came together in a mutually inspiring relationship as architect/client to create one of this century's great buildings, the Erdman Hall dormitory. It was my privilege as a young intern in Kahn's studio to witness and be involved in the process. • Creation is often a patient search. For over a year, Kahn and his assistants had been struggling to translate the college's design program of 130 student rooms and public spaces into a scheme. As in earlier works, he let geometry be the organizer ...but could not find a comprehensive form. When he finally freed himself from the rigid dictates of geometry, and *played* with geometry, the final design emerged. • The building became three square buildings, connected at their corners. The outer walls being formed of an interlocking of student rooms around three inner public spaces: the entry hall, dining hall and living hall. These spaces receive light from towering light monitors. And the building fits into the sloping site. • With skillful modeling of materials (concrete, slate, wood, copper, lead) and sensitive scaling of elements, Kahn produced a building which is at once in harmony with the campus tradition and yet a bold statement of its time. It soon achieved international acclaim and remains today one of the great creations of its architect."

Edward Davis Lewis

1 *Louis Kahn, 1972.*

2 Emma Bailey *(top)* studies in her dorm room at Denbigh Hall, designed by Walter Cope & John Stewardson in 1891, one of their many buildings on the campus. Her ornate facilities contrast with Eleanor Donnelly Erdman Hall, honoring a 1921 graduate, **3** *(below)*. It was designed by Louis Kahn in 1965. Kahn's philosophy stated: "A dormitory should not express a nostalgia for home. It is not a permanent place, but an *interim* place."

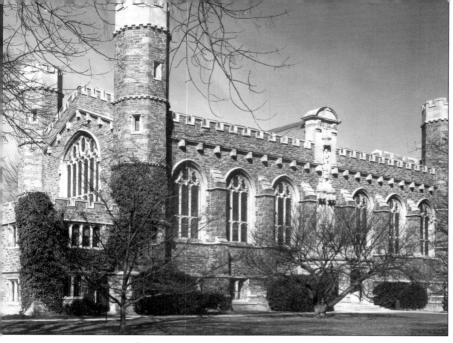

1 The Thomas Library (1903-1907) was another project by Cope & Stewardson. **2** The Great Hall (formerly the reading room) was a showpiece: cathedral ceiling painted with geometric Renaissance patterns; tall, lead-paned windows flooding the space with light. Ms. Thomas' cremated remains are in the courtyard cloister. The Great Hall today remains a grand space for lectures, concerts and other student gatherings.

3 President M. Carey Thomas

4 The Rhys Carpenter Library *(at left),* named for Bryn Mawr's late professor of Classical Archaeology, was designed by Henry Myerberg and opened in 1997. This astounding space is attached to the rear of the Thomas Library. The entrance is a four-story atrium...a comfortable, sun-filled place. Names of art and archaeology faculty are on the main wall, with a frieze of plaster casts from ancient Halicarnassus. The most inspired plan was to place most stacks, study areas, lecture halls and seminar rooms *underground.* With a roof concealed by grass, this creative design provides an improved and delightful background for the historic library.

2 Some founding nuns posed *(below):* Mother Dolores Brady, Rosemont's first president, is second seated nun from the left; Mother Mary Lawrence, who had a long and illustrious career on the history faculty, is fourth standing nun from the left. Her public lectures attracted a wide audience to the college. She brought to this country the English love of landscape gardening and the beauty of the campus was the result of that avocation. The original estate also contained a huge stable. The nuns converted it and created additional classrooms, science labs and an art studio.

3 Mayfield Hall dorm *(below, top right)* replaced the stables in 1929.

4 The Gertrude Kistler Library *(bottom right)* was erected in 1924, a memorial to a prospective student who had drowned in a swimming accident. Enlarged in 1934 and the 1990s, it retains its Gothic exterior yet provides a state of the art electronic learning and library system inside.

ROSEMONT COLLEGE was opened by the Sisters of the Holy Child in 1921 as a Catholic liberal arts college for women. The nuns had purchased the 32-room mansion **1** *(above)* of Joseph Sinnott for $250,000. At first the renovated mansion composed the whole college: dormitory space for students, a convent for the nuns, a chapel, classrooms, eating facilities and offices. There were seven students in Rosemont's first class...two were in the first graduating class in 1924. By 1931, the college had six buildings and 160 students. Rosemont still retains its original commitment to the education of women in its undergraduate liberal arts college. Beginning in the 1980s the first of six graduate programs, opened to both men and women, was introduced and in the 1990s an accelerated undergraduate program, also coeducational, was initiated.

168

1 The photo *(top)*, taken in the late 50s or early 60s, illustrates the then typical dress at Rosemont and the traditional habit of a Holy Child nun. Student dress codes underwent radical modification in the 1960s while, at about the same time, the nuns, influenced by the reform trends in the Catholic church, turned to conventional street clothes.

2 A member of Rosemont's language faculty *(above)* instructs a student on the use of computer software in Lawrence Hall's Conwell Learning Center. Opened in 1993, the Center provides equipment to enable students to work independently on course assignments and other projects. Although the Sisters of the Holy Child stand in a special relationship to the College, the overwhelming majority of faculty and adminsitrators are now lay men and women.

3 Some recent Rosemont students *(right)* exchanging thoughts just outside Rathalla, still the architectural center of the campus.

1 Dr. Barnes commissioned Paul Phillipe Cret, French-born architect who taught at the University of Pennsylvania, to design the structure that would house his foundation and its artwork. The three buildings Cret designed were in a simplified neo-classical style: a gallery *(above, center)*, the administration building, (at right), where the Barneses lived and the service building, (at left).

THE BARNES FOUNDATION was chartered as a privately endowed, nonprofit educational institution by the Commonwealth of Pennsylvania in 1922. Its stated mission was to promote the advancement of education, the appreciation of the fine arts and the study and the encouragement of arboriculture and forestry. The foundation, which one day would include one of the largest collections of Impressionist, Post-Impressionist and modern art in the world, was the brainchild of Dr. Albert Barnes, physician, self-made millionaire, collector and, above all, art educator. Barnes was born in 1872 in the working class section of Kensington in Philadelphia.

2 *(below)*. Early aerial view of the Barnes Foundation property.

1, 3 Dr. Barnes commissioned sculptor Jacques Lipchitz to carve seven reliefs for the exteriors of the buildings as well as a sculpture for the front of the Administration Building.

2 Barnes searched worldwide for just the right stone for the exterior. He had an old French quarry reopened and imported the stone.

Living in tough neighborhoods, Barnes learned to stand up for himself, a trait which he would maintain for the rest of his life. This determination, combined with a keen inquisitiveness, was his ticket out of Kensington. At age 13, Barnes won entrance to Central High School, one of the most academically rigorous and respected secondary schools in the country. A distinguished student, after finishing his studies at Central, Barnes continued on to the University of Pennsylvania Medical School, graduating with the class of 1892.

Choosing a career in pharmacological research rather than clinical medicine, Barnes went to Germany, then the world's center for the study of advanced chemistry. There he worked in experimental laboratories in Berlin and at the prestigious University of Heidelberg. While in Germany, he established a fortuitous partnership with the chemist Herman Hille. Together they refined a silver salt compound effective, primarily, in preventing eye infections and blindness in newborns.

Marketed throughout the world, Argyrol became a huge commercial success. In just three years, Barnes was wealthy enough to build Lauraston, a large home on Latches Lane named for his wife. (The home

is now part of the Episcopal Academy campus.)

With the leisure and money that came with success, Barnes could at last explore his fascination with art and aesthetics. His acclaimed collection of artwork started off modestly. Never one to believe that art was exclusively the domain of the privileged, Barnes took the unusual action of hanging paintings in the Argyrol factory as well as his home.

What's more, he used the paintings as an opportunity to educate his employees. He encouraged them to learn about and discuss with him the philosophy of art. Thus he attempted to create an environment where each employee could grow intellectually and creatively. Art was the medium and Barnes was the teacher.

In 1911, Barnes reconnected with a Central High classmate, the celebrated painter William Glackens. The next year, Barnes sent Glackens to Paris with $20,000, instructing him to purchase artwork. He returned with approximately 20 paintings from the then under-appreciated painters Van Gogh, Renoir, Cezanne, Picasso, and Pissaro among others.

These extraordinary paintings fed Barnes' desire for more artwork. Soon, Barnes ventured to Eu-

MEMORIES

Laura Leggett Barnes was born in Brooklyn in 1874. It was reported in her 1966 obituary: "While courting Laura, Dr. Barnes was tinkering with some chemicals on the Leggett family's stove. Those experiments led to his development of Argyrol. They were married in 1901. By the time he was 30, he was a multimillionaire. It's acknowledged that Mrs. Barnes' financial acumen was important to the business' success." • After their marriage, Barnes built a grand home on Drexel Road in Overbrook. Their next home was on Latch's Lane, over the city line, in Merion. In 1922, Barnes purchased the foundation's present 12-acre site from his neighbor, Joseph Lapsley Wilson. Wilson had begun an arboretum on the site in the 1880s and planted trees and specimen flora from around the world. Barnes agreed to keep the arboretum intact and to build his foundation on the site of Wilson's home. That arboretum *(above right)* became Laura Barnes' turf...she soon instituted classes in Botany, Horticulture and Landscape Architecture. A quiet, soft-spoken woman, she was a contrast to her husband, often called the "Terrible-Tempered Dr. Barnes." Laura died at age 92. Mrs. Barnes' former secretary, now 93, remembers: **"**Mrs. Barnes was a lovely 'elderly' lady (I thought then!) when I met her. She needed a secretary as the one who had been with her for some time was no longer able to continue. I forget how Mrs. Barnes heard of me, but I was delighted and was with her for some years. The Arboretum was flourishing. She knew every tree and bush by its Latin name. She had a marvelous man to help her ...also a horticulture expert. About a dozen young women attended her arboretum school. She insisted that they arrive on time and there was always much scrambling to make the 9 o'clock deadline. Some were young mothers. The later you were in arriving, the farther away you had to park... which compounded the problem. Being late was marked against your record. I took a sandwich with me, and would eat (along with Mrs. Barnes and the expert) in the kitchen of the little addition where we met. It was a great privilege to be with her. She was a really 'special' lady.**"** **Florence McElroy**

1 *(top)* Arboretum plan. **2** *(right)* Laura and Albert Barnes with their faithful dog, Fidéle, at the Barnes' summer home, "Ker-Feal."

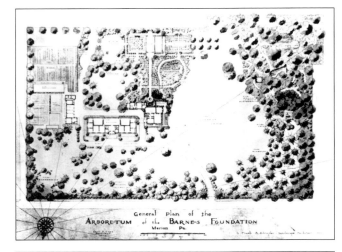

General plan of the ARBORETUM of the BARNES FOUNDATION Merion Pa.

rope himself in search of works for his collection. In Paris, he was a frequent visitor to the celebrated salon of art enthusiasts Gertrude and Leo Stein. There he learned to appreciate still more the artistic merit of Impressionist, Post-Impressionist, and Modernist painting. Before long, his many shrewd purchases of this under-appreciated (and often ridiculed) artwork became the talk of the auction and gallery circles.

Seeking a deeper understanding of the artwork he admired, in 1917 Barnes enrolled in classes at Columbia University taught by the philosopher John Dewey. Dewey's approach to education stressed the democratic and experiential aspects of learning. In this theory, Barnes found a philosophy that resonated with his own beliefs.

As his collection grew, Barnes' idea of founding an educational institution began to take shape. As he envisioned it, the foundation would consist of an art gallery which would house a school for the study of art. Incorporating his interest in horticulture, the foundation would also include an arboretum and school for the study of botany, horticulture and landscape architecture.

The Barnes Foundation was dedicated on March 19, 1925. Barnes appointed his friend and philosophical mentor, John Dewey, as the first Director of Art Education. Barnes

172

1 The interior finishes of the buildings *(left)* are austere yet rich, and never in conflict with the building's original intention: the display and study of artwork. Every room in the gallery has either a large window or a clerestory skylight to admit light.

2 *(below)* To give a unique character to the main entrance of the Gallery, Barnes commissioned the Enfield Tile Works to create tile adaptations of African sculpture to surround the main doorway.

used the gallery with its impressive collection of paintings as the extraordinary classroom for his students, who, in keeping with Dewey's democratic principles, came from all walks of life. Noteworthy students have included the acclaimed Afro-American painter, Horace Pippin; Richard Wattenmaker, Director of Archives of American Art at the Smithsonian Institution; and Fred Osborn, Dean of Education of the Pennsylvania Academy of Fine Art.

With the Foundation built, Barnes' mission was not yet finished. He wrote several books on art and collaborated with Dewey in his studies. He also expanded his art collection to include examples of man's creativity from many different cultures, traditions, and media. These include furniture, ceramics, ironworks, fabrics, antiquities, tapestries, and African sculpture.

He experimented with unique wall arrangements. For example, a series of ornamental door hinges and ironwork might be arranged with old master paintings, Post-Impressionist paintings, and African sculpture. Such groupings invite viewers to participate in understanding the creative process, and in finding parallels among diverse creative works.

In the mid-1940s, Barnes was considering the eventual fate of his foundation. It would be a difficult and lengthy process. His attempts to forge a relationship with the University of Pennsylvania and other schools were not successful. So, in 1950, Barnes chose Lincoln University, an historically black institution, to appoint four of the five trustees to the foundation's board. Nine months later, Barnes was killed in an automobile accident.

Today, nearly 50 years later, Barnes's educational legacy endures. The Barnes Foundation continues to hold classes in the philosophy and appreciation of art and in horticulture, botany, and landscape architecture. The Barnes Foundation serves as home to a collection of artwork which has no parallel in the world.

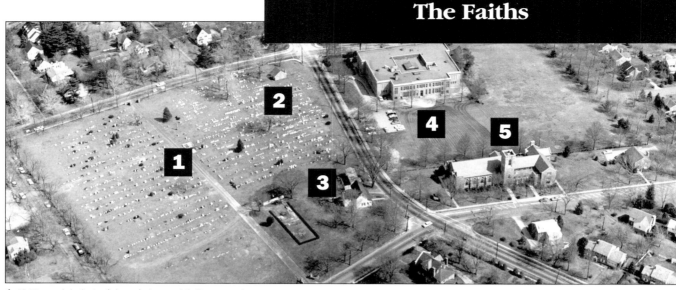

1 1940s aerial photo *(above)* shows: (1) Graveyard established in 1766, burial ground for 116 soldiers who fought in the Revolutionary, Civil and 1812 Wars; (2) Old Dutch Schoolhouse built in 1787; (3) Sexton's house, 1844, and the old parsonage, 1852; (4) Former Wynnewood Road grammar school, now Torah Academy; (5) The fifth church on East Athens Avenue and Wynnewood Road.

2 The Log Church, 1769 *(above),* a one-room building, served the early German Protestants, German Reformed and the Lutherans. **3** That was replaced by a sturdy stone one *(below)* on the same spot. Although economic times were tight for St. Paul's, the parish replaced it with the handsome, simple "Country Church" **4** *(right).* Note the old Dutch schoolhouse at the right rear. "Renting" of pews and sale of burial permits ($2) allowed the church to hire its first permanent pastor ($150 a year). Until 1890, St. Paul's was the only church in Ardmore and attracted a growing congregation because services were now in English.

ST. PAUL'S LUTHERAN CHURCH. Prior to the American Revolution, rural farms covered most of the Township. A 66-acre farm, the Atkinson Place, was bought at sheriff's sale (for $725) by a group of six German immigrants who sought land for a church and a burial place. Like their Welsh neighbors who fled their birthplace because of religious oppression, they also were welcomed by the colonies. The group erected a simple log church in 1769, then they attached to it a small stone schoolhouse in 1787. The disintegrating log structure was replaced by a stone one in 1800. As the parish grew (services were in German) there was a need for a larger place of worship. The simple white "Country Church" was built on the site in 1833 and a permanent minister was hired. As Ardmore's population grew, there was a need for a "Town Church." It was built in 1873-75 on Lancaster Pike in Ardmore. Despite the Depression, there was steady growth in the congregation and, when a farmland lot and a bequest were pledged by Charles Knox and sister Margaret Green, the present church was erected on East Athens Avenue and Wynnewood Road in 1940.

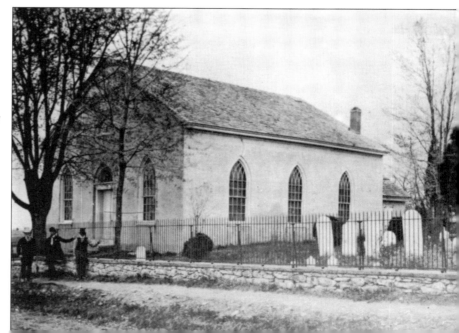

Ardmore was growing after the Civil War. There were 65 houses, 250 inhabitants, 4 stores, but no houses of worship. The village post office was called "Cabinet" and the railroad stop was "Athensville." With no available land near "The Country Church" the trustees of St. Paul's elected to look for a convenient location near the town center. Land at Lancaster Pike west of Church Road was given by Charles Kugler, whose father owned the famous Seven Stars Inn on adjacent property. **1** The "Town Church" *(left)* was dedicated in 1875.

2 The Church Council in 1915 *(left)* with Luther C. Parsons, seated, a devoted St. Paul's member and a church leader for over 50 years.

The ten beautiful turn-of-the-century stained glass windows were relocated from the Lancaster Avenue church to the present church **3** *(below left)*. The Good Shepherd Window **4** *(center)* was dedicated in 1915 to the memory of Sabina Green. Her mother and uncle, John Knox, had given the land for the fifth church. Though the new church had been in the planning stage for many years, it was stalled by the Depression. The dedication was in 1941. The Parsons Bell Tower, right of center, honored its long-time member. It was planned in the 1930s, finally built in 1957. The architecture reflects a Lutheran simplicity.

ST. JOHN'S EPISCOPAL CHURCH. Near Bowman's Bridge, "fronting on the road running from the Merion Turnpike to the Academy," the first service at St. John's was held on August 6, 1863, during the Civil War. The building was of board and batten construction. The church began because seven men, then members of the only Episcopal church in Lower Merion, the Church of the Redeemer in Bryn Mawr, voted that "the demands of this neighborhood require that an Episcopal church be organized without delay..." In 1864, a matching wooden rectory was built and by 1871 a Sunday school building of similar style was erected. In 1878, the Sunday school superintendent, John Marston, instituted Lenten Offerings for Missions. This was the start of Lenten Mite Boxes in Episcopal churches throughout the world. Millions of dollars have been raised over the years. For over 130 years St. John's has been a spiritual presence in Bala Cynwyd. The feelings of love and tolerance for all continue in this congregation today.

1 *(above)* Pen and ink sketch, c.1960, of St. John's Church at 404 Levering Mill Road, Bala Cynwyd, showing native stone church on left, parish house above and to the right of the archway, and rectory on the right. Most of the complex was built c.1900.

2 *(below)* The wooden church school, demolished c.1901. St. John's women and children pose in front, c.1890.

3 *(below right)* Breaking ground for stone St. John's rectory, May 1900. Wooden church building behind was demolished c.1901.

1 (top) Interior view of the wooden St. John's Church, Christmas 1897.

2 (right) Children of St. John's, c.1915, standing in front of Parish House entrance.

3 (below) Photograph of St. John's exquisite interior.

In 1900, the stone church which exists today on Levering Mill Road was begun. Stained glass was done by Nicola d'Ascenzo Studios of Philadelphia and Hardman Studios of Birmingham. In 1938, Dr. Herbert J. Tily donated money to purchase a M.R. Moller organ, still in weekly use. The organ screen and pulpit canopy are of oak, carved by Geog sel Erben of Oberammergau in 1911-12. The pulpit is Caen stone and Siena marble.

Recent charitable activities at St. John's are: preparing and donating food for the needy through Aid for Friends and St. Barnabas Church; parishioners volunteering time and money to an after-school, inner city arts program at St. Gabriel's Mission; participating in Habitat for Humanity; and buying and wrapping Christmas gifts for abused and neglected children in the Norristown area.

BRYN MAWR PRESBYTERIAN CHURCH, founded in 1873, has grown from the original greenstone chapel on unpaved, rural Montgomery Avenue to today's large campus passed daily by thousands. When the 1874 chapel became too small, the redstone church was built in 1886 with a Sunday School Annex added in 1874. Demonstrating a leap of faith, in 1927 parishioners built the present church with seating for twice the membership. The growth continued: 1931, the Education Building; 1940, the Mary Catherine Pew Memorial Chapel; 1964, the Activities Building; and 1990, the Ministries Center which created offices and spaces for large groups as well as incorporating Converse House (manse built for the Mutches) and the Activities Building into a unified whole. But the Bryn Mawr Presbyterian Church is more than a collection of buildings. Its current membership of 3,500 carries on the strong tradition of its 16 founders to be a community of faith that serves the church, the community and the wider world.

1 *(top)* The Bryn Mawr Presbyterian campus in the 1930s before the 1886 redstone church was razed.
2 *(left)* The magnificent sanctuary (pictured during a 1929 wedding) is not only utilized for worship, it is the site of today's more modest weddings, memorial services, musical vespers and forums that explore issues of significance for the vitality and well-being of the larger community.

178

In 1888 the church pledged to directly support two missionaries, one of whom was Dr. William Wanless (**1** *above*). In 1893 he established a clinic in Miraj, India. 106 years later, Bryn Mawr Presbyterian continues to support the Miraj Medical Centre. In addition, the church provides financial assistance to churches and mission workers in health, housing, education, community, and economic projects throughout the world, across the United States, and within the Philadelphia region.

The strength of Bryn Mawr Presbyterian Church lies in its preaching, teaching, music, and ministries to the many groups within the congregation as well as its outreach to the larger community.

2 *(top)* Rev. Andrew Mutch and his family aboard the *Caledonia* enroute to America in 1912. Daughter Ada is on the left.
3 *(above)* Dr. Mutch in later years after he became Pastor Emeritus in 1936.

4 *(above)*. One local project is the Tutoring Program, the oldest continuous volunteer program in the school district of Philadelphia. It brings together 120 elementary children from North Philadelphia and 120 high school tutors from Main Line schools. Since 1965 the program has involved approximately 4400 children, 3900 tutors and over 400 adults. It meets in the church's Education Building.

NOTABLE NEIGHBOR

"I was born in Scotland in 1905...I was seven when we came over to this country. On April 20, 1912, the week after the *Titanic* went down, we sailed from Glasgow to come to Bryn Mawr. We soon realized that we had a different accent from the other children...were very sensitive about it at school. I wondered why I used to get called on so often to answer questions. One of the teachers finally told me, 'I love to hear you talk.' • We came to live in the manse of Bryn Mawr Presbyterian Church...the first occupants of the new house. Father (the Rev. Andrew Mutch) had no way of getting around because in Scotland he had his horse and carriage to do his visiting. So he got a Model T. Ford. It was one you had to hand crank and he soon broke his arm because it kicked on him. • In 1918, we had this awful flu epidemic. It was terrible. People were dying right and left. Bryn Mawr Hospital didn't have enough beds so they decided to take the old Lancaster Inn (it had closed) and turn it into an emergency hospital. My older sister and I went down and volunteered. We scrubbed and got the vegetables ready; at noontime we fed the doctors and nurses lunch; served the tables. In the afternoon the visitors would come and I'd have to get them into gowns and masks. I had to get up on a chair to tie the mask on because they didn't know how. Then I'd take them up to the floors so they could see the member of their family. My father asked the doctor, 'Is there anything we should do or take to keep healthy?' And the doctor said, 'No, just be sure you get enough rest, get enough to eat, and wash your hands all the time when you're doing things.' And not one of our family came down with the flu. • My father and mother were very broadminded. On Friday night, since there were boarding students (next door at the Baldwin School) and my brother was at Haverford College...these friends came to our house. We had an orchestra of our own. So the manse was jazzed up on Friday night; we rolled up the carpets and danced. But on Saturday night we couldn't do that because he was getting ready for Sunday. And Sunday was the only day we were restricted in any way...no piano jazz...no ball games." **Ada Mutch**

[Ms. Mutch taught physical education, six of those years at Baldwin. After an appendix operation, she switched to nursing. Ada trained in New York and when World War II came along, went overseas with the Army. She was in charge of nursing at Headquarters Division in France and, after the war, was director of nursing at Lankenau Hospital.]

THE CHURCH OF SAINT ASAPH. On November 16, 1887, six gentlemen met at Pencoyd, home of George B. Roberts, and became the founding vestry of St. Asaph's Church. They chose Theophilus P. Chandler as architect, and he designed a building **1** *(above)* that resembles St. Asaph Cathedral in Wales, reflecting the origin of the Bala Cynwyd area's first settlers. The Robertses donated land for the church; ground was broken the following spring, interrupted by the "Blizzard of '88." The cornerstone was laid that May, and the Victorian Gothic building rose amid the fields, close to the still unpaved City Line Avenue and the Schuylkill Valley spur of the Pennsylvania Railroad.

2 The congregation worshipped in this temporary frame building *(above)* while the stone church was being built. T. Williams Roberts wrote of his childhood memories of parishioners dodging raindrops from the leaky roof, and of mischievous boys banging the lid of the coalbox during sermons.

3 The rectory *(right)*, was designed by Chandler, built during the summer of 1888 and funded by George B. Roberts in thanksgiving for the birth of his daughter, Miriam. The latter (future Mrs. Spencer Ervin) gave the funds for much of the Gothic embellishment of the church's interior in 1911, and celebrated her 100th birthday the year of the church's centennial.

1 *(left)* St. Asaph's in 1893.

2 *(below)* Chancel with Gothic carving and rood screen, 1943 photo.

The first service in the completed church took place on March 24, 1889. When the first rector, the Rev. Frederick Burgess, arrived in June, the money collected at his first service was sent to the victims of the recent Johnstown flood, beginning a history of outreach that continues to the present day.

St. Asaph's parish has had an active ministry in the 111 plus years since its founding. It has survived the Depression and two world wars, and weathered the liturgical changes in the Episcopal Church at large.

It has reached out to its community, including its close neighbors, Inglis House and Kearsley Home.

It shares its facilities with a Montessori school, a day care nursery and a boy scout troup, and has been home to two Korean congregations in past years. It celebrated its centennial in 1988, with the Dean of St. Asaph Cathedral and the Archdeacon of Wrexham visiting from Wales for the occasion.

It has had seven rectors, two of whom have gone on to become bishops, and two others of whom have each served for 33 years. St. Asaph's seventh and present rector, Ann Broomell, is the first woman to hold that permanent position in the Merion Deanery of the Episcopal Diocese of Pennsylvania.

3 *(above left)* George B. Roberts, first rector's warden, played the leading role in the founding of the church.

4 *(above right)* David Evans Williams, Roberts' brother-in-law, was involved with the church vestry for its first 50 years. Known fondly as "Uncle Dave."

5 *(left)* The parish house was completed and dedicated on October 6, 1891. To provide electric lighting for the evening's celebration, Mr. Albert Stadelman contributed a steam generator.

1 *(above)* Pen and ink drawing of the deceptively simple rubble stone exterior by Philadelphia architect Charles M. Burns, Jr. This view, looking northeast, shows the tower and south porch, important features of a High Victorian Gothic Revival church.

2 *(below)* 1905 photo of the Church of the Redeemer's entrance gates.

When **THE CHURCH OF THE REDEEMER** was established in Lower Merion in 1851 on the "north side of the Lancaster Turnpike, above the eight mile stone," it was the only Episcopal church between Philadelphia and St. David's. The parish quickly outgrew the small stone church, and in the late 1870s the vestry voted to move the burial ground and build a new church on a parcel of land in Bryn Mawr known as the "Parsonage Lot." The land was purchased in 1860 but deemed too costly an acquisition; the vestry tried to sell it. By 1870, they were resigned to its ownership and began to develop the grounds, building a rectory in 1872 and approving a plan for a cemetery in 1878.

In August 1878 N. Parker Shortridge, Chairman of The Committe on Plans, requested "Designs for A Church with Chancel and Tower in the Gothic Style of Architecture." The building was to be made of stone with a brick interior, to comfortably seat "not less than Five Hundred Persons and cost not more than Eighteen thousand dollars, finished complete except the upper Stages of the Tower."

The cornerstone was laid in November 1879 and the building, designed by Charles M. Burns, Jr., was completed in April 1881.

Gothic Revival Interior. From the stencilled ceiling and roof trusses to the polychrome brick walls and polished granite columns, the church epitomizes the ideals of Anglican reform movements.

Architect Burns designed the addition of a choir room in 1891 and he continued to serve the parish, designing various alterations and additions to the buildings through 1905.

In 1910, the west end of the church was enlarged by two bays and included a narthex, or vestibule. This addition, by the Philadelphia architectural firm of Evans, Warner and Bigger was the first of many alterations they would oversee.

Interior Changes. Smooth off-white Caen stone walls in the chancel, added in 1928, obscure the colored brick and tiles of the Burns era. This same stone marks the entrance to the Baptistery and defines the west wall, with its two colorful memorial windows. Decorative stained glass from several different periods and by many makers, including Tiffany, add to the overall visual appeal of the church.

A Classic Assemblage. The buildings and cemetery of The Church of the Redeemer give mute testimony to the enduring appeal of familiar architectural forms in tranquil settings and serve as reminders of the changing needs of parish communities.

1 *(above left)* Burns' 1881 drawing of the interior; view toward the east. **2** *(above right)* Photograph of the nave, c.1970.

3 *(left)* The cemetery and rear view of the church, showing later additions.

4 The rectory, or parsonage, probably designed by Philadelphian Addison Hutton; completed in 1872 and enlarged in 1914 by Evans, Warner and Bigger.

183

1 1922 postcard view of St. Matthias, the rectory at left.

2 *(above)* The original St. Matthias School, built of native stone to match the church and rectory. A convent for the Sisters of Mercy had the same architectural character. A new parish school was built in 1971.

3 *(right)* The sanctuary showing the 1930s ornamentation with the statuary and paintings added to the 1908 interior.

SAINT MATTHIAS. At the turn of the century, as Lower Merion suburban communities developed around station stops of the Pennsylvania Railroad, so did the religious institutions conveniently locate their parish churches. Typical of this growth pattern is St. Matthias Roman Catholic Church which was founded by Archbishop John Ryan on February 2, 1906. The first Mass was celebrated by Father Michael McCabe, the founding pastor, on February 2nd at the Lonergan home on Union Avenue and Conshocken State Road.

1 (left) Father Michael McCabe, the founding pastor. Rector from 1906 to 1918.

2 (center) His brother, Luke McCabe, followed him as pastor from 1918 to 1930.

3 (right) Sister M. Paula, beloved longtime principal of St. Matthias Parish School.

A New Parish. Following a generous gift of property on Bryn Mawr and Highland Avenues from John E. Lonergan, ground was broken and the cornerstone for the new parish church laid in October 1906. The church and rectory were designed by George I. Lovett and was the first example in the Archdiocese of Philadelphia of the monastery church style of the 12th and 13th centuries.

The new church was dedicated on November 8, 1908 by Archbishop Ryan. It was renovated in 1931 at which time the mural paintings were placed there.

The parish school and convent for the Sisters of Mercy were later built in the same picturesque architectural style, lending themselves to the beautiful suburban area. Total enrollment at that time: 19 pupils.

In the Chapel of the Crucified Christ (on the side of the church) are buried the first two pastors of the parish: Father Michael J. McCabe, the founding pastor, served from 1908 to 1918; his brother, Father Luke V. McCabe served the parish community from 1918 to 1930.

4 (above) May Procession, 1956, in Mary's Month.

5 (left) The first grade, 1955.

THE AFRICAN AMERICAN COMMUNITY. For generations African Americans relied on the church for leadership. Black churches led the struggle for human rights when African Americans were disenfranchised, unable to rely on politicans. As black people began migrating into the Ardmore community in the late 19th century, they were invited to worship at a local white Baptist church, located at Lancaster Avenue and Woodside Road. From 1875 to 1893, blacks and whites attended church together; children attended communal Sunday School services. As the black members of this church became more numerous, plans were made to create a separate facility; the Zion Baptist Church was chartered in 1894.

1 *(below)* Front view, c.1950, of Zion Baptist. The church is comfortably nestled within the residential community of South Ardmore. Earlier in the century, an addition to the existing facade gave the church its magnificent presence.

ZION BAPTIST CHURCH

Late in the last century, a meeting was called at the home of Caroline Strother to organize a new church for worship by blacks. Shortly thereafter, in March 1894, Zion Baptist Church was chartered under the auspices of Mother Zion Baptist Church of Philadelphia.

Until moving into their present site (West Spring Avenue in Ardmore), Zion's congregation met in a 10x15 foot room in a small frame building generously supplied by the First Baptist Church, located on the northeast corner of Cricket Avenue. Later in 1894, for the sum of $1,500, a 90x263 foot lot housed a 27x60 foot building utilized for worship until 1899.

During that time, worshippers undertook a massive construction project, completing work on a $7,000 addition (quite a sum in those days). The original frame building, used as a chapel upon completion of the addition, continued to serve members until it was destroyed by fire in 1913.

Since being chartered, Zion has enjoyed the service of nine Reverends and is presently led by Pastor James A. Pollard, Jr. Having recently celebrated its 100th anniversary in 1995, Zion continues as a beacon of light for the hard-working residents of South Ardmore.

1 *(above left)* Zion Baptist Sanctuary in 1981. The pulpit in Baptist churches is in the center of the chapel as a symbol that God is at the center...the focus...of the religious experience. The church choir normally sings to the right of the pulpit where musicians also perform. The altar is staged below the pulpit; holy communion is served during regular service every fourth Sunday in Baptist churches.

2 *(above)* Youth choir, c.1950s. Music is an integral part of the black church experience. Hymns are usually sung throughout services, with several choirs leading the congregation in song. Musicians often accompany choirs in renditions of spirituals. Song inspires an emotional release among members of the congregation, encouraging a joyous religious experience.

3 *(above)* Walnut Avenue view of Mt. Calvary in 1909. The original design of the church was disallowed at the call of protesting white neighbors. Current design plans are based on the original plans and would allow the church more room to build. Renovations added a larger entryway to make it easier for caskets to be brought into the chapel for funeral services.

MOUNT CALVARY BAPTIST CHURCH

Mount Calvary (Walnut Avenue in Ardmore) was organized during a meeting at the home of Mrs. Flora Woodson of Simpson Road, Ardmore, in January of 1906. First services were held later in that month under the direction of Reverend E. Luther Cunningham, who served for two years. The church gained official recognition shortly thereafter (April 1906) by unanimous vote of the Baptist Churches of Philadelphia and Vicinity.

Since establishment, nine reverends have accepted the pastorate. Of these men, Reverend F. M. Hedgeman had served the longest: 1913 to 1953! During his long tenure, the church grew in size and relevance in the Ardmore community; a new church was erected and dedicated (the mortgage was retired after only nine years), a new entrance and additional Sunday School facilities were added and a new pipe organ was installed.

1 *(above)* Sunday School 1956. Sunday School is an important way for youth to learn the Christian faith in a classroom setting. Learned adult members of the congregation serve as teachers; with the assistance of clergy, lessons are planned to introduce children to the Bible. Prayer and song complement the lessons.

Mount Calvary is presently led by Pastor Albert Gladstone Davis, Jr. Under his leadership, many new and successful programs have been instituted, including the Board of Christian Education, Christmas Candlelight Services, Holy Week Services and the Parents Ministry Group, which works to address issues in local schools.

Having recently celebrated their 90th anniversary in 1996, Mount Calvary boasts a steadily growing congregation of more than 300 members.

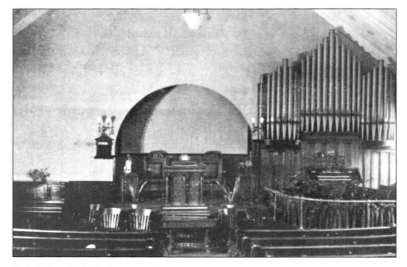

2 *(left)* Rev. F.M. Hedgeman who served as Mount Calvary's pastor for forty years. Under his leadership, church membership grew and capital improvements increased the physical capacity of the chapel.
3 *(above)* 1937 view of the interior. The pipe organ, originally installed, has since been removed. The magnificent ceiling was plaster-crafted by hand and contains a beautiful artistic canvas.

ST. LUKE UNITED METHODIST CHURCH. The first recorded meeting of area Methodists was in 1778, just as our nation was gaining its independence. That prayer service was held in the James Mansion House in Rosemont. A Class Meeting, in 1780, led to the founding of the log church in Radnor, known as "Methodist Hill." A few other infant congregations shared pastors who served the "circuit." The 1876 Centennial and the Pennsylvania Railroad's expansion of settlement in the area led the Methodists to build a more convenient house of worship in Bryn Mawr. Dedicated in 1879, the building cost $8,700. Originally called Bryn Mawr Chapel, the church was given the name St. Luke, beloved physician of the Bible and to honor the noted family of local physicians, the Andersons. In 1962, the "new" St. Luke sanctuary was consecrated. The church continues, after 200 years, to minister to the spiritual needs and fellowship of its people and the surrounding communities.

1 *(above)* The first St. Luke, built in 1879.
2 *(below)* Aerial view of St. Luke's and its grounds, The original church, now a chapel, is seen below the 1962 church.

THE JEWISH COMMUNITY. While it is true that most of the Main Line was originally comprised of people who were both Christian and white, in time certain minorities began to grow. Here, in territory that was founded in the 1680s and was steeped in Quakerism and Protestantism, a flourishing Jewish community has emerged. Beginning in 1884, the emigration of the Harrison family from Lithuania signaled a change, a change mirrored by communities as diverse as those in New York City and Auburn, Maine. Devoted to their faith, Jews worshipped in their homes until 1936 when the Main Line Hebrew Association was chartered. The houses of worship which ensued exhibit some of the finest modern architecture in the region.

1 *(right)* **Main Line Reform Temple-Beth Elohim (Reform).** Founded in 1952, the Temple is housed in a circular structure that was designed by Matthew B. Ehrlich and Ezekiel Levinson. It is the only Main Line congregation to have been founded by a woman, Mrs. Natalie Lansing Hodes, who headed a group of 16 families. It was dedicated in 1961. The stained glass windows were designed by Gabriel Loire, of Chartes, France. The Star of David, illuminated by the roof skylight, was designed by Joseph J. Greenberg, Jr., who also created the gold leaf ark and menorah in the structure's artistic interior.

2 *(right)* **Temple Beth Hillel-Beth El (Conservative).** It was founded in 1958 by 18 families meeting in the den of Frances and Gerald Chalal's home. Their structure, designed by Norman N. Rice, was built in 1965, dedicated in 1968. It resembles the Bath Houses in Trenton, designed by Louis I. Kahn, a classmate of Rice's. Constructed of Bermuda brick and concrete, it consists of three squares and a dome. The interior of the sanctuary is in modified Sephardic style with the pews facing an open court.

1 *(left)* **Temple Adath Israel of the Main Line (Conservative).** A rooftop cupola and a 12-sided structure serve as the centerpiece of Lower Merion's pioneer Jewish congregation. Their roots date to March 1936, the founding of the Main Line Hebrew Association by ten local businessmen. That original charter was amended in 1947. The structure, built in 1958-59, was designed by world renowned architect Pietro Belluschi and his associate, Charles Frederick Wise. It symbolizes the 12 tribes of Israel. The interior is dramatic, containing a screen on the bimah (altar) designed by noted sculptor George Kratina, an ark with sterling silver lettering and a unique candelabra. The base of the cupola forms a Star of David.

2 *(left)* **Lower Merion Synagogue (Orthodox).** Founded in 1954 by a small number of families, it is the Township's original orthodox congregation. It has always been known for "the spirit of its dedication to the perpetuation of authentic Jewish values." Two sanctuaries are both in use; the newer one, built in 1980 and designed by Gordon K. Palmer, is simplistic, preserving the traditional conventions of Judaism. The reading desk is in the center of the room and the ark is in the front...its doors symbolizing the gates of heaven. The main floor seats the men of the congregation, while elevated areas flanking the main floor form the Ezrat Nashim...the women's gallery, tribunal, or courtyard, like synagogues in days of old.

3 *(left)* **Har Hazaitim Cemetery.** Located on Greaves Lane off Conshocken State Road in Gladwyne is Lower Merion's only Jewish burial ground. It dates from 1893, when 15 beneficial associations purchased a site that had been a quarry to provide a dignified burial in accordance with Jewish law. The cemetery has been inactive since 1945. A nearby congregation has since assumed responsibility for it and will form a non-profit corporation for its care.

1 *(above)* View of the original part of St. Charles Borromeo Seminary built in 1871. Architects Addison Hutton and Samuel Sloan designed this building which reunited the preparatory college and theology divisions.

2 *(above)* Original farmhouse (1860s) still located on the campus. This house was part of the purchases in Lower Merion made by Archbishop James F. Wood, starting in 1863.

SAINT CHARLES BORROMEO SEMINARY was founded in 1832 by the Most Reverend Francis P. Kenrick, third Bishop of Philadelphia. The initial location of the Seminary was the home of Bishop Kenrick on Fifth Street in Philadelphia. Circumstances dictated the subsequent moves to the northwest corner of Fifth and Prune (now Locust) Streets, to St. Mary's Rectory on Fourth Street, and eventually to the southeast corner of Eighteenth and Race Streets in Philadelphia. For an 11-year period the preparatory division of the Seminary was located at Glen Riddle in Delaware County, Pennsylvania. In 1863, Archbishop James F. Wood made the first of three purchases of property just outside Philadelphia in Overbrook. Today these purchases in Lower Merion Township comprise the Seminary campus.

Architects Addison Hutton and Samuel Sloan designed the building where the preparatory college and theology divisions were reunited in September 1871. In December 1875, the Chapel of the Immaculate Conception was formally dedicated by Archbishop Wood. Subsequent Archbishops of Philadelphia have made improvement on the campus: Archbishop Patrick J. Ryan: Library (1911); Archbishop Edmond Prendergast: student residence hall; Dennis Cardinal Dougherty: the college building as you enter the main gates; John Cardinal O'Hara: indoor swimming pool; John Cardinal Krol: residence hall for theology students and multi-purpose building dedicated to St. John Vianney (1971). The buildings that consist of the current Theology Division and the Ryan Memorial Library stand at the western end of the campus. The Seminary College is located at the eastern end.

1 *(below)* Open house at St. Charles Seminary (1999).

2 *(below)* Aerial view (1930s) of the grounds of the Seminary bordering Lancaster Avenue and Wynnewood Road. The original buildings are to the left in the photo and the large college building and St. Martin's Chapel to the right.

3 *(below)* Interior view of Immaculate Conception Chapel, formally dedicated by Archbishop Wood in 1875.

Mission. The fundamental mission of Saint Charles Borromeo Seminary is the formation of Catholic men of the Archdiocese of Philadelphia, of other dioceses, and of religious communities for pastoral service in the Roman Catholic priesthood. The Seminary is committed to providing a unified college and theology program of formation in priestly spirituality, pastoral ministry, celibate witness, emotional maturity, intellectual integrity, and physical wellness.

This program is complemented by personal and community prayer, a comprehensive academic program of liberal arts and theological studies, and a program of pastoral preparation designed primarily for parochial ministry.

Offering its resources to the larger church community through its Religious Studies Division, the Seminary provides a variety of academic and pastoral programs to serve the needs and interests of priests, deacons, and the religious in parochial and other ministries, other parish ministers, teachers of religion and interested lay persons. The Seminary is committed to serving the need for on-going formation and preparation for pastoral ministry.

1 *(left)* Early engraving of the Seminary from the 1870s.

Structure. The seminary is a fully accredited college and graduate school of theology. It consists of three divisions: College, Theology, and Religious Studies. Potential candidates for the Roman Catholic priesthood pursue a program which consists of a four-year liberal arts curriculum followed by a four-year curriculum within the professional school of theology. The seminary offers the degrees of Bachelor of Arts, Master of Divinity, and Master of Arts.

Seminarians of the Archdiocese of Philadelphia and several other dioceses participate in the College Division's Spirituality Year Program in Northampton, Pennsylvania as part of the normal preparation for the Theology Division. These programs are envisioned as parts of a single uniform program of formation for the priesthood which gives the Seminary its distinct identity.

In addition to its responsibility for the formation of candidates for the Roman Catholic priesthood, the Seminary also serves as a center of theological education for laity and the religious in the Greater Philadelphia area and around the country. Its Religious Studies Division conducts evening and summer courses on both the graduate and undergraduate levels in Catholic theology, Sacred Scripture, and related fields. The Religious Studies Division offers a fully accredited Master of Arts Degree Program. All programs are designed to foster greater knowledge and deeper appreciation of the Catholic faith and keener awareness of the religious needs of all men and women.

Examples of art work in the Seminary's Collection:
2 *(top left)* Monsignor Patrick J. Garvey by Thomas Eakins.
3 *(top right)* Archbishop James F. Wood by Thomas Eakins.
4 *(above left)* Archbishop Jean Jadot by Alice Neel.
5 *(above right)* John Cardinal Krol by Philip Pearlstein.

1 *(below)* Interior view of St. Martin's Chapel.

Within the Larger Community. The campus provides the setting for numerous activities in the course of the year. While not directly related to the Seminary program, events such as prayer meetings, clerical and professional conferences, alumni reunions, vocation weekends and a summer camp for children give evidence of the Seminary's spirit of openness for the sake of service. In addition, a number of Archdiocesan offices have been located on campus: the Vocations Office for Diocesan Priesthood, Family Life Office and the Office for the Permanent Diaconate and Church Ministry Training Program. The various educational projects and workshops conducted on campus together with the services that the Ryan Memorial Library extends to the larger community create a spirit of vitality and outreach for the Seminary.

MEMORIES

"My great grandfather, James, and his brother, Michael, were saddlery and harness makers and in 1881 they owned 300 acres in Penn Valley, which we inherited. Father used to go out monthly to visit Mr. Stretch, who was the tenant farmer on the property, to collect the rent. Mr. Stretch was a dairy farmer. Mother never liked to come out here because there were only about two roads and the roads were awful. Just mud heaps. • Our home was built in 1899 and in every room of the house we had combination fixtures, both gas and electric. Electricity was expensive. Gas was not. So every evening a maid would go around with a taper and light all the gas lights in the common rooms and halls. Later on, if we were all in one room, the gas would be put out and we'd put on the electric lights ...but they were sort of a luxury. • What boys liked to do in my youth? Of course, in the wintertime it was sledding...we went over to the hills on property of the Overbrook Golf Club. My brothers and I had wind-up trains, large gauge known as 1 or G-gauge today, and at this time our family had no live-in maids. So there was an empty room and this is where I would have my trains because it took a whole room. And my friends would come over, and they all had modern electric trains, Lionel standard-gauge. They didn't have any use for wind-up trains because they'd go around three or four times and then you'd have to pick up the engine and wind it up again. After a bit I got some O-gauge trains so I could compete more favorably. And this started my interest in trains. So I'm a little boy who never grew up." **George Magee**

[George Magee is married to Betty Wynne, a direct descendant of Dr. Thomas Wynne, physician to William Penn. Before he retired, George had a publishing business and later was proprietor of a hobby shop featuring electric trains. His collection of trains ranges from coffee table size to giant ones.]

2 *(above)* The focus of life at St. Charles is to prepare for the priesthood. An example of the social life is seen in this photo of street hockey.

THE REVOLUTION TOUCHES LOWER MERION

In 1776, the capital city of the colonies was Philadelphia. In 1777, George Washington moved his army south from the Hudson River tracking British General Howe who had embarked his army to sail south and enter Chesapeake Bay where they landed at Elkton (then known as Head of Elk) and headed into Pennsylvania.

Washington and Howe and their two armies clashed at Brandywine Creek on September 11, 1777, and Washington's men lost to the redcoats. The Americans retreated toward Philadelphia, crossed the Schuylkill, avoided the town, moved north, camped near Falls of Schuylkill and Indian Queen Lane for a day's rest, then on to Roxborough/Manayunk.

The Continentals in Lower Merion. On Sunday, September 14, Washington's army waded the Schuylkill at Levering's Ford (near today's Belmont/Green Lane Bridge). Before dark they climbed the hill, followed Meeting House Lane, entered the road to Lancaster just behind Merion Friends meetinghouse, turned right and deployed into open fields for the night.

Officers probably slept at the Buck Tavern (on Lancaster Avenue where Haverford and Bryn Mawr merge) about three miles ahead. Next day, September 15, General Washington at the Buck wrote a letter to Congress pleading for supplies. Help was not likely; congressmen were packing to flee west to Lancaster then to York where the Continental Congress would reside September 30 to June 27, 1778. Washington continued his march west partly to deflect the British from a supply depot at Reading.

Two Minor Battles, Then Came Germantown! If reconstruction of events is correct, the British and Americans clashed in the first battle after Brandywine on September 16 outside of Lower Merion Township, near White Horse tavern off Goshenville Road. It was the "Battle of the

1 1876 Centennial engraving depicts one of the Revolutionary soldiers.

Clouds" when torrential rain wet ammunition and the patriots again bowed in defeat.

The next encounter in the same vicinity, known as the Paoli Massacre, occurred September 20. General Wayne and 1,500 men on a mission apart from the main army met disaster, with many killed. Discouragement for Washington culminated on October 4 with the Battle of Germantown when autumn fog fouled plans, and the Americans lost again. Meanwhile, the British were happily ensconced in Philadelphia.

Lower Merion: No-Man's Land. In such fine country as the Welsh Tract, lying as it did between two enemy armies during the War for Independence, its farmers did not escape the forced requirements of both the British and the Americans, each side

helping itself freely to food for men and hay for horses.

Lower Merion became a no-man's land that neither side controlled and was repeatedly raided by foraging parties. Some said the British were more welcome to the goods because they paid in cash, whereas the colonials paid only in notes or orders which were usually quite worthless.

It is true that the American forces were more demanding of the Quakers as several severe orders came from Valley Forge aimed at the farmers who wouldn't fight and were accused of being Tories. These Welshmen were not people who went out and publicly defended or fought for a cause. In their quiet and dignified manner they favored the patriots, but the Society of Friends preached non-violence and the elders, at least, opposed any active part in the war.

Younger Quakers, however, were not so strict in their views. Many served in the Philadelphia County Militia (their Seventh Battalion was recruited in Upper and Lower Merion) and many young men gave up membership in the Society of Friends so they could fight against British tyranny.

Cornwallis vs. The Militia in Lower Merion. It was the search for "necessaries of life" that created the only other Revolutionary War episode in Lower Merion. While Washington's men camped at Whitemarsh in November-December 1777 recuperating from losses in the Battle of Germantown, forage parties prowled on both sides of the Schuylkill for both armies. Pennsylvania militiamen were posted in Lower Merion to keep the enemy at bay.

1 Troops rest along the way through Lower Merion.

The morning of December 11, 1777, Washington ordered his army to leave Whitemarsh and march down to Matson's Ford (Conshohocken) to cross the river on a makeshift bridge of wagons to regroup in the Gulph ("hollow between hills") and move thence to Valley Forge. Apparently by coincidence that same day, early in the morning, General Cornwallis and 1,500 (numbers vary) dragoons left Philadelphia on a foraging expedition into Lower Merion.

Following is a report by patriot General James Potter of what happened:

> "Last Thursday, the enemy march out of the City with a desire to Furridge; but it was necessary to drive me out of the way; my advanced picquet fired on them at the Bridge; another party of one Hundred attacked them at the Black Hors [Black Horse Inn, Old Lancaster Road and City Avenue]. I was encamped at Charles Thompson's place [Harriton House] where I stacconed the Regiments who attacked with Viger. On the next hill I stacconed three Regiments, letting the first line know that when they were overpowered the(y) must retreat and form behind the second line, and in that manner we formed and Retreated for four miles; and on every Hill we disputed the matter with them. My people Behaved wel...."

But the day was conclusively lost when patriot General Sullivan, engaged in moving divisions across the makeshift bridge toward the Gulph, looked up at the hills (where his scouts had spotted redcoats chasing Potter's men) and, uncertain of enemy numbers, decided to withdraw.

The infuriated Potter wrote:

> "Had the valant Solovan covered my retreat with the two Devissions of the army he had in my rear, my men could have rallied, but he gave orders for them to retreat and join the army who were on the other side of the Schuylkill...about a mile and a half from me...[this left the enemy to] plunder the Country, which they have done without parsiality or favour to any, leave none of Nesscereys of life Behind them that they conveniantly could carry or destroy."

Of the episode, Washington wrote "...we...intended to pass the Schuylkill at Madisons (Matson's) Ford where a bridge has been laid across the river." But based on "best accounts we have...4,000 men under Lord Cornwallis, possessing themselves of the heights of the road leading from the River and the defile called the Gulph..." it was deemed too great a risk to proceed.

Instead, Washington directed his army, 11,000 men, to cross the river farther upstream at Swedes Ford (Norristown), and march back to Gulph Mills. By the time they arrived, the British marauders had vanished back to the balls and dinners of Philadelphia.

Tradition says that Cornwallis returned along Gulph Road as far as Harriton, then found his way to Haverford Road and spent the night at Pont Reading, house of the Humphreys family. Meanwhile, Washington and his men bivouacked in the hollow of the Gulph from December 13 to 19, 1777, and from there marched to Valley Forge.

1 *(top)* 1900 photo shows Hanging Rock with Griffith's Mill in the background.

2 *(center)* Recent painting by local artist Robert Knight shows the troops' retreat through Gulph Mills toward Valley Forge.

3 *(below)* The hard winter at Valley Forge.

THE CIVIL WAR ERA IN LOWER MERION

To Arms! To Arms!
The Rebels Are At Your Doors!!!
*Men of Pennsylvania, your homes are in
actual danger. Your harvests are to feed
rebel invaders unless you arouse to save
them by driving back the ruthless invader.
Already they have made desolate one of the
fairest valleys of our good commonwealth.
Up then! Drive the invaders back!*
*Companies of sharp shooters are
wanted from our mountains, and mounted
infantry from our farmers to find their own
horses for the use of which they will receive
40 cents per day and paid for if killed,
injured or lost.*

Arouse! Arouse!
A.G. Curtin
Governor and
Commander-In-Chief

Volunteers Recruited. The Main
Line was alarmed by the approaching
Confederates and Philadelphia threw
up earth fortifications (especially at
the site of the 30th Street Station) and
dug trenches. The above call-to-arms
was issued by Governor Andrew
Gregg Curtin *(2 right)* just before the
battle of Gettysburg.

In April 1861, President Lincoln issued orders for a militia to
defend the capitol at Washington and
75,000 volunteers to put down the
rebellion. Pennsylvania's Gov. Curtin
relayed the call to the cities, the
towns, and the villages in his state.
Lower Merion men were eager to
respond. Most of the enlistees were
farmers' sons.

The state legislature passed
an act for the organization of the Re-
serve Volunteer Corps to consist of 15
regiments: 13 of infantry, one of cav-

alry, one of artillery. The men were to
be enlisted for three years.

Complying with the act,
prominent Lower Merion citizen
Owen Jones (1819-1878) began raising a company of cavalry, the first unit
the county sent to the army.

Lower Merion was a good
field for cavalry recruiting, since a
large part of the population was
accustomed to dealing with horses.
Recruits were mustered into service
in August 1861 at Athensville (the
former name of Ardmore).

Owen Jones became a Ma-
jor, then Colonel, and the regiment
saw vigorous service with the Army
of the Potomac and in the Shenandoah
Valley.

Discharge Center. While the war
was at its height, and the terms of
many of the first enlistments were ex-
piring, the U.S. government established the state's mustering-out camp
in Lower Merion in October 1864.
The site selected was a summit on the

west bank of the Schuylkill. The post
bordered the locale of today's Riverbend Environmental Education Center off Spring Mill Road in Gladwyne.

The area was at the crown of
the hill above the houses on Kritner's
Farm. The outlook commandeered a
view down the Schuylkill River to
Flat Rock, the Whitemarsh valley,
and, in the other direction, a ridge
with a view of Bryn Mawr beyond.

A large group of men lev-
elled the rough, uneven surface. They
then constructed a quadrangle of
buildings with a parade ground facing the river. Water was piped from
an old spring near Hanna's Farm and
transportation was over the Reading
Railroad on the east bank of the river.
A large sentry box *(3 below)* served
as the camp's Schuylkill entrance.

One month later (Novem-
ber 1864) the camp was ready for the
reception of soldiers. It was chris-
tened Camp Spring Mill, but later
known as Camp Discharge.

Many of the men being mustered out came from Andersonville
and other southern prisons and hospitals and were in sick and miserable
condition. Their records were put in
order and pay was prepared as they
recovered their health prior to discharge. No man was released until he
was well, properly clothed, and provided for.

In July 1865, with the end of
the war, the War Department dis-
banded the post.

NOTABLE NEIGHBOR

Eldridge Reeves Johnson (1867-1945). You may not remember the Victrola, once a synonym for "phonograph," but you may recognize Nipper, the dog, listening to "His Master's Voice," trademark then and now of RCA-Victor. • Eldridge Johnson of Dover, Delaware, was once considered too stupid for college and was apprenticed to a machine repair shop in Philadelphia. There he devised for the Berliner Gramophone, rival of Edison's invention, a spring-driven motor to play a flat disc instead of a cylinder, with a governor to control the speed of revolution, and improved sound reproduction. Many patents later, in 1901, age 34, Johnson became president of the Victor Talking Machine Company and his factory in Camden began selling world-wide a huge selection of styles of his record player.
• In 1903 he, Elsie his wife, and Fenimore their only child, moved to Merion on part of the Baird estate. By 1919 he was one of the most heavily taxed (read: richest) men in the nation, owner of yachts, benefactor of the University Museum in Philadelphia where he served as board chairman. To that museum he gave Chinese treasures and helped fund archaeological excavations. Later he established the Johnson Foundation for Research in Medical Physics at the University of Pennsylvania, gave the Free Library and Deaconess Home in Camden, the Community church in Dover, the Moorestown, N.J. Community House, and the Merion War Tribute House in Merion.

1 Eldridge Johnson. **2** "The Chimneys," razed to build Merion Tribute House.

THE MERION TRIBUTE HOUSE. One week after the Armistice ended World War I in 1918, a committee in Merion voted to consider a "Peace Memorial Community House." By the following April subscriptions were coming in slowly. Civic Association board members were urged to underwrite the fund, and five dances at the Overbrook Golf Club were planned to raise money. Suddenly two "angels" materialized in the form of Mr. and Mrs. Eldridge Reeves Johnson, residents of Merion, made rich by his very popular Victrola and wax records to play on it, products of the Victor Talking Machine Company (later sold to RCA). America and the world danced to Victrola's music. The Johnsons offered to give their house, carriage house, and $250,000 to cover design and construction of a new building and to double the $70,000 already collected as an endowment. It was estimated that maintenance of the Tribute House would cost $7,089 per year, and income from the fund would be $7,150. The Johnsons' gifts were accepted with gratitude, and the deed of trust was handed to the newly organized Merion Community Association as trustees, in May 1922. The Johnsons thereafter moved to New Jersey to be nearer his Victrola plant.

3 Memorial plaques and military symbols in the main hall.

1 *(top)* The Tribute House from the front.
2 *(below left)* The Lounge, c.1927, a comfortable gathering place for teas, socials and meetings. **3** *(below right)* The Legion Room, c.1932, a sanctuary for American Legion Post 545 members (Merion World War I veterans for whom the building was dedicated).

Local architects Livingston Smith and Walter Karcher, who lost a son in the war, went to work and developed a set of plans. Edward Bok, president of the Civic Association, with only a tinge of jealousy perhaps, declared the drawings "so ornate, so palatial...I cannot endorse or recommend them," which delayed matters. But Johnson's son, Fenimore, insisted on this "most beautiful structure of its kind" and ended the argument.

The old Johnson house, The Chimneys, was demolished. The driveway of the original house was partially preserved, a massive granite front step became the lintel over the door from the porte-cochere in the new building, and the limestone balustrade of the Johnson home was transferred to the new flagstone terrace. Stone for the building was shaped on site, unusual in modern times and mullions and jambs were

1 *(below)* Edward Bok.

NOTABLE NEIGHBOR

Edward Bok (1863-1930) came as a boy from the Netherlands to Brooklyn, New York and steadily advanced without much more than a primary education, to become smart, rich, generous, bossy, famous and most importantly for our purpose, a resident of Lower Merion.
• Selected by Cyrus Curtis to edit his popular Ladies' *Home Journal* in Philadelphia, Edward wooed, and later won, 15-year old Mary Louise Curtis, built her a house in Merion and fathered two worthy sons, Curtis (later a judge) and Cary. Mary Louise, when domestic life became less demanding, founded the Curtis Institute of Music in 1924.• For thirty years editor of America's most significant women's magazine, Edward Bok recruited famous authors for articles, including Theodore Roosevelt, who in the course of time wrote a pamphlet, "Model Merion" to boost his friend's Merion Civic Association, originally organized in Bok's living room. Mary Louise's devotion to music prompted Edward's first philanthropic efforts, following his many World War charities, namely his fifteen year campaign to place the Philadelphia Orchestra on firm financial footing. He was the quintessential man of influence for improving things. • *The Americanization of Edward Bok,* a glowing autobiography, won the author a Pulitzer Prize in 1921. That done, Bok established the Philadelphia Award of $10,000 given annually to a contributor to the community (examples: Leopold Stokowski, conductor; Russell H. Conwell, founder of Temple University; Samuel Yellin, artisan) and, finally, the American Peace Award (a.k.a. the "Bok Peace Prize") for a practicable plan to achieve and preserve world peace. • His final resting place is now a National Historic Landmark: Bok Tower Gardens, 157 acres in central Florida, a sanctuary of music, flowers, birdsong and beauty to this very day.

2 *(top)* Community Red Cross Ladies roll bandages in the Tribute House Legion Room during World War II. **3** *(below)* A horse drawn snow plow clears a path on a Merion Street in 1923 to assist homeowners with snow removal. The Merion Civic Association began this service in 1913 and continued it for 30 years.

cut by hand. The tower is embellished by three lifesize figures in high relief: a soldier, a sailor and a marine in battle dress. Below, in the main hall, memorial plaques list men of Merion who served in both wars.

On May 12, 1924, the Tribute House was dedicated. The building was conceived as a gathering place for the residential community around it, with a tearoom and a small kitchen, meeting rooms, ballroom/ movie theater/concert hall with organ and, outside, a playground. A director originally lived in the bunga-low built behind the parking area, now rented, and Scouts still use the old carriage house.

Today the tearoom, organ and movie projectors are gone, while weddings, corporate gatherings, bar mitzvahs and occasions of all sorts are celebrated by renters from miles around and community service meetings are frequent. Air conditioning makes for pleasant summer use and two fireplaces lend atmosphere in winter. The Merion Tribute House hosts more than two hundred events each year.

The Services

THREE TOWNSHIP TREASURES. Lower Merion owns and maintains three beautiful old buildings that span a period from the early 1700s to the late 1800s. Appleford, Ashbridge House and the Bryn Mawr Community Building are used for offices of various nonprofit groups in the Township and are available to rent for meetings, community events and social occasions.

1 *(above)* Appleford, 1728 portion.
2 *(center)* rear. **3** *(below)* A parlor.

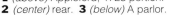

APPLEFORD

A beautiful 22 acre Villanova estate, Appleford (named for the surrounding apple orchards) started as a simple, one-and-a-half story stone farmhouse, built in 1728. A two-story section was added in 1780. In 1798 the next owner, prosperous Peter Pechin, increased the building further and located his tannery in a separate outbuilding.

In 1867, Moro Phillips, a Philadelphian in the chemical and fertilizer business, bought the property for $15,375. The family soon amassed over 800 acres in Villanova. This 113 acre estate was inherited by the son, Frederick Phillips, and then the ownership passed to Samuel G. Smyth in the early 1900s.

Subsequent owners, Anabel and Lewis Parsons, contracted an important colonial revival architect, R. Brognard Okie, to integrate and expand the estate in 1926-27. Earlier stone work was replicated; wood siding and partially stuccoed stone facade is characteristic of Okie's "colonial" style.

In the 1930s an important landscape architect, Thomas Sears, worked with the Parsons to design the gardens and recapture the formal setting seen today. Upon Mrs. Parson's death in 1973, she passed Appleford to Lower Merion Township as a perpetual trust.

203

1 The Ashbridge estate in an early 1900's photo.
2 *(below)* Ashbridge today.

ASHBRIDGE HOUSE

Built of multi-colored field stones with Georgian period proportions, Ashbridge House was erected in 1769 by Rees Thomas III and his father, William. A datestone above the present front porch, marks the event with their names and their wives' initials: "E" for William's wife, Elizabeth and "P" for Rees' wife, Priscilla. The house rested on part of an original land grant of 625 acres purchased by the grandfather, Rees Thomas after 1683.

By 1845, George Dunn had purchased the house and 155 acres. Five years later, Peter Pechin bought the property at "public vendu." Pechin's daughter, Rebecca Emily, inherited the farm and married Joshua Ashbridge. The Ashbridges subsequently purchased other nearby acres from the Thomas heirs.

Around 1863, Joshua gave land for a passenger station to the Pennsylvania Railroad to be named Rosemont. Through the generosity of their daughter, Emily Ashbridge, the house and grounds were left to Lower Merion Township in 1940. The grounds and specimen trees are a memorial to the soldiers of World Wars I and II who were from the community.

The Township provides space for the Library and Museum of the Lower Merion Historical Society on the sceond floor of Ashbridge House. The first floor is used as a public meeting place for groups in the Township.

The story of Ashbridge House parallels the stages of growth in Lower Merion Township. From large holdings of Welsh Quaker settlers in the 17th and 18th centuries, the land has systematically been divided by future generations. A few estates, such as Ashbridge, are now prized for their open space and their use by the whole community.

1 *(above)* The Black's spring-house, in the rear, today houses the Lower Merion office of the Montgomery County Office of Aging and Adult Services.

2 *(left)* The Upland estate as it appeared in a c. 1896 photo.

SAMUEL BLACK'S UPLAND

The Bryn Mawr Community Building was once the estate of Samuel Anderson Black (1820-1890), a major owner of farmland in this and surrounding counties. A prosperous lawyer, he was long associated with the Pennsylvania Railroad. Black himself designed the gracious stone home he called Upland, near the corner of Bryn Mawr and Lancaster Avenues. Much admired, it was hailed as one of the first "modern" residences in town.

A generous man, he gave both a new house and land to many of his relatives, a descendant reported. After his death, his estate (on four acres with two outbuildings and a springhouse) passed to his widow, Elizabeth C. Black. She and her family lived at Upland through the turn of the century.

The house was enlarged and drastically restyled c. 1908. It remained in the Black family through the mid-1920s. The property then passed to the Township and by 1926 it was the Bryn Mawr Memorial Association War and Community House.

Today it sits beside Luding-

ton Library and houses two vital non-profit groups: ElderNet senior assistance services and the Retired and Senior Volunteer Program. The Montgomery County Office of Aging and Adult Services is housed in Upland's old springhouse in the rear.

The facilities are available to the community for diverse uses: civic gatherings, AA meetings, chess and bridge matches, conferences and non-profit group get-togethers.

3 *(above)* The building now is a Township facility used by ElderNet and R.S.V.P. The public rooms are available for various community needs.

LOCAL TRADES

Change at Warp Speed. Some say there was a trading post for exchange of goods between Swedish settlers and local Indians along a trail to the Susquehanna River that became the road to Lancaster (now Montgomery Avenue). Welsh Quakers and others began to arrive in 1682-3 and could buy venison and fowl from the Indians in their dooryards once they had house, door and yard. Taverns, the gathering places, began almost immediately, some even in the early "caves" in Philadelphia. But the yoemen farmer and his wife grew the raw material and processed it or trained a hired-hand to do the work...or did without.

1 Edward S. Murray's Feed Mill and Coal Yard, built in 1887, was located at Lancaster Avenue and Woodside Road. In doorway: Edward S. Murray and Joseph Golden, bookkeeper. Standing: *(left to right)* Morton Carr, John McCall, a child and Cowagon Connelly. On the wagon: Fran.

Philadelpha Trades. Stores, as we know them, were slow to appear in Philadelphia because merchants and artisans were limited to selling in stalls in the city market at High (Market) and Front streets and, after 1693, at Second Street. Market days were Wednesdays and Sundays, though some vendors sold there all week long. Tailors, tanners, chandlers, pewterers, goldsmiths, weavers, coopers...on and on goes the list...made a living. Ready-made shoes were evidently non-existent, and the cordwainers (shoemakers), who had their favored customers, were early to organize but were tried at court for "conspiring to raise their wages."

Gradually, in Colonial Philadelphia, luxury goods came into the port and ladies flocked to milliners, glove makers, stylish fabric merchants...but still farm wives would not or could not show interest.

Farm Trades. There were not many wagons in use until the Revolution, and horses transported food and raw materials to town and carried items for farm wives...possibly coffee, tea, household items...back to the farms.

Most commerce was carried on near the wharves. Diarist Joseph Price, a carpenter and builder, but also a farmer with a scholarly bent, had to go into Philadelphia to buy boards, screws, window glass, nails, paint, glue, varnish, hardware. For the household, he purchased a coffee mill, sugar, salt...for the farm, a plow... and for his own education, books (and eyeglasses).

Cloverseed he was able to buy at the Buck Inn. Farmers hereabouts slaughtered their own hogs, bought produce from each other, brought flour from the local mills and were fairly self-sufficient.

1 *(top)* Morris Kane's Blacksmith Shop, built in 1876, on Lancaster Avenue, west of Ardmore Avenue.

2 *(center)* Franklin P. Azpell, Harness Maker. His shop, built c.1879 was located on the north side of Lancaster Avenue, just west of the intersection with Ardmore Avenue.

3 *(below)* The other side of Azpell's shop served as the office of the Justice of the Peace; photo c.1890.

Country Progress. Fifty years later, toward the end of the 19th century, changes came thick and fast. Communities had coalesced, usually around a tavern, and blacksmiths picked locations on principal roads. With the advent of more wagon traffic, the wheelwright set up shop, sometimes side by side with the blacksmith.

One hundred years ago, more or less, Lower Merion Township had two restaurants, one grocery, two confectionery shops, one provisioner, three flour and feed stores, three drug stores, 14 general stores and a dozen assorted other emporia, two coal-yards among them. We may smile at so few shopping opportunities, but in those days Lower Merion had nine hotels. Today? None.

Fare and Transport. Among businesses listed by William J. Buck in 1884, food and transportation with their adjunct services accounted for most of our commerce. Sometimes the two categories coincided.

For many years and into the post-World War II era, the well-to-do sent their butlers or maids to the railroad station in the morning to hand up a list of needs...principally groceries...to the conductor, and in the afternoon, came back to collect the bags and baskets of provisions at the station.

Savvy shopkeepers then stepped in to supply and deliver telephone orders; roving meat, butter and eggs, bread and milk men made the rounds to homes. Such service ended by the 1960s, bowing to the inevitable...the supermarkets.

Modes of locomotion fascinated the first photographers as our collection of pictures show. And closely behind transportation came gastronomy. 'Twas ever thus. 'Tis ever so.

1 (top) McIntyre's horse-driven grocery wagon.

2 (center) John Stretch's express delivery on wheels.

3 (below) Dominic DeLucia dispenses ice cream from his wagon, c.1940s.

1 *(right)* Main Line Sea Food, c. 1934; Autocar plant in rear.

2 *(above, left)* Samuel F. Stadelman's Pharmacy, built c.1868; the first drug store on the Main Line; southwest corner of Lancaster Pike and Mud Lane (now Cricket Avenue). First telephone switchboard in the area installed in 1885.

3 *(above, right)* Haverford Pharmacy, early 1900s, on the south side of Haverford Station Road, between Montgomery and Lancaster Avenues.

4 *(right)* Gingerbread House, 10 Cricket Terrace, Ardmore, home of Hartman's body and fender business; shows his Model A Ford pickup.

FARMERS' MARKETS

Today's local shoppers may not realize they are following an early colonial custom. In 1683, the first market was established by William Penn on High Street (Market Street) in Philadelphia. As the city grew, additional stalls were added, allowing Jersey farmers to cross the river with their produce. New Market Square (1745) survives today at Pine and Second Streets in Philadelphia.

The availability of fresh produce spread later into our township.

• Albrecht's Farmers' Market (**1**, *top),* built in 1928, housed the family's flower business that started in 1914. In recent years, the building was developed to feature many produce stands.

• Ardmore Farmers' Market (**2**, *right)* opened as the Suburban Theatre in 1937. By 1980, it was converted to a food market called the St. James Market... and two years later changed to the current name. • At both markets, suburban shoppers delight in the availability of a fresh supply of farm-grown vegetables and fruits, choice meats and poultry, a variety of dairy products, baked goods, flowers and many other local goodies.

MAPES 5 & 10

Mapes (originally Davis') was started by Charles E. Davis in 1897 on Main Street in Narberth. In 1908, his brother, Howard Eugene Davis, bought the store. He ran it with his wife, Sarah, and son Eugene until his death in 1954. • The glory days of Davis' store were during the era of Narberth's National Football League commissioner Bert Bell (in office 1946-59) when what had been a regional sports hangout and "hot-stove league" gathering place around the cracker barrel during the pre-World War II period when the town's semi-pro baseball team won most of the pennants in the Main Line League suddenly captured the national limelight attracting sports writers, coaches, athletes (and their fans) for discussions with Bell. • Bert Bell held forth there daily in conversations that often started in front of the general store and then moved to the soda fountain or booths with a crowd of regulars to talk football. He even made some of his NFL policies based on those talk sessions. • (**3**, *left*) In the early 1960s, William Mapes, a retired textile salesman from New York City, purchased the business. His friendly personality and traditional ways fit the small-town character of Narberth until his death in 1973 at age 97. Mapes' manager, Frank Hess, became the owner that year yet considered selling the business at his retirement. Then Raymond Benner, a long-time patron, invested in this cherished family-style Narberth fixture.

WISCONSIN HOUSE

Back in 1876, almost all the states built houses to show their native products and to serve as headquarters for visitors from home at the great International Exhibition in Philadelphia's Fairmount Park...a huge celebration of the nation's centennial. • Wisconsin built a wood house, "a simple structure, not pretty, merely useful..." It stood several blocks back of Ohio House, which still stands, corner of Belmont Avenue and South George's Hill Road on its original spot. • The Simes estate bought Wisconsin House when the giant fair closed. But when it was being moved to Lower Merion, the transporter broke down on Conshohocken State Road near Belmont Avenue and left the house in the middle of the street where it was an obstruction for more than a year. Eventually it was installed, minus part of its porches, near what is now the intersection of Union Avenue and Conshohocken State Road (not far past City Avenue), approximately where the present Bala Cynwyd post office is situated. The neighborhood around the building was known locally as "Wisconsinville." • It became a hotel operated by Phipps and Bair, then by Dan Titlow, and finally was owned by William H. Doble, a noted horse trainer, followed by his son William, Jr., whose brother Budd carried his father's skills with horses even further, and generally was recognized as the greatest trainer and driver of trotting horses. • Around the bar at Wisconsin House, "trotter" enthusiasts, as distinguished from "pacers" (who gathered at the General Wayne Inn in Merion), toasted their favorites. Budd Doble made his fortune with winning horses, most famous of which was *Nancy Hanks,* the horse that won three world trotting records (best time: 2 minutes, 4 seconds) around the mile oval at the Belmont Driving Park. Mrs. Adelaide Doble, widow of William, Jr., lived in Wisconsin House, no longer a hotel, almost to her death in 1960. The place was visibly run-down, a worry to the Union Fire Association men as a fire hazard. It and eight small rental houses behind it were sold for $40,000 in 1961, and razed.

HAVERFORD HOTEL

From 1913 to 1973, parents attending graduation ceremonies at local colleges found gracious lodging at Haverford Hotel. In those days, 50 rooms were available at "The Main Line's Finest." • Located at the corner of Montgomery Avenue and Grays Lane, management advertised with pride: "Garage on Premises. Air Conditioned Lounge and Restaurant." The hotel was a welcoming place with a columned porch and porte-cochère. The bedrooms had Chippendale desks, Chinese art, mahogany cabinets, brass sconces and flattering lighting. • President Eisenhower's granddaughter enjoyed her wedding reception here, and many a party brightened spacious public rooms through those 60 years. (A lady who wouldn't dream of lunch at a bar, could, and often did, enjoy a glass of wine here with a meal at midday.) • After a "house sale," when many neighbors bought items for souvenirs of happy times gone by, the building was torn down and a condominium on Gray's Lane, designed by Vincent Kling, was built on the site.

1 *(top)* Photo c.1900 of the first Bryn Mawr Hospital, established in 1893, designed by Frank Furness.
2 *(below)* Rare 1890s photo of a horse-drawn ambulance.
3 *(bottom)* Motorized ambulance, c.1909.

BRYN MAWR HOSPITAL

The actual beginnings of the plan to build the hospital, which had long been a desire of Dr. George S. Gerhard, an Ardmore physician, took shape at a tea party hosted by Mr. Rodman Griscom of Merion Square. After some initial fund raising, they then applied for a charter in January of 1892. It was duly accepted and incorporated two months later.

Bryn Mawr Site. Next, from the initial contributions, was the purchase of a two acre lot on the corner of Bryn Mawr Avenue and County Line Road from C. Warner Arthur for $7,900. This location was chosen because Bryn Mawr was a favorite town for people from the city to visit in the summer. The Bryn Mawr Hotel, the Summit Grove Hotel, the Buck Tavern and the Whitehall Hotel were some of the best known establishments in the area.

The generosity of the members of the community was exceptional and the actual construction of the hospital was oversubscribed. It must be noted, in addition to cash gifts, many generously donated various hospital supplies to outfit their new institution.

A Furness Classic. The new building, designed by Frank Furness, was ultra-modern with an elevator and electric lights. Henry Frorer's construction firm used native gray stone in the construction of this important addition to the Main Line. When the hospital opened, Dr. George S. Gerhard and Dr. Robert C. Gamble were in charge of the public's needs. In 1905, a medical laboratory was installed and a school of nursing opened.

Today, the Gerhard Building, the first Main Line hospital for the general public, stands surrounded by new and larger buildings that make up the Bryn Mawr Hospital complex with its multitude of up-to-date medical services.

1 *(below)* 1920s view of a ward in the Bryn Mawr Hospital.
2 *(bottom)* 1947 rendering of the Bryn Mawr Hospital complex.

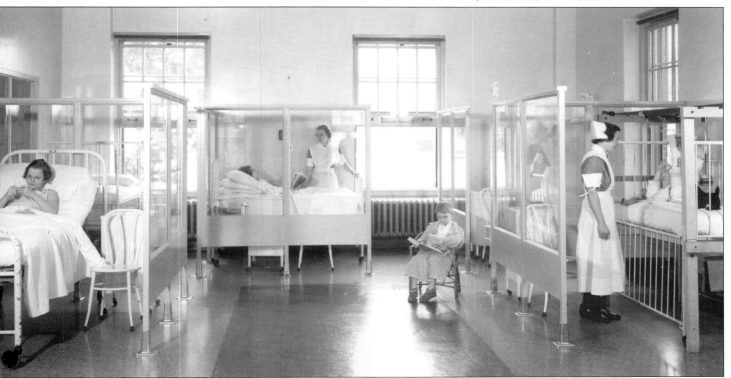

LANKENAU HOSPITAL

In the mid-19th century, the economic and political turbulence in Germany which followed the Napoleonic Wars prompted a flood of German migration to Philadelphia. Many of the immigrants arrived ill, penniless, speaking no English. The German Hospital of the City of Philadelphia was chartered in 1860 to provide a place where the German speaking populace could be treated by persons speaking their own language.

Deaconesses from Germany. Also imported from Germany, in 1884, was a band of seven Lutheran deaconesses to take charge of the hospital's household and nursing service. Trained at Kaiserswerth (where Florence Nightingale also received her training) the deaconesses soon earned for the hospital a reputation for superior nursing care.

1 *(top)* c.1980 view of the Lankenau Hospital compex.

2 *(above)* John D. Lankenau in an 1889 photograph.

Philadelphia Sites. The first home of the hospital was a converted residence at 20th and Norris Streets. In 1872, it was moved to its second location at Girard and Corinthian Avenues. By the turn of the century the hospital occupied an entire city block. The name changed in 1917 to honor John D. Lankenau, a German-born Philadelphia merchant, President of the Board for 27 years and a longtime benefactor.

Move to Lower Merion. By the mid-20th century, the hospital plant was aging; it was necessary to rebuild or relocate. Relocation was the choice; the 93 acre Overbrook Golf Club was chosen as the site. In 1953, the hospital moved to Lower Merion and into handsome new buildings which won a first place award in architecture for the designer, Vincent Kling.

Lankenau today is first among its peers in patient care, education and research.

1 (above) Science lab, c.1950.

2 (below center) Sister Amelia Schaeffer, head of the Nursing School, consults with Ada Mutch, Director of Nursing Services,

3 (bottom) Nurses congregate at the new building, mid-1950s.

OUR PROTECTORS

Suburban police and fire protection have always been led by the concern and kindness of local volunteers. Herewith, a charming collage of photographs from the Society's collection that seems to show their spirit and camaraderie years ago.

1 *(right)* The Col. Owen Jones Fife and Drum Corps, Bryn Mawr, c.1903. **2** *(center)* Lower Merion's police force, established in 1900, wore Spanish war hats and uniforms. They got around on bicycles and on horseback. Photo c.1904. **3** *(bottom left)* In 1901, space was leased from the Merion Fire Company for a lockup in the rear of their Lancaster Avenue firehouse. The escape, in 1904, of a prisoner led to a scandal that involved their police chief. **4** *(bottom right)* A big parade, winding through Lower Merion, was held on June 1890 to demonstrate the emergence of the Merion Fire Company. This 1905 photo shows their headquarters in Ardmore.

216

1 *(top)* The Lower Merion Township Pumping Station, c.1905, located in Ardmore at Lippincott and County Line Avenues.

2 *(center)* The volunteer Merion Fire Company of Ardmore poses for a photographer c.1907.

3 *(below)* The Lower Merion Police, Department, c.1910, gets wheels!

1 *(top left)* 1914 photo demonstrates the company's Simplex Machine.

2 *(top right)* The Merion Fire Company relaxes on July 4, 1916.

3 *(center)* The Merion Fire Company parades in 1915.

4 *(below)* The Township Police Force with autos, 1926.

1 (left) The first all-Eagle Scout Patrol in America, led by W. Lawrence Saunders II, standing at center, in October 1914. Flanked by, from left: Alexander H. Holcomb, Jr., Joseph H. Keefe, John Winters, John Rinkenback; seated: Isaac Kershaw, Jr., Harry Ingram, Harry Pierriera. 2 (below left) Troop Bala One scout camp scenes; formation, c.1912. 3 (below right) First Aid training, c.1930s.

TROOP BALA ONE

Citizenship Through the Years.
Troop Bala One has a long and glorious tradition in both the Boy Scout movement and the Lower Merion community. In 1907, General Robert Baden-Powell, an English Army officer, took a group of lads to Brownsea Island, England. This was the first Boy Scout Camp. In 1908, he wrote a book called *Scouting for Boys* which had an international, instantaneous impact. Troops and patrols sprung up in England and, shortly thereafter, in Europe.

An Unofficial First.
The Boy Scout movement was slower to transition to the United States, except in the tiny town of Bala, Pennsylvania. Here, in 1908, a group of community leaders, headed by insurance executive Frank Sykes, organized America's first group of boys under the principles of scouting as set forth in Baden-Powell's book. Troop Bala One thus became the first unofficial Boy Scout troop in the U.S.

The national umbrella organization, The Boy Scouts of America, was officially organized in February 1910. The following year, Troop Bala One was officially inducted with the alternate name of Troop 16. At that time, President William H. Taft was Honorary President of the Boy Scouts of America and former President Theodore Roosevelt was Honorary VP.

The Saunders Initiative.
In 1914, a young man by the name of W. Lawrence Saunders II, became Scoutmaster and raised himself and seven other members of the Troop to the rank of Eagle Scout. Troop Bala One dominated all regional scout competitions in Cobbs Creek Park and was the first in the United States to be awarded the prestigious honor of "Bucktail Troop."

Mr. Saunders is now remembered as the dedicator of the beautiful Saunders Woods, a Lower Merion park in Gladwyne which is used to this day for Cub Scout and Boy Scout camping.

The Early Years. During World War I, troop activities became limited as both older scouts and leaders were called to serve their country. During the Depression, the troop endured although camping trips had to be limited because of lack of equipment. During World War II, Troop Bala One was continually involved in projects and services to aid the troops overseas and their families at home.

Continuing Activities. Troop Bala One still maintains an active schedule of camping, canoeing, backpacking and educational outings. The troop still carries the torch, lit by Baden-Powell and followed by the early local leaders, to promote personal growth, leadership, fun, safety and self-reliance in outdoor settings.

Libraries Today. There are six community-based libraries which service the Lower Merion Library System. Their histories parallel the social customs of an era in which women's clubs and volunteerism figured prominently in the promotion of library endeavors.

1. The history of **The Ardmore Free Library** is bound to that of its loyal benefactors, the Women's Club of Ardmore. In 1899, the club rented a room in the old Merion Title and Trust building and equipped it with a library not only for the use of club members, but for the community.

2. The Bala Cynwyd Library began in 1915 as an ambition of the Women's Club of Bala Cynwyd. Since space was not available at the Academy building, the Bala Cynwyd Library Association used part of the Union Fire House as their home.

3. In 1916, Bryn Mawr witnessed the emergence of the Community Center Library which was located in the old Public School building on Lancaster Pike. **Ludington Library,** today, is the main branch of all the community-based libraries.

4. The Penn Wynne Library dates its beginnings to a 1929 donation from the Penn Wynne's Women's Club.

5. The Gladwyne Free Library opened its doors in 1930 at the front of the Gladwyne Community Building. This library is the only one to have remained in its original location.

6. Belmont Hills Library. In 1935, three women opened a library in St. Andrew's Chapel. Named West Manayunk Free Library, it was a branch service of the Bala Cynwyd Library run under the auspices of the Girls Friendly Society. In 1941, the library moved and was renamed.

2 (above) **Bala Cynwyd Library's** early home was in the Union Fire House. After 47 years at their next home on Levering Mill Road, the library relocated to Old Lancaster Road in 1974, where it continues to serve the community.

3 (below) **Penn Wynne Library.** It's first home was on the corner of Henley and Manoa Roads from 1929 to 1949; it then moved to its present location on Overbrook Parkway.

THE LIBRARIES

The Beginnings. Education expanded beyond the walls of the Lower Merion Academy into the community when, in 1842, the Trustees established the Lower Merion Library Company which resided in the third floor Committee or Library Room.

In 1876, the entire collection of 1,400 volumes was relocated to the Union Sunday School building.

With the construction of the Cynwyd Elementary School in 1914, students transferred from the Academy into their new building. The Union Sunday School was removed, leaving the library without a home. The entire collection is now with the Lower Merion Historical Society,

1 *(below)* **Ludington Library.**
1927 photo, when it was dedicated by Charles H. Ludington to the memory of his wife, Ethel Saltus Ludington.

2 *(below)* **Gladwyne Free Library.**
Early interior view; note basketball markings on the floor. The chest in the right foreground housed the children's collection.

3 *(bottom)* **Belmont Hills Library.**
Its forerunner was the Bird Library, located on Ashland Avenue from 1941 to 1969, when the library was moved to Mary Watersford Road.

MEMORIES

"Lower Merion gave me, and our very close family, a sense of roots and community for which I have always been grateful. We had only two homes: a row house on Kenilworth Road in Merion and then a small but freestanding house at 228 Avon Road in Narberth, where my maternal grandparents lived. Each street was a community. At Kenilworth, we played on the street and awaited the daily arrival of the man who delivered ice and the popsicle man, Louie. We used the great open space of nearby Shortridge Park to sled in winter. Avon Road was a real community that led from the large Scheffey estate (in the 18th century, Joseph Price's Locust Hill) where everyone played, to the center of Narberth where almost every day we went into Davis' store. • The Philadelphia Athletics were in decline and the Phillies had not yet risen from the cellar; so we idolized the Narberth baseball team as it took on the rest of the Main Line League. We particularly liked the 55-year old first baseman who specialized in getting cheap hits into the willow tree that hung over the field just beyond first base on the old Narberth playground. • My father was perpetual Judge of Elections at Merion School and my greatest teacher. He filled No. 228 with used books from Leary's store and my mother was the heart of the Avon Road community. Whenever a new family moved into the neighborhood, she baked a loaf of bread for them. My parents' remains lie in All Saints Church in Wynnewood, which played a major part in my life...as did a host of teachers in Merion School, Bala Cynwyd and Lower Merion High. • No challenge was greater than 'swimming the English channel'...being able to give the answer to simple arithmetic problems inside two minutes for Miss Duke's Second Grade Class. I always remember that one of the school leaders several classes ahead of me, who died in action during World War II, carried into battle his very few effects: the little candy life-saver with a blue ribbon that Miss Duke awarded to those who made it to the other shore."

James H. Billington

[Dr. Billington serves as The Librarian of Congress in Washington, D.C.]

1 Illustration of the original Merion Cricket Club (1865-1873) in Wynnewood.

1873-1880

2 The club relocated to Ardmore in 1873 and remained there for seven years.

THE MERION CRICKET CLUB. The historic sport of cricket has been a part of Lower Merion since it was first played at Haverford College in 1834. In 1865, fifteen young Main Line enthusiasts first played cricket on the grounds of Colonel Owen Jones' estate in Wynnewood; next on new club property acquired on Cricket Avenue in Ardmore.

Since the move to Haverford in 1892, Merion Cricket Club has a long history of involvement with other sports: lawn tennis (1879); bowling (1895); golf (1895), the cricket and golf clubs separated in 1942; soccer (1896); squash racquets (1900); field hockey (c.1900); badminton (1937). For many years, the club has hosted important tournaments in these various sports and an impressive group of its members have become national champions.

Merion Cricket, after 134 years, continues to support a vital program of family-oriented athletic and social programs within its fine facilities in Haverford: fine sportsmanship, good fellowship.

3 The space was soon inadequate for the club's number and enthusiasm, and they built a new clubhouse, in 1891, on Cricket Avenue in Ardmore. A destructive fire damaged it the next year.

A NEW LIFE

When Merion Cricket moved out of their Ardmore location after the fire (left page), the property was purchased by Hamilton & Yarnell in 1892. **1** Despite the fire, they enclosed the porches and established St. Mary's Laundry (left). **2** The driving force behind this ambitious project was Emily Borie, Mrs. James Rhodes (right) who, with her husband, organized the laundry to give work to the women of St. Mary's Parish who were devastated during the hard times that followed the national panic of 1893.

3 Following the 1892 fire, the "Main House" (above) was constructed that same year. **4** "The Cricket House" (left), along Montgomery Avenue, was connected and had showers and locker facilities and sat beside a stable and shed structure. Another era ended again when the massive "Main House" was completely destroyed by fire in January 1896. Valuable documents were also lost– the original founders' papers of October 1865 along with valuable club pictures, trophies, and other relics.

The 1896 fire of "The Main House" was a total loss. Only the chimneys and some bearing walls remained. But work was immediately begun on a larger house, a substantial brick and terra-cotta structure **1** *(above)* that was set back toward Grays Lane, designed by the prestigious Philadelphia architects, Furness and Evans. The new site provided a much larger field for both cricket and tennis.

There is a description of the new clubhouse in Hotchkin's 1897 book, *Rural Pennsylvania* ..."porte-cochère and recessed porches, two separate hallways for men and women– a large central hall for general use, and on one side the café, library, and billiard-room for men, and on the other the ladies reception and tea-rooms. Below stairs are bowling-alleys and shuffle-board rooms, store-rooms, ladies' tennis-rooms, cricket dining-room, lavatories, etc. The second floor contains a large main dining room, private dining-rooms, bed-rooms for men, bath-rooms, etc., and a large theatre with dressing-rooms and a separate entrance. On the third floor are more bed-rooms for men, kitchens, sewing-rooms and rooms for employees. The whole house is heated by one large boiler, and lighted with both gas and electric lights. It is supposed to be the most complete and largest country-club house in this country."

2 Incredibly, in the fall of 1896, tragedy struck once again! *(center)*. Local papers deemed the September blaze of mysterious origin. At a $150,000 loss, they reported that the fire could have been caused by "rats gnawing at matches." The photo shows the bucket brigade, who bravely (and elegantly) fought the blaze at four in the morning .

Thanks to a good water supply and the dedication of local volunteers, a large part of the building was saved. Once again, the stalwart directors of the club acted decisively and the clubhouse was restored within half a year. **3** The rebuilt club *(right)* remains today, an active part of the sport and social community in Lower Merion.

1 *(above)* The Indian Olympic Field Hockey Team vs. the U.S. Olympic Team, August 1932, at the Merion Cricket Club. A club member recalls: "We played them on the front field before four or five thousand people. It was one of the most colorful sights with the Indians in their turbans and their ability to play the game." The Indians handed terrible defeats to the U.S. team...24-1 at the Olympics and 17-2 at Merion. **2,3** *(below)* Active scenes at Merion Cricket.

"A GENTLEMAN'S GAME"

Haverford College took to cricket from the beginning. It was introduced there in the 1830s by William Carville, an English gardener brought over to landscape the new campus. In 1834, the first cricket club, made up entirely of American youth, began one year after the college opened. Haverford's Quaker founders weren't sure about the effect the game's excitement would have on students who were encouraged to study and behave with fitting decorum. But even the staid members of the Society of Friends recognized cricket's historical appeal: the game has been traced as far back as the Middle Ages. *Creagh* was one of its early forms, played around 1299. In the colonies, prior to 1776, cricket was known as a "gentleman's game."
• In cricket's heyday, from the 1860s to the 1920s, many schools had teams. The sport then entered a period of low interest, but is now undergoing a renaissance in America with increasing numbers of cricket teams in major universities...95 in New York, 31 in Miami, for example.
• Haverford College, however, is the only one granting varsity letters to its cricket team.

225

BELMONT PARK.

Gate Ticket

Admission $1.00

Gentlemens Road Race

THE BELMONT DRIVING PARK

A mile-long oval race track for harness racing was created in 1876 on land where Washington and his troops, after crossing the Schuylkill, had camped on September 13, 1777 on a site called Price's Field.

Built during the Centennial in Philadelphia, the track was on 72 acres along Meeting House Lane, just down the road from Merion Meeting. Horse racing was a popular sport since Colonial times, so these sulky races drew many sportsmen, racers, and spectators. Droves of tourists came by carriage from the city and filled local inns, rooming houses, and the General Wayne.

The clubhouse **1** *(top)* was an elaborate three story building with wide verandas and a second floor porch. Ladies with their escorts sipped claret lemonade, and the men cheered the sulky races from porches below and the nearby grandstands.

2 Sign *(left)* at the Montgomery Avenue and Meeting House Lane corner pointed the way to the track: "Belmont Driving Park. Licensed. Open to the Public. Draft Beer," (perhaps to the chagrin of some members of Merion Meeting).

1 *(left)* Marker at Albrecht's denoting Washington's encampment. **2** *(right)* Miss Marker, in her sleigh, ready for a winter drive around the track grounds.

Favorite horses like Star Pointer, the Guideless Wonder, Jay Eye See, May Queen, and Maude S. Smuggler were featured stars. For the Grand Circuit of 1917, racers and trotters came by train from stables in New Hampshire, Kentucky, Ohio, and Massachusetts, arriving at the Cynwyd rail station. A half-mile track, within the original oval, was added in 1890.

At one time there were 300 members of the Belmont Driving Club. Joshua Evans, the president for many years, was succeeded by the second (and final) one, Frank Bower. But interest in sulky racing began to decline, and even races of automobiles and motorcycles no longer attracted many crowds.

In the fall of 1924, the entire acreage was sold to a construction company for $300,000 (a 200% profit for the stockholders).

With plans for 374 lots, paved streets and sidewalks, and a number of fine homes, Merion Park became a substantial residential community where, ironically, many of its homeowners never heard of the exciting sulky races of the past.

3 *(above)* Stock certificate, five shares, owned by Belmont president Frank Bower. **4, 5** *(below)* When the track was razed in the mid-1920s, the clubhouse was divided and moved within Merion Park. Both sections remain today as private residences.

OVERBROOK GOLF CLUB

It was in 1900 that the Overbrook Golf Club was incorporated and the golf course built on some 93 acres of land leased from the owners of the Greenhill Farms Plantation. There were still great trees and green hills as well as a flowing stream at the site. Originally deeded by William Penn to Thomas Lloyd in 1682, the tract had increased to over 300 acres by 1714. Wistar Morris, whose mother had inherited the property in 1799, spent his life on the property. His stone mansion, built in 1863, is now owned by Friends' Central School.

The golf club remained on the site until 1948, when it was sold for $500,000 to developers. Then the club moved west to Sproul Road where it intersects Godfrey Road in Villanova. On its former site we now find Lankenau Hospital.

THE PHILADELPHIA FIELD AND CYCLE CLUB

Philadelphia and its Main Line, including the social and athletic movers and shakers, enjoyed to the full the advantages of the countryside– its trails, roads and rivers–from the late 1700s on. The invention of the cycle, the high-wheeler, gave anoth-er risky pleasure, followed by the bicycle which gave safer riding and greatly increased the number of cyclists.

The two oldest clubs, the Germantown Club and the Philadelphia Field and Cycle Club, were born in 1879. The site of the Philadelphia Club was on the corner of Church Road and Lancaster Pike in Ardmore. Early in this century, the cyclists had rehabbed a summer residence at that location called Green Gables.

THE VON TRAPP FAMILY IN MERION

The Maria von Trapp life story, immortalized by the 1959 Rogers & Hammerstein musical *The Sound of Music*, had a lively Merion chapter. Baron Georg von Trapp, Baroness Maria, their two sons and seven daughters (ages 7 to 27) arrived in 1938 at 252 Merion Road virtually penniless. As singers seeking refuge in America after fleeing the Nazi takeover of Austria, they settled in that comfortable house lent by Merion lawyer and music patron Henry S. Drinker, Jr., an authority on Bach. There the family's tenth and last child Johannes (who became the clan's charismatic leader) was born in 1939.

While there, the family learned to become self-sustaining and regained its financial stability, which enabled it to buy the Vermont farm where it moved full-time in the mid-1940s (and still owns).

The von Trapps already had a jump-start in turning their singing hobby into a successful profession in Europe. Over here, singing soon became a way of life for them. Yet from baking to house-cleaning, like the Swiss family Robinson, they did every chore, made all their own clothes, shoes, furniture, pottery.

At Merion, the distinctive Tyrolean garb of dirndls and lederhosen they all wore daily for reasons of thrift, soon became a Trapp Family Singers signature. One of the concert field's most heavily booked attractions, they performed as a group for 25 years.

The 1965 film of *The Sound of Music* won the Academy Award for best picture of the year and was for several years the all-time top money earner, even beating out *Gone With the Wind*. And an estimated 600,000 people worldwide still see *The Sound of Music* each year.

1 *(above)* The von Trapps with the family priest, Father Franze Wasner, at left, who also conducted the twelve singing Barons and Baronesses.

2 *(right)* The von Trapps stayed at a house at 252 Merion Road from 1939 to 1943.

3 *(below)* Regularly, at four in the afternoon, the adult von Trapps gathered for the traditional Austrian coffee hour in Merion.

ALEXANDER J. CASSATT'S
CHESWOLD

One of the best known Main Line figures is Alexander J. Cassatt, who became nationally known as president of the Pennsylvania Railroad. His house set the style for summer retreats for wealthy Philadelphians in these western suburbs.

Cassatt began Cheswold in 1872 on his 54-acre parcel of land off Montgomery Avenue. About $50,000 went into the construction of this Queen Anne style villa with the notable Philadelphia architects Furness & Evans incorporating a boldly paneled walnut hall, stained glass windows, and plentiful bedrooms and baths for the family.

There was great energy to the design and details, and wonderful textures to the materials used, appropriate to a railroad officer and art connoisseur. Cassatt's frequent travels to Europe, especially to Paris to

1 *(above)* The Cassatt's summer residence in Haverford.

2 *(left)* A.J. Cassatt, president of the Pennsylvania Railroad.

3 *(below)* Pastel portrait of Mrs. Cassatt, the former Lois Buchanan, by her sister-in-law, Mary Cassatt, in France, 1883.

visit his sister Mary, already a well-known artist, expanded his collection of furniture and art on a continuing basis. Soon they overflowed his Rittenhouse Square residence and Cheswold.

Furness & Evans returned several times to do alterations and additions. Cassatt was also increasing his involvement in Lower Merion Township as he paid to have Montgomery Avenue paved, established a gas plant, and purchased a significant share of the Lancaster Turnpike.

By the 1880s, his passion for horse racing and fox hunting had grown and since the area around Cheswold had begun to develop (as he had hoped) he also purchased Chesterbrook Farm in Berwyn, about 600 acres. Cheswold's sub-division began in the late 1930s with Walter Durham designing charming colonial style residences on a more modest but still elegant style.

1 *(top)* Cassatt with his granddaughter Lois, 1900 photograph.

2 *(center)* Monument honoring Cassatt, an enthusiastic sportsman, at the Merion Cricket Club, where he was elected President in 1891.

3 *(below)* Only Cheswold's gate lodge survives today.

LOWER MERION HISTORICAL SOCIETY

Founders of the Society were Edward H. Snow, principal of the Ardmore Junior High School, John M. Nugent, staff writer for the *Philadelphia Evening Bulletin*, and Douglas C. Macfarlan, M.D., ear/nose/throat specialist. In October 1949, eighty-five citizens of the Township were invited to hear State Historian S.K. Stevens praise their enthusiasm for the preservation of local history. They organized in time to celebrate the fiftieth anniversary of Lower Merion as a First Class Township.
• Principal missions of the Society are the collection and preservation of records, artifacts, evidence of the past, and to educate young and old about local history. The Society regularly presents programs and events featuring speakers and visits historic places in the area. • Each year the Society provides, without charge, special talks and bus tours for school classes, and cooperates with students of all ages in research.
• Journalists and home owners use the growing library of the Society to find background material on property, institutions, events in the Township as well as neighboring Narberth.
• The library is housed in historic Ashbridge House, Rosemont. Two histories and a study of architectural treasures of the region are Society publications. • The Lower Merion Historical Society lives up to its promise...to preserve the memory of the past. **Ted Goldsborough**

1 The Wheeler villa, built in 1873. Many years later, it was destroyed by fire.

2 (below) Pembroke's charming gate house is now a private residence.

CHARLES WHEELER'S PEMBROKE

Charles Wheeler's Pembroke, in Bryn Mawr, originally looked out over 100 acres bounded by Fishers Road, Morris Avenue and New Gulph Road. The Wheelers were among the first of the prominent families to build in Bryn Mawr after several seasons of staying at the Bryn Mawr Hotel.

Wheeler, president of the Pascall Iron Works and a founder of the Central National Bank, hired Quaker architect Addison Hutton to design his summer house which was built in 1873. As it first appeared, it was a square Gothic villa with large verandas and a porte-cochere...a modest summer cottage.

Wheeler died in 1883, and in 1890 his widow decided to move to Bryn Mawr year-round. Her family wrote of the many excursions out from Broad Street Station to Bryn Mawr in the fall and winter season when party-goers journeyed for an evening at Pembroke. Reports are that guests took whole passenger cars and festivities began as soon as the train left the station. Coaches would meet the formally attired guests and drive them the mile to Pembroke where they would enter the large hall and find a roaring fire.

Perhaps influenced by houses on the Isle of Wight in England, where Mrs. Wheeler spent July and August, she expanded the house into a vine covered, picturesque old English manor.

Around 1903, her son hired Wilson Eyre to redesign the billiard room, this time in the style of a Tyrolean chalet. Extensive gardens were highlighted by formal elements near the house and natural features moving down the hill towards Morris Avenue.

The family began selling off parcels of the land as early as 1910, but the house remained for many years until it was destroyed by fire. Its gate lodge survives along Fishers Road, and dotted over the former gardens and farmland are houses designed by Walter Durham.

1 Massive and squared rather than picturesque, Olinda was a five-bay, three-story suburban villa that took inspiration from the Classic Revival in a restrained way. Built shortly before 1859 for Blair McClenachan's daughters, it was acquired that year by the honorary consul for Brazil in Philadelphia, Edward S. Sayres, Sr., who graced it with its Portugese name, Olinda. The house's Classic Revival features were not self-consciously fashionable. They were a low-slung bracketed gable roof with flat projecting cornice, emphatic lintels and sills and a pert cupola.

WILLIAM McDOWELL'S
OLINDA

William L. McDowell (1824-1897) symbolized the entrepreneurial spirit that swept into Lower Merion in the post-Civil War era with the lightning speed of a fast trotter.

The countdown for America's 1876 Centennial in Philadelphia had already begun when McDowell became the moving force behind establishing and operating Belmont Driving Park, the harness race course that lured Centennial throngs and decades of visitors to 73 acres where Merion Park now is. He quickly acquired a major farm as track location, formed a syndicate of backers and held its mortgage. McDowell also provided upscale off-track accommodations in a former Price colonial mansion, calling it Maplewood (later named Brookhurst Inn).

This self-made man, born in Philadelphia, was hired as a youth to be a manufacturing firm's entry clerk. He rose rapidly to become a partner and, in 1869, became its president. Leibrandt & McDowell Stove Company employed 208 people.

Settled at Olinda on 51 acres in Wynnewood c.1872, the William McDowell household in 1880 comprised wife Mary Abbott and himself, six of their seven children, a son-in-law, grandson, mother-in-law and three Irish servants, before the children built nearby homes of their own.

2 *(above)* The side view showing rear wings and large barn at left.
3 *(below)* Willliam L. McDowell.
4 *(right)* The entire McDowell household poses out front, c.1894.

1 Rose Hill, home of Charles E. Hires, on Highland Avenue and Montgomery Pike, Merion. The house sat on 20 acres of parklike grounds with five acres of lawn. It is now the site of Temple Adath Israel. Hires later lived on Buck Lane in Haverford.

2 Charles Elmer Hires (1851-1937)

3 Charles Hires' first wife, Clara Kate Smith Hires (1852-1910), mother of his six children.

CHARLES E. HIRES' ROSE HILL

Charles E. Hires is best known as the originator of Hires Root Beer, a soft drink which gained great popularity in the 1870s. Hires began his career as a pharmacist and sold a variety of health remedies and flavoring extracts before introducing root beer as a healthful and refreshing alternative to beer.

He also sold ginger ale which was called champanale. While soft drinks were at the heart of his enterprise, he was a pioneer in manufacturing condensed milk and had factories in towns near dairy centers including Malvern, Pennsylvania. His Purock Water Company distributed spring water around the region and Hires water coolers were found in many Philadelphia area buildings. Hires' sugar plantations in Cuba supplied his bottling plants around the country.

Hires is seen as one of the pioneers of modern advertising, using trade cards and then magazine,

newspaper, and radio advertising to sell his products. Hires Root Beer was a staple of most soda fountains and an item popular for home production.

Hires' first wife was Clara Kate Smith, a Quaker lady, who was the mother of his six children. Their children attended local Quaker schools...his sons rode horseback to Haverford School. After 35 years of marriage, Clara died and Charles went through an agonizing period of grief.

After his second marriage to "Miss E," Emma Waln, member of a prominent old Quaker family, Hires financed the restoration of Merion Friends Meeting, wrote a history of that historic house of worship and was actively involved with Friends' Central School's move to Lower Merion Township.

Hires' five children pursued various careers. His son Charles worked his way up through the company to become its president in 1923. His home was on Remington Road in

1 The clan gathers, c.1925. Charles *(seated right of center)* holds grandson Bill. Emma Waln Hires, in floral hat, is to the right.

2 A fishing trip with the boys, c.1930. *(from left)* John Edgar, Harrison, the captain, Charles, Jr., and father Charles.

Wynnewood. Harrison worked for the family company but also had a lively interest in the arts, writing several books of poetry. Son J. Edgar was an engineer and in the 1920s and 30s lived on Linwood Avenue in Ardmore. Next door lived his sister, Linda, a graduate of Wellesley who was trained as an architect. The youngest daughter, Clara, became a botanist.

3 Charles E. Hires, c.1930s.

NOTABLE NEIGHBOR

"My grandfather, Charles E. Hires, had 21 acres in Merion Station, acquired it in 1894 and the name of the property was Melrose. There's now a synagogue there, Adath Israel (Old Lancaster Road and North Highland Avenue). • When I remember him, of course, he was living on Buck Lane (Haverford) after 1906 or so. His first wife, Clara Kate Smith, died in 1910 and he married his second wife, Emma Waln, a Quaker. She had been a teacher at Friends' Central School and had taught Aunt Linda Hires. Grandfather was very much in sympathy with Quakers, but he didn't sign up as a Quaker until he remarried. • I started my school career at Friends' Central in third grade and grandfather was one of the people instrumental in having it move out to City Avenue...the old Morris house. • Grandfather had started the business back in the 1870s. My father was in the root beer business, too. I remember he told me that his first job was summer employment. I worked one summer, after I was in first year of Montgomery School, and father said, 'Now I'm starting you off at $12 a week. *My* father started me off at $8 a week.' In those days, this was 1936, you worked half a day on Saturday too. There was this line of bottles that kept coming toward me on a moving platform, a metal conveyor belt. And right in front of me would be boxes coming along, and I'd take two bottles out and put them in and when you filled the box you pushed the box on, and another box would come into place. All day long. Someone said, 'Treat this guy just like anybody else, and forget about the fact that his name is Hires.' I remember being called to task at lunchtime, because I was so exhausted I would lie down whenever I could at lunchtime. They said, 'You don't want to do that. That's not setting a good example. You want to get out there and play baseball with the other guys.' • I worked for the Hires Company for a year after a year at Harvard." **William Hires**

[After Mr. Hires' service during World War II, he graduated from Haverford College in 1949. He was called back to duty during the Korean conflict and served as a psychologist in Virginia. After thirty years in the military, his post-retirement stint was dean of academic studies at Curtis Institute.]

FREDERICK PHIILIPS' and later J. KEARSLEY MITCHELL'S RED ROSE INN & STOKE POGES

Red Rose in Villanova was almost the site of an arts colony such as Rose Valley near Media or the Roycrofters in East Aurora, New York.

In the early 1900s, Frederick Phillips purchased 800 acres off Spring Mill Road with several 18th century farm houses. He named the property Stoke Pogis (sic) after William Penn's family home in England and remodeled one farm house into the style of a colonial inn, calling it The Red Rose.

Here he planned a community of artists and craftsmen who shared common tastes and the simplicity of old stone buildings. These would be individuals of modest means, kindred spirits who would work in their studios during the day and then come together at night to dine, drink, and socialize.

Phillips' early death dashed this scheme and soon after pieces of the 500-acre holding were sold off, many to be developed by the architect/builders Baily & Bassett with sizable Tudor and colonial style houses.

The largest parcel, 194 acres, was purchased by the financier J. Kearsley Mitchell and his wife, the daughter of one of Philadelphia's richest men, Edward Stotesbury. It included the old Red Rose Inn, farm buildings, stables, and Phillips's studios. A large half-framed Tudor manor, designed by Cope & Stewardson, was built in 1911 for the Mitchells at a high point of land.

Terraced gardens were designed by well-known landscape architect Beatrix Farrand which, like Wheeler's Pembroke, integrated a formal arrangement near to the house and then flowed out to the farmscape of old buildings and rolling pasture.

Later, Mitchell's son would occupy the farm buildings which were remodeled as a comfortable and unassuming house...quite a leap from his grandfather's 125-room mansion, Whitemarsh Hall, in Wyndmoor.

Once again, Walter Durham was the developer when most of Red Rose was sold, and Brynllawn Road encompasses both Durham's designs of the 1950s and readapted Red Rose outbuildings.

HENRY C. GIBSON'S
MAYBROOK

Along Penn Road in Wynnewood, distiller Henry C. Gibson's Maybrook was designed by the Hewitt Brothers and built in 1881. Described variably as a Gothic or Elizabethan house, it was clearly English in inspiration and built to impress its visitors.

To have the work done properly, English stonemasons were brought over. When it was completed it had cost $200,000, a grand sum for that era. A 72 foot tower served as a striking landmark to be viewed for miles around. Fountains splashed in front of the house and Victorian gardens with thousands of annuals were its setting.

The suggestion may have been great age, but the comforts were modern...hot-air furnaces and plenty of hot running water. Later, a baronial room which had a court about 60 feet long with a 50 foot ceiling was added. Stained glass windows by Violet Oakley lit the cloistered court, giving it a feeling of part ballroom, part cathedral.

The house was purchased from Gibson's daughter by John Merriam who built the Thomas Wynne apartments on part of the land. The estate remains in private hands.

1 *(top)* Henry C. Gibson.

2 *(above right)* The striking facade of the English-inspired Maybrook.

3 *(right)* The 60 foot ballroom.

1 Dolobran, the Haverford estate of Clement A. Griscom, the work of Furness and Evans between 1881 and 1895.

2 Clement Acton Griscom, President of the International Navigation Company's American Line; Director of the Pennsylvania Railroad and many other institutions.

CLEMENT GRISCOM'S DOLOBRAN

The 1900 book, *Fads and Fancies* describes Clement A. Griscom:

"Few men possess more divergent tastes; he is president of a company that operates one of the largest transatlantic fleets; he is a member of a club devoted to agriculture and breeding blooded cattle; he has been commodore...of a yacht club; he sows and reaps his own crops, and takes prizes at county and state fairs for his horses, cows, and sheep."

The remainder of the article speaks of his various national and international honors, but little of his amazing estate.

An Evolving Mansion. The house is the work of the firm of Furness and Evans between the years of 1881 and 1895. During this time, there was constant construction, as the plan and variation of styles shows a distinct evolutionary trend.

Much of the building occurred to house his growing collection of Old Master and late 19th century paintings. After his death, the inventory of an auction of his collection lists works by Rembrandt, Canaletto, Constable, van Dyck, Monet, and the sister of one of his neighbors, Mary Cassatt.

The Dolobran estate grew to almost 150 acres over a 15 year period. The grounds contained formal and informal gardens, farm buildings and pastures, and a golf course. The main house shows Furness working in the "stick style," a mode favored for resort architecture, and practiced by his mentor, Richard Morris Hunt, in his Newport cottages.

Hunt was the first American architect to study at the Ecole de Beaux Artes in Paris, and Furness studied at the studio Hunt established in New York in the 1850s. Allen Evans was the son of a doctor and land speculator who bought property along Gray's Lane in Haverford. He developed the land for himself and others, notably Alexander Cassatt. Evans began his apprenticeship in 1872, and became his partner in 1881.

By the mid-1880s, the house had doubled in size and was sprouting towers and the Furness trademark chimneys. By 1890, the "shingle and stick styles" were giving way to more substantial stone construction.

Dolobran encompassed a floor area of over one-half acre spread across five levels as the house rambled across the gently sloping site. The building that remains is a fascinating chronicle of changing tastes of the late Victorian era.

Upstairs. Downstairs. Just as the exterior evolved from earlier less formal resort styles to a more classical mode, so did the interior changes. For a house of it's overall size, the individual rooms are not particularly large, except for the 40 x 50 foot gallery/ballroom addition at the rear.

Throughout the home were collections from Griscom's world travels: exotic glass, porcelain, Delft tiles, a painted canvas ceiling in the manner of traditional Oriental art, intricately carved wood paneling.

238

The upper floors contained a master bedroom suite with two bathrooms, and bedroom suites for each of the Griscom's five children. A three story service wing contained a warren of servant's rooms along with a large kitchen and larder with three built-in tiled ice boxes.

Clement Griscom lived in the house for over 30 years, but when he died, the landholdings and ancillary structures were rapidly sold off, and most demolished.

The main house, hopelessly out of style in the Colonial Revival age, sat empty for many years. Many objects were stored in the sub-basement. During the restoration preceding the Vassar Showhouse of 1990, many original pieces were re-installed, and the exterior was returned to its original appearance with wood shingling, green trim, and a copper-edged roof. Since the house was commissioned by such a prominent Philadelphian, and reflects so many periods in the architectural practice of Furness and Evans, it is a priceless relic of the Gilded Age on the Main Line.

1 *(top)* The entrance hall is finished in dark paneling that sets off the blue and white Delft tile murals. The main staircase is narrow and steep. **2** *(bottom)* The fireplaces, such as this one in a second floor bedroom, have exquisite Furness ornaments with variations on stylized flowers.

MEMORIES

"Now at that time, 1927-28 or maybe earlier, the [Narberth] fire company had no money. They had one little building and one engine. We used to give a big party once a year to raise funds...a dinner. And the women cooked everything. Nothing was bought. And the food was delicious. A wonderful meal. And the fire company people were invited as guests, but most people paid, and that money went to the fire company. • This is when Mr. Nulty was the chief of the fire company. Now Mr. Nulty was the driver and chauffeur for Dr. Barnes of the Barnes Foundation. And you know Dr. Barnes was called all kinds of names, but he got very much interested in our fire company through his chauffeur. Dr. Barnes came to one of our meals and he liked apple pies. And he said to Mrs. Mueller, 'You don't have enough dishes, what's the matter?' And she said, 'Well, we don't have enough money to buy dishes, but we're doing the best we can.' So he said, 'How much do you need for a set of dishes?' and she told him, so he pulled out a check and said, 'Now here, you get some dishes.' So she conscientiously put it in the bank so she could draw it out to get some dishes. But the bank closed! The famous closure of the famous bank *[Merion Title.]* The money for our dishes was in the bank. So Dr. Barnes said to Mrs. Mueller, 'Did you buy the dishes?' and she said, 'Oh the money was in the bank that failed.' And he said, "I didn't tell you to put that money in the bank; you should have bought those dishes.' So he gave us another check for the dishes."
Marguerite Sessler Goldsmith

239

1 Ballytore at the turn of the century.
2 Isaac Hallowell Clothier.
3 (below) One of the outbuildings.

ISAAC CLOTHIER'S BALLYTORE

Its battlements make Isaac H. Clothier's Wynnewood residence, Ballytore, a castle, and its present use (with some structural changes as a sanctuary), make it a church.

Originally, this towered stone fortress of a house by architect Addison Hutton bristled with a turret, cren-elated walls, a semi-encircling covered porch (instead of a moat), and a porte-cochere, its piers topped by what appear to have been a sentry gatehouse at each of its four corners. Still intact is a four-tiered square defensive tower. Instead of being walled solid, it has narrow "lookout" windows on each level, as does its turret. The steeply peaked roof is another Hutton signature.

The Clothier castle was constructed in 1885, the same year and by the same architect as another large mansion, Torworth (in Germantown) for Clothier's business partner, Justus C. Strawbridge. Hutton also designed, and repeatedly worked on, the co-partners' Strawbridge & Clothier de-

partment store building in Philadelphia. So the two mansions were a natural next step.

Addison Hutton was commissioned to design a castle in Wynnewood on 60 acres for his personal friend, Clothier, the department store magnate and philanthropist. On property that had been Henry Morris' Maple Grove farm, this assignment

doubtless had special significance for Hutton, "the Quaker architect of Bryn Mawr," who was at the apex of his career.

Henry Morris, Clothier's son-in-law (by then living next door at Fairhill) had been Hutton's first client and earliest patron. Morris saw to it that the architectural career of this rural upstate lad was launched three

decades earlier: he had young Hutton design the Morris family "cottage" at Newport.

Earlier, in 1878, Morris built three cottages of dressed stone, their low-slung roofs covered with red diamond-shaped tiles and having secret passages below ground. This picturesque and eccentric group, Red Roof, was built on what became Ballytore ground. While Hutton might have been involved in the design of the round-towered lodge house, one suspects that Henry Morris himself was the creator.

Morris, a widely traveled amateur architect, probably designed these quaint houses which were the forerunner of all the "English villages" in this country. He had used themes brought home after trips abroad and put into practice his own great love of fine handcraftsmanship in every aspect of the construction. Morris' Red Roof group remains a handsome harbinger of the Arts & Crafts Movement that blossomed in the 1880s on this side of the Atlantic.

Agnes Irwin School was located at Ballytore from 1933 to 1960. In 1963, Saint Sahag & Saint Mesrob Armenian Church, ministering to over 300 members in the tri-county area, relocated there from the Cobbs Creek section of Philadelphia. Following some structural changes, Ballytore was converted into a distinguished sanctuary. Clothier's mansion continues to have a vital legacy.

1 (*top*) The stables at Ballytore.

2 (*center*) One of Morris' Red Roof group.

3 The estate today functions as the Saint Sahag & Saint Mesrob Armenian Church.

ALAN WOOD, JR.'s
WOODMONT

The Towering Estate. Alan Wood, Jr. was the grandson of James Wood, who founded an iron rolling mill in Conshohocken in 1832. Alan was to become president of the huge Alan Wood Steel Company.

Mr. Wood now owned many acres on what may be the highest point along the river in Lower Merion Township. There was a 15 to 20 mile panorama of the Schuylkill valley, including a view of the Wood steel mill down in Conshohocken.

Wood commissioned the noted Philadelphia architect, William L. Price, to design Woodmont. The house was constructed between 1891 and 1894 in the style of a French Gothic chateau.

Price took advantage of his spectacular site with an architectural confection unmatched by any of his previous work which had been stylistically eclectic, plumbing the various revival styles, sometimes in new ways, but generally typical for the day. At Woodmont, he stretched the series of buildings across the ridgeline, beginning with the barn, a lodge and then the manor house. It owed some inspiration in the French Gothic revival of Richard Morris Hunt, but the combination of forms and massing was unlike any predecessor.

Using locally quarried stone with limestone trim, Price combined the academic detailing of pinnacles, crocketed dormers, gargoyles and buttresses with a tall red pyramidal roof over a great hall. This roof is the tallest peak of a small mountain range consisting of turrets, gables and tall chimneys. An overscaled porte-cochere projecting from the center front

1,2 *(top)* Alan Wood, Jr. and his Woodmont estate. **3** *(right)* One of the Victorian bathrooms. **4** *(below)* The baronial great hall, dominated by an elaborate Caen stone fireplace, grand carved stair and encircling balcony give the entrance space a distinct medieval character. 1895 photo.

1 Another 1895 photo shows one of the classical first floor parlors.

2 Visitors, in more recent years, admire the Peace Mission's Chapel Dining Room.

anchors the building to the ground, while an octagonal study and semi-circular porch with their attendant roofs are the foothills of the composition. It is truly a precocious building for a 30 year old architect, no doubt encouraged by a client who didn't mind ostentation.

The interior continued the baronial theme in the great hall by an elaborate Caen stone fireplace, grand stair and encircling balcony. The stair, railings, doors and ceiling are carved, stained oak, with a distinct medieval character.

Mrs. Wood thought the house was too isolated and sold the property to a nephew, Richard G. Wood. In 1929, he subdivided 73 acres, which included the manor house and five support buildings, and sold it to J. Hector McNeal, a corporation lawyer known also for his horsemanship. The interior of the main house underwent renovations.

The Peace Mission. The estate was neglected for a number of years after the death of Mrs. McNeal. In 1953, the house and acreage was sold to the followers of Father Divine. They established the country estate of Father and Mother Divine as The Mount of the House of the Lord and spent a little over one year restoring the 32

3 (above) Mother and Father Divine.
4 (below left) The Peace Mission hosts a "day in the country" for city children.

rooms. The Palace Mission, Inc., is one of the incorporated churches under Father Divine's International Peace Mission Movement and serves as their spiritual headquarters.

Woodmont is open to the public on Sundays from April through October, without charge. Guests can enjoy the first floor of the manor house and visit Father Divine's shrine.

The property is cared for by consecrated co-workers who live communally, some on the property and others in Peace Mission Homes in Philadelphia. The movement's dynamic leader, Mother Divine, is also active in the local community.

In 1998, Woodmont was designated a National Historic Landmark. Today the property reflects the extraordinary care it has received from this religious community. It is a masterpiece of a striking estate, formal gardens, wooded hills, a pond, a lake, streams...and peace.

5 (above) Father Divine's Shrine to Life, set among the Manor House gardens.

243

1 (left) Rathalla's spectacular facade.
2 (below) Joseph Sinnott, c.1902.
3 The main hall of Sinnott's estate.

come a long way from his arrival in 1854 as a 17-year-old immigrant. He had been born in County Donegal, Ireland to a family that could trace its roots back for 700 years...when the first "Synnots" arrived with the Anglo-Norman invasion of Ireland in the 12th century (during the reign of Henry II). One descendent, Susan Synnot, came to America in the 17th century and married George Nixon. Their grandson, John Nixon, gave the first public reading of the Declaration of Independence at the State House on July 8, 1776.

Sinnott joined the distillery firm of John Gibson's Son as a 20-year old bookkeeper. After a brief stint as a private in the Civil War, he began to move up in the business. In 1884,

JOSEPH SINNOTT'S
RATHALLA

In 1889, Joseph Sinnott, owner of the Philadelphia distillery, Moore and Sinnott, purchased 40 acres in Rosemont...land once part of the Ashbridge estate called Rosemont Farm. By summer of 1891, a 32-room house designed by Philadelphia architects, Hazlehurst and Huckel, was ready for occupancy. The house was named Rathalla which in Gaelic means "home of the chieftain upon the highest hill."

Joseph Francis Sinnott had

Gibson retired and Sinnott and Andrew Moore took over. With Moore's death in 1888, Sinnott became the owner of one of the largest distilleries in the country.

When Sinnott and his wife moved into Rathalla, they had six boys and three girls ranging in age from 27 to 13. In addition, there were seven servants in residence: cook, assistant cook, two chambermaids, seamstress, laundress and groom. Mr. Sinnott died in 1906, his wife in 1918. The house stood empty until its purchase by the Sisters of the Holy Child in 1921.

In 1980, the property was placed on the National Register of Historic Places.

1 (above) Rear view of La Ronda.
2 (below) Mr. Foerderer ("Mr. Jefferson").
3 Entrance to the estate today.

PERCIVAL FOERDERER'S
LA RONDA

Percival E. Foerderer (1884-1969), a successful Philadelphia businessman, retired in his early 50s to contribute his energy, affection and support to public service. For 33 years he was the backbone of the growth of the Thomas Jefferson University Hospital. His significant contributions earned him the nickname, "Mr. Jefferson."

Percival Foerderer was the third generation in the family leather business. His grandfather was a curer of hides in Prussia. His father expanded the company in Philadelphia and invented the "chrome process" of treating goatskins to manufacture soft, pliable leather. Their Vici Kid factory, in 1892, employed 2,300 who turned out quality leather kid gloves and shoes.

Foerderer attended Penn Charter School and entered the University of Pennsylvania in 1903 with the desire to be a doctor. His father's serious illness forced him to abandon a college career and he entered the family business to learn the trade from the ground up.

In 1910, Foerderer married Ethel Brown, daughter of a Philadelphia textile machinery maker. For the next 26 years Percival was president of the largest leather manufacturing

business in the United States, perhaps in the world.

There was unemployment and unrest during the Great Depression, and after a strike at the Foerderer factory in 1936, Percival chose to close the plant and retire.

After World War II service, he returned to the home that he and Ethel had designed on a 6+-acre plot in Merion.

Foerderer's success in the stock market allowed him to dream of a larger home in Lower Merion, but not in the popular Colonial or Tudor Revival styles that flooded the Main Line. Percival and Ethel yearned for another home with Spanish and medieval character.

Who else to turn to but Addison Mizner, designer of flambouyant homes in Palm Beach in the 1920s? Foerderer and Mizner, a great team, created La Ronda in 1929, a vast residence on 233 acres. 51 rooms (21 bedrooms) included an elegant mixture of styles: Spanish towers, Gothic porticos, Venetian stained glass, Italianate monastery cloisters and flags, plus European formal gardens.

With the help of 27 employees, Ethel and Percival raised their three daughters in these unique European surroundings.

Ethel sold La Ronda in 1968 and moved to a smaller house in Haverford. She succumbed at 96. Mr. Foerderer died in 1969 at age 84.

WALTER LIPPINCOTT'S ALSCOT

Publisher's Son. Early in 1892, when his only child was 11, Walter Lippincott (son of noted Philadelphia publisher J.B. Lippincott) began the purchase of his 20-acre summer estate on Fishers Road in Bryn Mawr, between the Wheeler and Fisher estates.

Part of the Lippincott property near the corner of Pennswood and Fishers roads included the Lovell farmhouse which was later enlarged and named Greenway. A concrete walkway wandered through specimen trees between Greenway and the service buildings on the Avon Road end of the property.

During the war, Greenway was the site of frequent large parties for wounded servicemen held by Lippincott's daughter, Mrs. Stricker Coles. Mrs. Coles won the Gimbel Award for helping the wounded and founding the United Service Club in Philadelphia during World War I. About two years before our involvement in World War II, the 50-room mansion was demolished.

Alscot. Lippincott named the mansion house, Alscot, after Alverdiscott (pronounced Als-cot) in County Devon, England, where the Lippincott clan had been living since the 16th century.

1 *(top left)* Alscot estate in Bryn Mawr
2 *(above)* Mr. and Mrs. Lippincott with 6-year-old Bertha, Germany, 1886.
3 *(below)* Greenway, c.1920, before stucco was added to the upper walls.

Walter Lippincott's vast Main Line estate also included a guest house he named The Annex. East of the main house was a cluster of 13 buildings: dog kennels, garage, stable, carriage house, tool house, duck house, two hen houses, a greenhouse, a laundry/workshop, a power house (used for heating the main house, still standing), Colony Cottage (still standing) and Hillside Cottage (where foreman Hatton lived). Two other buildings across Avon Road remain: Sunnyside Cottage and Haven Cottage.

Daughter's Marriage. In 1908, Walter and Elizabeth (Bessie) Trotter Horstman Lippincott's only child, Bertha, married Dr. Stricker Coles. Their wedding reception was held at Alscot. The couple lived next to her parents on Walnut Street in Philadelphia (a common-wall joined the two residences) but at some point the family gave up city living and made Alscot their main home. Summers were spent at Jamestown, Rhode Island (favored by the wealthy Philadelphia Quakers over Newport) and on their yacht.

The Annex. Nestled at Alscot's back door, this was the guest house used for parties. In 1932, Dr. and Mrs. Coles' son Walter and his bride, Frances Sadtler, spent their honeymoon night at the Annex and lived there for three years. They subsequently moved with their toddler into Greenway for a couple of years until a new stone house, Colesbrook, was built for them on Avon Road.

1 *(top)* The barn was one of the 13 outbuildings on the Alscot estate.
2 *(center)* Mrs. Walter Lippincott with daughter, Bertha and Arthur Jarvis,

family coachman since 1880, at Alscot's barn in the summer of 1897.
3 *(bottom)* Mrs. Lippincott at the front of Alscot with coachman Jarvis.

MEMORIES

"Back eighty years ago, the people in Gladwyne were mostly farm workers. It's interesting to me how their houses were built on lots 60 feet across the front and 200 to 300 feet back. They're all that way up the street. • Everybody had to be self-sufficient in those days, so everybody needed a plot of ground in the back where. well, first of all, they had a toilet. Nobody had a bathroom in his house or if he did, it was not as we think of bathrooms today. So everybody had one of those 'privies' surrounded by lilac bushes, or a yellow bush that we called a 'privy bush.'
• Everybody had chickens, and they all had a garden. They all had a grapevine because mother made grape jelly, you know; there was nowhere else to get it. Some families had an apple tree or two, maybe a pear tree or some other kind of fruit tree. • The women who were always at home were never idle, because they always had fruit to be canned and stored away or jellies to be made. Another thing they had was rhubarb; they made pie from it. Everybody had a little bed of rhu-barb because rhubarb came up every year. It was no trouble at all. • Fathers who worked around the countryside in the farms came home in late afternoon and when they'd had their dinner they worked in their own gardens. They didn't have anything to listen to or watch, or anything. And so this became a real nice type of place where everybody was friendly with everybody else." **Margaret Doran**

1 *(above)* The vast Penshurst estate and gardens. 2 *(below)* Percival Roberts.

PERCIVAL ROBERTS' PENSHURST

This mansion is truly a Main Line legend, both for the scale of the house and gardens and because of the manner of its demise.

Beginning in 1890, Percival Roberts began amassing farmland in which is now Penn Valley and Gladwyne. By 1898, he had accumulated 539 acres. He had also significantly increased his fortune, leading the Pencoyd Iron Works through its evolution as the American Bridge Company to make it the leading supplier of steel for bridge construction in the country.

By 1901, it made the next profitable leap, merging with the giant U.S. Steel Company, with Roberts becoming one of it directors. Soon after the merger, Percival and his wife Bessye began to plan their house.

They drew on the architectural firm of Peabody and Stearns of Boston, perhaps because Bessye was a Bostonian, or perhaps because families like the Da Costas and Biddles in Philadelphia had already employed this talented partnership.

The newspapers argued over just what inspired the 75 room house...Fountainbleu? Hampton Court? Sandringham? Probably it had elements of each, including a strong dash of Hardwick Hall and Longleat.

The reception hall was marble; the floors were teak. A great balcony surrounded the hall. Much of the interior paneling was antique, brought from England. Newspapers speculated on cost...millions many thought, but it would appear from Roberts' secretary's notes that $525,000 for the basic structure was more the reality.

But that was just the beginning. The house had to be decorated and furnished. An electric generating plant was built along Mill Creek. Landscape architects, the Olmstead Brothers, had to lay out miles of drives and create the great screen and gates along Conshohocken State Road which looked up the hill past fountains and terraces to the house and beyond, capped by an impressive brick water tower at the highest point of the land.

Millions were undoubtedly spent. The house, when completed, was the centerpiece to a vast working farm where dairy barns for the Ayrshire herd were immaculately maintained, with veterinarians on staff, and dozens of farm workers.

But while Penshurst may have fulfilled a role signifying both business and social prominence, it never was used to its fullest. The Roberts did very little entertaining. Sadly, their sons died at an early age probably of scarlet fever or diphtheria. Thereafter Percival and Bessye led quiet, relatively unpretentious lives considering the luxury of their setting, and seem to have found their greatest pleasure in the gardens and farm.

1 *(left)* Bessye Roberts. **2** *(above)* Penshurst's entrance. **3** *(below)* The remaining gates.

The legend continues. By the late 1930s, Mrs. Roberts was quite ill. Roberts commented on how nobody could afford to live in a house like this anymore. He grew increasingly angered as he heard of plans for an incinerator whose tall smoke stack would be in his view. Although he tried to block it, he was not successful. When the incinerator was built in 1939, they moved to a large suite at the Bellevue Strafford Hotel in the city, where live-in nurses and servants attended to their needs.

That year Roberts filed for a permit to demolish the house. He made good on his threat, first selling interior paneling and the artwork, but leaving elements of the garden...

summer houses, fountains and gates.

At his death in 1944, the land and his estate were bequeathed to the Roxborough Hospital and the Children's Seashore Home. The hospital in turn sold it to Home Life Insurance Company, whose owner for many years maintained the Japanese rock gardens, a favorite place for a Sunday stroll by Lower Merion residents.

In the 1950s and 60s, much of the land was developed; Welsh Valley School was built. Today all that remains are the gates along Conshohocken State, a large mid-19th century house and several farm buildings and outbuildings.

1 Yorklynne's main hall.
2 *(below)* Dining Room corner.

3 Another view of the main hall.
4 *(below)* Library.

5 John Gilmore, photo c.1902.

JOHN O. GILMORE'S YORKLYNNE

In 1900, City Avenue was still an unpaved country lane. The road itself had only been re-surveyed in the mid-1850s to more exactly determine the boundary between Philadelphia and Montgomery County. Moving south from the Schuylkill River, the road was lined with farms and some new large estate houses.

William L. Price had been one of the principal architects for the builders Wendell and Smith at Overbrook Farms in the mid-1890s. Known as the "Quaker architect," his practice was entering a phase that included more large residences, with many being located in Overbrook and Merion.

The Snuff King. The largest house by far at this time was Yorklynne, designed by Price in 1899 for John Odgers Gilmore. A Philadelphia native and educated in the public schools, Gilmore was a member of the firm of W. E. Garrett & Sons, the largest snuff manufacturer in the world.

At the turn of the century, Philadelphia was the largest, and one of the most diverse manufacturing centers in the country. Fortunes could be made in products ranging from snuff, men's hats, umbrellas, to steam locomotives.

Gilmore planned a move from a modest speculative home in

1 The mammoth Yorklynne estate of John Odgers Gilmore on City Avenue.

Wayne and launched a competition for architects, a rare custom. Many of the top names in the profession competed, but Price's eclectic blend of European medieval styles won. The house is said to have cost more than $200,000, but with the designer's decorative arts program for the interiors (including furniture designed by Price) the cost was certainly greater.

Stylistically, the exterior was similar to his other designs, with coursed rubble stone contrasting to the carved limestone trim. Flourishes such as gargoyles, an immense red tile roof, and terra cotta *fleur de lis* gave it a French flair.

A House of Crafts. The interiors were a museum of the craftsman's and artist's work. The paneled 20 x 40 foot living hall created an Elizabethan impression. All through the house there was a vibrant mix of contemporary arts set off against furniture and interior architecture that had medieval overtones. This was consistent with the Arts and Crafts movement, also contemporary, that looked back towards a guild system and handwork as a contrast to the mechanization appearing everywhere at the turn of the century.

The upstairs contained a large living hall and suites of rooms for Gilmore, his wife, and children.

Topping off the interior was a huge open room under the roof. Jack Gilmore, grandson of John Gilmore, said that his father had especially enjoyed roller skating around the large room.

In his later practice, architect Price was promoting the ethic of craft work (he would be co-founder of an artist's colony in Rose Valley); his office was at the forefront of modern building technology, as in his reinforced concrete Jacob Reed's Sons store in Philadelphia and the Blenheim and Traymore hotels in Atlantic City.

In 1921, seeking to reduce its debt by selling its building on a valuable Center City lot, the Episcopal Academy purchased the entire property for $225,000 and moved the school to the suburbs.

For most of the 50 years the school occupied the building, it served as the Upper School. It was demolished in 1973 after a new consolidated building was constructed behind the Latches Lane mansions that housed the Lower and Middle Schools. Yorklynne was one of the last of Price's great eclectic houses, and certainly was the centerpiece of the grandest estate on City Line.

PERCY CLARK'S WILLOUGHBY

Percy Hamilton Clark (1873-1965) was descended from the Clarks who emigrated from England to Boston in early 1600s. His family had long resided in Germantown. A successful lawyer in Philadelphia, Percy married Elizabeth Roberts in 1904. Elizabeth was one of five children of Pennsylvania Railroad president George Brooke Roberts and his wife Elizabeth (Pyle Williams) Roberts. George was a descendant of one of the first settlers in the Welsh Tract, John Roberts, who settled in 1683 on a grant of land from William Penn. That became the family estate, Pencoyd, in Bala.

In 1908, Percy and Elizabeth Clark received property on the Roberts tract along Belmont Avenue. They commissioned a cousin, architect Clarence Clark Zantzinger, to design their home, to be called Willoughby. The gracious residence would eventually hold their growing family (eight children) and a large staff (houseman, cook, scullery maid, waitress, governess, a nurse, chambermaid, and others).

They also built a handsome barn and chauffeur's cottage because this was to be a working farm: seven cows, one horse, and 400 chickens. Two gardeners, a farmer, and a driver added to Willoughby's retinue.

John Clark remembers his parents as a "perfect team." Father: patient, thoughtful, dedicated, an enthusiastic outdoorsman; Mother: outgoing, energetic, humorous, dedicated to others, and a good executive who not only ran the large household, but was an involved, loving mother. "There were never any serious 'tiffs' among us eight. We were very involved with our many Roberts cousins who lived nearby. There is still a strong bond between those who remain," John recalls.

Percy Clark, determined that his six boys should learn how to handle money, established a paper corporation, The Clark Brothers Chicken Co. Every day, after returning from the Montgomery School, the boys gathered eggs from the barn, which were then delivered (by the chauffeur) to the neighboring relatives and friends.

In 1951, the estate was sold to The Mary J. Drexel Home. A tribute to Mary J. Drexel Lankenau by her husband, John, the facility provides a unique caring residence for older adults. It is part of the social ministry of the Evangelical Lutheran Church in America.

1 (*top*) Willoughby when it was the Clark family residence...now The Mary J. Drexel Home.

2 (*above*) The charming Clark barn remains on the Belmont Avenue property.

3 (*right*) 1904 wedding photograph of Percy and Elizabeth (Roberts) Clark at the portal of the ancestral Pencoyd estate.

1 *(top)* 1904 wedding party of Percy and Elizabeth Clark.
2 *(above)* In later years, the large clan gathers for Christmas dinner in 1946.

MEMORIES

"I claim to be a descendant of the second settler of Pennsylvania, Sven Schute. Pennsylvania's birthday is April 8, 1643 when the first permanent settler landed in what is now Pennsylvania. That was when the first Swedish boat landed on what is now Tinicum Island. When the boat landed, Johann Printz was captain of the ship; he came down the gangplank first and my ancestor was second in charge...he came down second. His name was Sven Schute.
• The Swedes had a very good relationship with the Indians. No Swede lost a night's sleep from the war whoop of an Indian. My ancestor, Tench Coxe, was the interpreter under that so-called elm tree where William Penn made the treaty with the Indians. That treaty was due to one word, *netappi* ...Indian direct dialect for 'our kind of people' or 'our people.' This is what the Indians called the Swedes. My ancestor Coxe said, 'These are netappi' and the Indians made the treaty.**"**
Samuel Booth Sturgis, M.D.

Dr. Sturgis (1891-1983), patriarch of Township doctors, was born in Belmont Hills (then called Ashland Heights), within 15 miles of the spot where Swedish ancestor, Sven Schute, landed in 1643. From 1918 Dr. Sturgis practiced medicine on the Main Line. His collection of medical prints is now at the Philadelphia College of Physicians. Dr. Sturgis was 90 years old when this interview was taped.

IDLEWILD'S EARLY HISTORY

Originally, the land that became Idlewild Farm, bounded by "the Road leading through the Black Rocks," was part of over 400 acres in the Welsh Tract which was deeded in 1698 to Welsh farmer Robert Lloyd (1668-1714). Lloyd married Miss Lowry Jones when he received his land. Around 1700, on his tract, Lloyd built a one-room-with-loft stone farmhouse with a walk-in oven and an exterior beehive oven (restored), still visible in part in the rear of the existing house. By the time of his death in 1714, the Lloyds had eight children. The inventory filed with his will clearly shows that it was a working farm producing wheat, rye, oats and barley. There was considerable livestock, several servants and "Negro Joe." • Mrs. Lowry Lloyd married again soon after Robert's death. Tradition has it that around 1717, but probably later, the westerly portion of the present two-story house was built in front of Lloyd's small house. These buildings were connected c.1825. The two-story house, later expanded to the east, had two front doors and a pent roof across the front. Also, an 18th-century log barn behind the house was replaced with the present stone bank barn around 1825. • In the early 1800s, the farm passed briefly to several owners until 1834 when John Williamson purchased it. After his death in 1864, it was partitioned to his two sons: Garret and Samuel G. Williamson. In 1868, Garret sold his share to Samuel who then added a kitchen wing on the east side of the farmhouse. The stone stable (carriage house), new spring house and probably the farmer's house also are from this period.

LAWRENCE AND DOROTHY SAUNDERS' IDLEWILD FARM

The Saunders Purchase. In 1897, Mrs. Frances Baugh Saunders (1858-1937), wife of Philadelphia medical publisher Walter B. Saunders (1858-1905), purchased the newly-named Idlewild Farm (or Idylwild) from Samuel G. Williamson. Her purchase along Williamson Road, Bryn Mawr, included the nucleus of farm buildings and 87 of Williamson's 104 acres. Around 1900, Mrs. Saunders converted Idlewild to a dairy farm and summer house.

When Frances Saunders purchased the farm, she acted independently, using her own inheritance. Although their home was in Overbrook, the Saunders family spent summers at the farm. It was a place for work and play, especially for the children: William L. Saunders II (later Lawrence, "Larry") and Emily.

Flight from Philadelphia. The period at the turn of the century was one of migration by affluent Philadelphians from the industrial city to the farm areas of the Old Welsh Tract. Many of these rural estates became "country gentlemen's estates" or

hobby farms, with mansions or greatly remodeled homes.

Mrs. Saunders preferred to retain the old stone farm buildings, remodeling the main house as little as possible. By 1900, she added a herd of Ayrshire milking cows, a milkhouse, plus a large wing and bull pen to the bank barn. She also purchased three adjoining properties, increasing the farm to 167 acres by 1920. Although she was completely deaf, she ran the dairy business from the farm or home until 1927, selling high-quality raw milk to Suplee Dairies.

Lawrence and Dorothy. In 1923, while on a visit to New York, Lawrence Saunders (1890-1968) met Dorothy Wynne Love (1902-1992), a Vassar College student. She was the daughter of cotton factor William Love of Memphis, Tennessee, and his wife Mary. Lawrence and Dorothy were married in 1924 at Princeton, New Jersey, where Dorothy's mother resided. The couple took up residence at Idlewild Farm.

In 1927, Frances Saunders deeded the farm buildings and 70 acres to Lawrence, and the remainder of the land to her daughter, Emily. Although Frances had made limited changes to the farmhouse, the young couple undertook a partial remodeling and renovation in order to make it a permanent residence. The facade was modified to give a more formal appearance; stucco covering the building was removed, and the beautiful old locally-quarried fieldstone was repointed.

Family Growth. The years which followed were busy ones as the Saunders raised their five children. In 1937, Lawrence became Treasurer of the family publishing company, later President and Chairman of the Board. The couple was also active in the community, particularly in matters concerning the environment.

1 *(above)* 1939 aerial view of Idlewild Farm. The residence, (c.1700, 1740, 1910), is at the center, surrounded by the carriage house/ stable and farmer's house (1870); bank barn (1825); dairy barn, milk-house and bull pen (1905); wagon house (1827); spring-house (1860). In 1924 the pool was added, a garage in 1950, the chicken house in 1975. **2** *(left)* The Saunders family, c.1949. (Standing, from left): Morton, Nancy Gayle, Patsy. (Seated): Lawrence, Dorothy, Sally Love, Grier.

In 1927 Dorothy and Lawrence, with a group of property owners in the area, began Bridlewild Trails Association. It now has a large membership of families who enjoy riding or hiking on over 30 miles of marked trails.

In 1951, Lawrence created Saunders Foundation, a private group to maintain Saunders Woods (also known as Little Farm), a 26-acre property he had purchased in 1922 on Waverly Road, Gladwyne, for the public enjoyment, recreation and preservation of its natural beauty.

Dorothy at Idlewild. After the death of Lawrence in 1968, Dorothy purchased Idlewild Farm with 26 acres from his estate. It was a working farm and Dorothy enjoyed farm life in all seasons. She would later incorporate her feelings about its rolling pasture lands, woodlands, lovely old trees and quarried stone walls into a book of poems, "Unbroken Time," published on her 80th birthday. In her later years, graduate students stayed at the farm to help her. Dorothy made all who came to live or visit Idlewild feel welcome.

An Active Life. Despite failing eyesight and other infirmities in later life, Dorothy kept active with social events, travel and writing poetry. Uppermost, however, was her need to fulfill a long-time dream: to find a way to protect her beloved Idlewild Farm for the enjoyment of future generations.

Beneath her warm and gentle manner, this soft-spoken woman had the strength and determination to protect this property which had been in the Saunders family for almost 100 years. The first step, the research to substantiate Idlewild's history pursuant to a National Register nomination, was for Dorothy a fascinating study of this, the oldest operating farm in the township.

National Register Nomination. In 1983, Idlewild farm with its farmhouse, outbuildings and 26 acres was

1 *(left)* Facade of residence before 1927 remodeling. Stucco covered the locally-quarried fieldstone and was removed. **2** *(center)* Idlewild Farm's springhouse (1860). **3** *(below)* Hay wagon. **4** *(bottom)* Remodeled front elevation is seen in 1980 photograph.

entered on the National Register of Historic Places as an excellent example of a turn-of-the-century country gentleman's estate. Over the ensuing years, with the aid of the Natural Lands Trust, a private, non-profit corporation, Dorothy's preservation and conservation dreams came to fruition. In 1988 she conveyed Saunders Woods to the Natural Lands Trust for its protection and maintenance. In 1990 she conveyed 21.2 acres of Idlewild Farm, including farm buildings, to be kept as a preserve. The main house was sold and the remaining lots were sold to create an endowment for this purpose.

Dorothy Love Saunders passed away in February 1992 at the age of 89, having spent the last years of her life at The Quadrangle in Haverford. This remarkable woman had accomplished her goal: to leave for the enjoyment of future generations a lasting gift of unspoiled landscape.

1 *(above)* Recent photograph shows the westerly side of the house, shed porch (at right) removed. The earliest portion of the house is in the middle section, later expanded, roof raised. Current owners had made additions and renovations.

2 *(right)* Dorothy Love Saunders, c.1975. Along with her devotion to Idlewild Farm, her efforts in support of local land preservation have made a significant impact on the landscape of Lower Merion Township.

"UNBROKEN TIME"

(from a book of poems written by Dorothy Love Saunders, published in 1982):

THE PEAHEN

Your consort was so dazzling a companion
but he has not been alive for several years.
You are our lone peacock at Idlewild.
Tell me, would you rather live at the zoo?
There would be other peacocks for company,
but here is where you were born and we'll
    feed you always.
But tell me, would you rather live at the zoo?
              –December 10, 1969

SONG

A mockingbird lives somewhere
    at Idlewild Farm
and sings and sings and sings.
A favorite perch is the tippy top
of the hemlock down by the springhouse.
You can clearly see him as he pours out
    his beautiful song.
On and on with such volume
that the whole meadow and field around
are alive with glorious music.
             –September 22, 1970

A SUNSET GLOW

What do I see? A mass of glowing rust color
in the bare trees, now dead of winter.
These trees should have no color
other than the black of trunks and branches.
How can it be?
I see the buttonwood
rising glistening white above the others
like a silver birch.
The woods are transformed.
The setting sun has done its magic
with the help of newly washed air,
    and is playing tricks on us.
    And I love tricks!
             –January 28, 1979

IDLEWILD

They say the universe
is contained in a grain of sand.
This expanse of rolling meadow
to me symbolizes all spaciousness.
It brings to my mind
the endless wheat fields of the Middle West
or those limitless views of our Far West.
It is like the ocean calm at sea
or an arc of sky.
It has the feel of uninterrupted time.
As I gaze,
I no longer feel confined.
             –April 18, 1982

1 *(top)* 1925 aerial view of the James Crosby Brown Estate known as Clifton Wynyates, designed by William Price and M. Hawley McClanahan in 1903 for William C. Scott. Under Scott's ownership, the estate was often labeled on maps as The Dipple. The masonry half-timber mansion was connected to the carriage house by a passage built over the driveway.

2 *(above)* Compton Wyngates, the British Tudor castle in Warwickshire, England, once home of Henry VIII; c.1920 postcard. The building served as an inspiration for the Price design and other American estate homes of the period.

JAMES CROSBY BROWN'S CLIFTON WYNYATES

A 1915 newspaper clipping reads "James Crosby Brown, of the banking house of Brown Bros., has purchased Clifton Wynyates, the estate of Mrs. William Carpenter Scott at Ardmore [Gladwyne]. The estate was valued at $500,000 and was sold at a figure close to that price. Clifton Wynyates comprises 200 acres, a house of 50 rooms, garage, dairy, stable, numerous other outbuildings and a large riding ring. It is one of the most extensive private estates in the vicinity of Philadelphia."

The Brown Estate. James Crosby Brown, the son of John Crosby Brown of Brown Bros., merchant bankers of Philadelphia and New York, took a position with the Philadelphia office in 1904. He later married Mary Agnes Hewlett of Long Island and they had two sons.

The estate he purchased in 1914 had been designed in 1903 by William Price. Brown called upon the original architect to make changes and improvements. The site incorporated various early farm buildings, mills and mill worker's houses from the former agricultural and industrial

lands bounding Mill Creek. Those structures served as housing for servants and over 25 farm hands who worked on the gentleman's farm. Because Brown's wife suffered from asthma, Brown continued to expand his land holdings to protect her from the smoke of burning leaves. Unfortunately this served little purpose, for she died of an attack while out of state.

In 1921 Brown married a widow, Aurelia Jenkins, former wife of a Yale classmate. Together they combined a family of five boys and two girls. In 1925 their own daughter, Aurelia (called Thistle) was added to the family.

The Market Crashes. The lavish life of this Golden Age family changed radically after the stock market crash of October 1929. Brown apparently lost half or more of his investments. At age 56, a heart attack caused his death while walking home from his neighbor and financial associate, Joseph N. Pew. Despite his losses, Brown's

estate totaled nearly 1.5 million dollars (including the 194 acres in Gladwyne, 1,000 acres on Pasque Island in Massachusetts and two yachts in Brooklyn).

The widow and family moved to a small property in Sugartown, leaving the Gladwyne estate to be sold by his executors to create a family trust.

A Large Subdivision. By 1933 the land was being subdivided through Brown's widow and his brother, Thatcher. Walter Durham and James Irvine, a leading architecture and development team in the township since 1926, became the chief collaborators. Of all the Main Line estates that Durham & Irvine developed , this was the largest. Subdivision plans changed from 20 large tracts in 1934 to 43 parcels by 1948.

Durham designed and built new houses on 25 parcels. He adapted or altered existing buildings on three others. He also converted Clifton Wynyates into two residences and the garage into a third. What was significant about this development was the care and consideration given to the landscape through a 3-acre lot size and deed restrictions. Despite the estate's need, the land was not plundered for profit through a high density development of four to five houses per acre.

Durham's Architecture. Eight of Durham's new houses typified his early, classic Pennsylvania farmhouse pattern (derived from the 18th-century vernacular Welsh homes of the area). Two buildings mimic the British picturesque masonry manor house. Fourteen others range from *moderne* to new eclectic designs using regional architectural patterns that Durham initiated after World War II.

The Brown Legacy. The Brown estate and the Durham & Irvine team left the township with a quality development using spacious lots with sensitivity to the Mill Creek Valley. Their forward-looking land conservation goals have enabled 192 acres to appear as undeveloped wooded hillsides even today.

1 *(above)* Clifton Wynyates' baronial entrance, photographed in the mid-1930s. The English Gothic revival style mansion featured a ballroom, a chapel and a banquet hall. Massive walls and buttressing were part of the original design to retain the house on the hillside and create terraced areas. **2** *(below)* The large two-story, timbered entrance hall, photographed during the Brown's ownership.

From the Brown family album: **1** *(top)* James Crosby Brown and Aurelia Jenkins Brown with their five boys and two girls on the steps of Clifton Wynyates in the 1920s.

2 *(center)* Thistle Brown in her donkey cart.

3 *(below)* The Brown and Jenkins families mounted and ready to ride. The family owned eight to ten horses and rode frequently to hunts in Radnor and Whitemarsh.

NOTABLE NEIGHBOR

Eugene J. Houdry (1892-1962), a French-born engineer, was originator of several methods using catalysts, generally called the Houdry Process, to speed up conversion of petroleum components to useful products such as high-octane gasoline. He was employed by the Sun Oil Company which put into operation the first large-scale commercial catalytic cracking plant and produced Blue Sunoco, first of the high-octane gasolines. • In 1937, during the subdivision of the Brown estate, Clifton Wynyates was divided into two residences, separating the carriage house from the main building. Houdry purchased 9.8 acres that included the distinctive mansion house. He had the architect Walter Durham add peaked roofs to the round crenelated tower and named it *Le Mesmil,* meaning little farm. The interior was also greatly altered to French taste.
• At one time Houdry's neighbors objected when he conducted experiments in his garage related to the catalytic cracking of petroleum. Joseph N. Pew, Sun Oil president, became the first owner of the carriage house. A recent restoration of this by Robert A.M. Stern introduced a lap swimming pool into this elegant residence. • Subsequent owners of *Le Mesmil* have been Frank Goodyear, entertainer Mike Douglas, and soul singer Teddy Pendergrass.

1 *(top)* 1936 aerial view of the Ludington estate in Gladwyne. Clovelly, at left, is the Colonial Revival home designed by Seeler (alterations and additions by Sellers and later by Durham) for Charles Ludington. The 1933 modern Court House, at right, was built by Durham for C. Townsend Ludington on the former squash court adjacent to the formal gardens.
2 *(left)* Mill Creek, by Furness, Evans & Co., originally on the site of Clovelly, was built in 1887 for Dr. Henry C. Register. The building burned in 1897. 3 *(below)* Carriage house of Henry C. Register built by Furness, Evans & Co. in 1887 and converted to a residence during the 1950s. Pictured here before its demolition in 1998.

CHARLES LUDINGTON'S CLOVELLY

Charles Ludington stemmed from Old Lyme, Connecticut, and was a graduate of Yale Law School. He married Ethel Saltus in 1895 and they lived in Manhattan where Charles practiced law. In 1901, he took the position of secretary and treasurer of the Curtis Publishing Company in Philadelphia and the Ludingtons moved to the Main Line.

Mill Creek Valley. A ten-acre hilly tract with a mansion, carriage house, artist's studio and spring house on Old Gulph Road in Gladwyne (formerly Ardmore) was purchased in 1905. Their estate, named Clovelly, was cherished, remodeled and newly built on for over 50 years. The 19th- and 20th-century architectural history of the property represents a microscopic tale of the aesthetics, social life and development of the Main Line from the founding fathers to the present.

1 *(above)* The south and east facades of Clovelly, built by Edgar V. Seeler on the site of Dr. Register's Mill Creek after a fire in 1897. The Furness and Evans carriage house remained with some changes.

2 *(below)* The Ludington family on the south porch of Clovelly, c.1918. Charles Henry Ludington, Wright, Nicholas, Townsend and Ethel. The boys grew up at Clovelly, but as teenagers, each was sent to a different boarding school.

Furness and Evans. The first house built on this hillside east of John Roberts' residence and grain mill on Mill Creek was one for the prominent dentist, Dr. Henry C. Register, designed by Furness and Evans. After fire destroyed most of the building in 1897, Edgar V. Seeler, architect for the Curtis Publishing Company, rebuilt the house in a Colonial Revival mode. The estate was newly named Clovelly after an English town.

When the Ludingtons took possession of Clovelly in 1905, Charles became actively involved in Philadelphia educational institutions and academies, served as treasurer for the Bryn Mawr Presbyterian Church and was a member of many social clubs.

As was the tradition of the day, Ethel served her family, home and social causes. Her strong leadership, enthusiasm and a zest for life won her many friends. An extensive formal garden adjoining a squash court became her pride and joy.

3 *(left)* Old photo of the estate's beautiful gardens. In addition to the colorful flower beds, Clovelly boasted sweeping lawns and unusual specimen trees.

262

1 *(far left)* Ethel Saltus Ludington in a 1909 painting.

2 *(left)* Mid-1920s photograph of Charles Ludington.

3 *(below)* In 1926 Charles gave $50,000 to build a library as a monument to his beloved Ethel, a tribute to values they both held dear. Additions in the 1950s, 60s and 80s have enveloped the original building *(see Libraries)*.

4 *(bottom)* Portrait of Charles Ludington (c.1920s) in Bryn Mawr's Ludington Library.

During 1913-14 the estate was remodeled by another local architect, Horace Well Sellers. The west porch wing was extensively expanded, adding new charm for both family and visitors. The joy of the remodeled home was dampened by the diagnosis that Ethel was suffering from tuberculosis. Despite her illness, the family maintained an active travel schedule both in America and Europe. Sanatorium stays in the west and Saranac Lake did little to curb Ethel's disease; on September 7, 1922, she died after a valiant battle at the age of 51. No one was more devastated than her husband, her most devoted follower.

Memorial To Ethel. Thanks to his wealth, Charles Ludington was able to turn his wife's untimely death into a philanthropic cause to memorialize her life. A small book told of her community efforts, spirit and intelligence. A new infirmary was built for the Saranac Lake sanatorium. Funds went to the Ardmore Library, and $50,000 built the new Ludington Library in Bryn Mawr. Ethel Saltus Ludington's name became prominently attached to the built environment.

The Ludington estate's architecture and open space remains reminiscent of the dedication of a former Main Line family to the community.

J. HOWARD PEW'S KNOLLBROOK

Knollbrook, a 13 acre estate owned by J. Howard Pew during his lifetime, sits high on a hill at Grays Lane and Mill Creek Road. It was built on land owned by John Roberts, the miller. In 1845, Samuel Croft, who also operated mills, purchased 35 acres to be used for farming. In 1883, he sold his acreage to his friend and attorney, I. Layton Register. Register built Lynhurst, designed by noted Philadelphia architect, Frank Furness, in 1890.

Giving about 5-1/2 acres to each of his children, Register built Knollbrook for his son, Albert Layton Register. Completed by 1908, the home was one of the very few country houses built of brick and was unusual in having the regularity of Georgian design. Philadelphia architect, Lindley Johnson, planned the early Knollbrook.

Records indicate that J. Howard Pew rented the house before buying the 8.29 acre estate from Register's three sons in 1917. The Pews soon brought in another architect, William Woodburn Potter, who planned the additions.

At first Knollbrook was a relatively small, block-shaped colonial with typical center-hall design. In the following half century it was more than doubled in length and so embellished that it is now one of the outstanding Georgian homes on the Main Line.

When Mr. Pew bought Knollbrook, the land was mainly open fields which had been pastureland for Register's sheep. Some of the old sheep pens, stables and farm houses were still to be seen on the property into the 1970s.

1 *(top)* Lynhurst, designed by Frank Furness in 1890 for attorney I. Layton Register.

2 *(above)* Knollbrook entrance, early 1970s.

1 J. Howard Pew, 1947 photo, became president of Sun Oil Company at age 30.

J. Howard Pew was immensely interested in his property. He transformed the grounds into three immaculate terraces which drop with the hillside, complete with putting green and swimming pool. Courtyards were created with a fountain, as were paths, springs with little bridges, a rock garden and a greenhouse.

At the time of Pew's death in 1971, the estate contained 65 acres. Much of these holdings have been subdivided. Three other Register houses, Lynhurst, Gray Grange and Dove Lake Farm, are still in existence. The present owners of Knollbrook have renamed the estate, Camelot.

2 Knollbrook today, nestled in foliage on its hillside setting, is barely visible from along Mill Creek Road.

CONTRASTS

THE LOG HOUSE. At the end of a long lane in Gladwyne is a simple dwelling, probably built for a worker on Herbert's farm between 1698 and 1700. Nothing is known of its history in the 18th or 19th centuries until the 1860s. William Booth bought part of the Herbert farm, adjacent to his mill, and included the cabin. Booth's farmer, John Doran and his wife, Martha, lived in the one-room building. In 1872, it was made into a six-room house to accommodate the Dorans' growing family. They lived there until 1892.

• One previous owner relates, "Laurence Jordan, a black handyman, used to live in the cabin. He grew melons in the field by the cemetery (Har-Hazaitim) and also had a couple of cows. There was a date stone in the north peak of the cabin: 1698. It was stolen! The cement between the logs was made of hair. I think it's the oldest standing structure we have on the Main Line."

3 Gladwyne's Log House.

1 *(above)* Marriott Smyth's Brentwood estate survives today as Sydbury House.

WILLIAM L. MC LEAN, JR.'S SYDBURY HOUSE

In February 1906, an announcement appeared in the *Philadelphia Inquirer* regarding a house rising on Cherry Lane. Plans were completed and contractors were chosen for "a handsome three-story stone residence." The land, with some old farm buildings on it, had been part of a property called St. Mary's Farm owned by Harry Shoch, just across Cherry Lane from the larger, 167-acre holding of Louis Wister.

The Furness Touch. The new house was designed by the venerable Philadelphia architectural firm of Furness, Evans & Company, whose principal partner, Frank Furness, had by then reached his mid-sixties. Whether he was still directly active as its designer is uncertain; the house adopted the guise of the fashionable Colonial Revival that was sweeping the suburbs, casting commuters in the guise of 18th-century country gentry. Such academicism was something of a rebuke to the bold, inventive and expressive spirit that marked Furness' most celebrated works of the 1870s and 1880s.

Still, there are marks of the old vigor: a distinctive breadth and massiveness, a resistance to the new fluidity, lightness and academic correctness and an unconventionality in plan that seems to recall the old lion's hand, even if it may have operated here through his influence over others in the office.

The architect's client was Marriott C. Smyth, a businessman in his early sixties who had lived in Philadelphia. Smyth was president of companies that made wheels and other parts for trains, the Latrobe Steel Company. His own commute was to an office on Broad Street. He was an active clubman both in the suburbs and downtown. During the tenure of Smyth and his extended family, which lasted until his death in 1919, the house and surrounding estate of 33 acres was called Brentwood.

The Lippincott Purchase. Following the Smyths, in the early 1920s the house came into the hands of Walter H. Lippincott, a broker, and his wife Edith D'Olier, who renamed their home Sydbury House.

In 1926, the Lippincotts hired landscape architect Thomas Sears to work on their grounds, which included the design of a formal garden, a pool and tennis court. He also added a library to the house and removed an original porte-cochere.

The McLean Era. The house subsequently became the home of William Lippard McLean, Jr., who had succeeded his father as publisher of the Philadelphia Evening Bulletin. McLean's father had purchased the newspaper in the late 19th century, then reportedly the smallest of the city's 13 daily papers, and transformed it into "the most profitable evening newspaper ever published in this city of state," according to a 1941 account, with a circulation that at one point topped a half million.

The new owners hired another renowned Philadelphia architectural firm, Mellor & Meggs, to renovate and alter the house. In the late 1930s, William Jr. and his wife Eleanor Bushnell McLean moved here from a house in Chestnut Hill, and she survived him to live nearly fifty years in the house, until 1986. Their son, William III, worked at the Bulletin until 1980. In a recent interview he recalled the house and neighborhood.

"The house, quite naturally, was the product of the Victorian era, and you have to take yourself back

1 (below) A fountain in the gardens by landscape architect, Thomas Sears.

2 (bottom) The McLean family in 1949. From left, Bill, mother Eleanor, sister Ray and father William McLean, Jr.

into those times to understand it. It is a monstrous rockpile with three floors in front and four floors in back [to fit in lots of servants]...The house was built for five children and their bedrooms were all on the second floor [prompting one visitor to call it 'the motel']...When we moved into Cherry Lane in 1938 there was no traffic light on Montgomery Avenue. But then it wasn't needed...When my father bought this place, it was staked out in building lots, 33 of them, and it was something less than 22 acres".

In 1954 William III married landscape historian Elizabeth Peterson and they moved into "the little white house" on the property. These younger McLeans recalled the staffing and service buildings of the main house in the years before World War II.

"Pre-war, there was a lady's maid upstairs and a downstairs maid. There was a chauffeur who lived in an apartment over the garage. This was a garage that could hold six carriages or six automobiles...it was attached to a horse stable. It had right below it a little cow barn. There was a gardener who lived on the place...he had an assistant. There was a house man, a headwaitress, [an old family retainer] and an assistant waitress...there was a cook and a kitchen maid. There were people crawling out of the woodwork.

After the war, that got cut back. Times change. The house man went. A couple of the maids went. But right up to the end, Mother had the headwaitress, the lady's maid, the upstairs maid; she had a chauffeur and a gardener; both lived on the place. And a laundress; she cleaned the back of the house, not to be confused with someone who cleaned the front of the house. This is just the way things were in those days."

With all the formality of that, to put it in perspective, [William III's] mother felt very close to all of them,

and she referred to 'the girls.' "They could have been 60, but they were 'the girls.' She was very fond of them. She worried about them and had one chauffeur who drank. She stuck with him; she worked with him. He went to AA. And she saved him. She was like that. All the maids, all the formality gives you one picture, but I think the way she dealt with them gives you a different picture."

In 1968, the McLeans had a new house built for them on a corner of the property. In the late 1980s, the land around the old house was subdivided into a minimum number of lots that became sites for new houses designed by Lyman Perry.

1 *(right)* The Megargee home, known as Pen-y-Bryn, designed by Minerva Parker Nichols about 1893. The roof shape, window details and uncovered porch create a unique architectural design.

2 *(above)* The ruins of the three-story mill workers' double house located on the former Nippes mill property. The building is likely c.1825.

3 *(right)* Irwin N. Megargee (1862-1905) on his horse at Folly Farm. The Megargee family of Philadelphia spent summers at the farm where their five children mastered a knowledge of horsemanship.

ROLLING HILL PARK

The Walter C. Pew Estate purchased by Lower Merion Township in 1995 for passive recreation and a nature preserve was the last and largest Township park acquisition of the 20th century. The tract in Gladwyne is significant for its lineage as three significant parcels of land that had originated from three different Welsh patent holders under William Penn: John Roberts, Robert Jones and Richard Harrison. At one time miller John Roberts held two of the three parcels. Two parcels had corners crossing Mill Creek, and on each of these the clear, rapid water supply encouraged construction of a mill.

Early Mills. Frederick Bicking built a paper mill by 1762 at the western end. This site evolved into a textile mill by the end of the 19th century. Benjamin Brooke established a forge or gun powder manufactory at the eastern end in 1794. This became a rifle factory under the Nippes family and was later converted to a wool carpet yarn mill. The enlarged mill still stands outside the park.

Above the creek on the adjoining hillside and peak, farmland was cultivated by other settlers to serve local residents or Philadelphians. These parcels served as both agricultural land and for milling industries for nearly two centuries.

Megargee's Folly Farm. By 1852, a large agricultural tract descending from the Roberts Family was subdivided to a 43-acre parcel. In 1892, a Philadelphia industrialist and paper merchant, Irwin Megargee, developed the site as an elaborate gentleman's dairy and horse farm called Folly Farm. It featured a caretaker's cottage, a large stone barn, stables, macadam drives and a swimming basin. Minerva Parker Nichols, a young woman architect, redesigned the early farmhouse for Megargee, who renamed it Pen-y-Bryn ("top of the hill").

Hagenlocher's Purchase. When Paul C. Hagenlocher, an investment banker, purchased the farm from Megargee's widow in 1909, he hired the architect Clyde Smythe Adam to design an elegant new stone Colonial Revival mansion for the same site. Hagenlocher continued the gentleman's farming tradition and added then-modern concrete farm buildings that included a silo and hog barn (still extant). The stock market crash caused Hagenlocher to sell his farm and it was purchased by Walter C. Pew in 1929.

Pew's Rolling Hill Farm. Walter Pew, grandson of the founder of Sun Oil, renamed the property Rolling Hill Farm, but he focused less on agriculture and instead expanded his land holdings to create a significant suburban estate. He added tennis courts and a swimming pool west of the house designed by the noted landscape architect Thomas Sears of Gladwyne.

By 1938, Pew had added sections of the Bicking and Nippes mill parcels along Mill Creek, land with at least four stone residences for mill workers built prior to 1850.

The Pews and their two children lived at Rolling Hill Farm until the 1950s, but by 1958 family members had left the residence unoccupied. While it was being dismantled in July 1958, a blow torch set the building in flames.

The remains were demolished and the Pews never used the site again, though the caretaker continued to live in the cottage.

The Township's Rolling Hill Park. When the property of the Pew Estate was put on the market in 1994, there was an immediate effort in the Township to acquire this special tract of open space with its remaining farm buildings and mill residences neatly bounded by Rose Glen Road and Mill Creek.

Through Montgomery County Open Space funds, a Township bond issue and contributions raised by Lower Merion Preservation Trust from the community at large, 103 acres of open space was purchased for $4.37 million and renamed Rolling Hill Park.

1 *(above)* Stone mansion designed in 1911 for Paul C. Hagenlocher. The property became Walter C. Pew's suburban residence in 1929.
2 *(below)* The farm cottage seen in 1936. Built c.1895 for Megargee's brother, it was later home for caretakers of the ensuing owners... and will now serve Lower Merion Conservancy.

A Natural Refuge. Rolling Hill Park is now a cherished nature preserve and cultural resource as well as part of a National Register Historic District. The park is used to teach the history of early Quaker settlement and industry in the Township and to provide opportunities for bird watching, hiking, horseback riding, fishing and picknicking. The farm cottage built for the Megargee's caretaker is being restored by Lower Merion Conservancy, where they will work to protect open space, historic resources and clean streams throughout the Township.

TWO RECYCLED ESTATES

Several of the Township's large properties have been saved for adaptive reuse. There seemed to be rivalries among some of the local railroad barons to see who could erect the most impressive castle. The estate of **Samuel Rea, 1** *(top)*, President of the Pennsylvania Railroad (1913-1925) now serves as Waverly Heights, a lifecare community in Gladwyne. **William L. Austin** was President of Baldwin Locomotive Works. His property, **2** *(above)*, is also a lifecare community, Beaumont at Bryn Mawr.

TWO MODERN CLASSICS
Frank Lloyd Wright's concept for Suntop Homes in Ardmore, **1** *(top)*, was
to be a prototype for affordable cluster housing constructed with inexpensive
materials. This 4-unit dwelling was built in 1939, but the war blocked plans
to develop more. A striking example of the International School of architecture
is the broadcast center on City Avenue, **2** *(above)*, built for station WCAU.
Designed by **George Howe** and **Robert Montgomery Brown,** it was a state
of the art facility when it was constructed in 1952.

DERIVATION OF LOCAL NAMES: TOWNS, ROADS AND LANES

Academy Road: Named for the Lower Merion Academy, built in 1812.

Ardmore: A small town in Ireland on the Atlantic coast.

Armat Avenue: Named for George Armat, a Philadelphia merchant, who owned a 100 acre farm in the area,

Ashbridge Road: Named for Joshua Ashbridge family that lived in Thomas House (built in 1764), now called Ashbridge House.

Athens Avenue: Classic Greek names, styles, etc. were popular during Napoleonic age and Ardmore was given name Athensville.

Avon Road: From Haverford estate of Charles E. Mather, called Avonwood Court.

Baird Road: After Matthew Baird, proprietor of Baldwin Locomotive Works, through which his estate, Bardwold, was laid out.

Bala: Town in Gwynedd, Wales. Derived from the Celtic "belago" meaning the efflux of a river from a lake.

Ballytore Road: After Isaac H. Clothier, Philadelphia merchant and philanthropist, who built his castle and called it Ballytor.

Bangor Road: Town in Gwynedd, Wales. Derived from Celtic "ban" meaning a bond or strengthening, and "cor" meaning woven.

Barmouth: Town in Gwynedd, Wales. An Anglicized form of "abermaw," "bar" being a mutation of "aber," the mouth of the river Maw. "Maw" means broad.

Belmont Avenue: "Pretty mountain" or "beautiful mount" was the name given by the father of Judge Richard Peters to his mansion on the Belmont Plateau in West Fairmount Park, by which the road runs.

Berwyn: Name of a mountain range forming the border between Merioneth and Montgomery counties in Wales.

Black Rock Road: From igneous black rocks that are found in the vicinity.

Bowman Avenue: Named for Roger Bowman who settled in locality in 1798.

Brookhurst Avenue: From Brookhurst Inn, which catered to frequenters of Belmont Driving Park.

Bryn Mawr: Name given to his plantation by Rowland Ellis after his home in Wales. Means "high moor," or "great hill."

Buck Lane: From Old Buck Tavern which dated to 1730.

Cheswold Lane: From Cheswold, ("chestnut woods"), the estate of A. J. Cassatt.

Chichester Lane: Once part of the Wister farm of 190 acres. G. M. Chichester married a Wister daughter.

Conestoga Road: Derived from the Conestoga Indians and applied to a river and, in turn, to a valley. The road got its name because freight was carried in Conestoga wagons.

Conshohocken: Lenape word meaning "pleasant valley," "at the long fine land," "at the place of the great land."

Coulter Avenue: For Lewis Coulter whose farm was divided into building lots.

Cricket Avenue: Originally the farm lane from Lancaster Avenue to the Sheldon farm (popularly known as Mud Lane). In 1880, a parcel of the farm was sold to the Merion Cricket Club which was located here until 1889.

Curwen Road: Originally part of Walnut Hill, the large estate of the Curwen family dating back to 1787.

Cynwyd: Town in Gwynedd, Wales. Personal name of a Welsh saint/confessor.

Daylesford: Named for a tourist resort in Australia.

Devon: Named for a tourist resort in England.

Dove Lake: Dove paper mill, which used outline of dove as watermark, was located here in colonial times.

Dreycott Lane: Meaning "secluded spot" or "secluded retreat" is the name of a village in England founded in 825 A.D.

Eagle Farm Road: From Eagle Farm of John Suplee.

Elmwood Avenue: Elm was the old name of Narberth.

Fishers Road: Road opened in 1846 through the 81 acre farm of William A. Fisher.

Flat Rock Road: Road leading to Flat Rock Ferry across Schuylkill below Flat Rock Dam.

Floyd Terrace: Named by Frank S. Floyd who developed this and Markee Terrace.

Ford Road: Vestige of a once major highway which connected Old Conestoga Road (Montgomery Avenue) with the falls of the Schuylkill.

Gladwyne: In 1887, the Lower Merion Post Office renamed this area from Merion Square to Gladwyne, which was borrowed from a nearby freight station of the Reading Railroad.

Glanrafon Creek: Glanrason, through which the creek flowed, was the plantation of Kate Jones who came to Lower Merion in 1683.

Glenn Road: Ancient road leading to Mill Creek, named after Edward Glenn, local historian, who had his home on it.

Grays Lane: William Gray owned about 70 acres of land south of Trout Run and the lane that led to Montgomery Avenue to his home had this name.

Grenox Road: Combination of Green and Knox, brother and sister, who owned farms through which the road runs.

Greystone Road: Name of estate of Joseph B. Townsend, real estate lawyer. Blancoyd and Raynham, the nearby homes of his sons, furnished the name for two other roads in the locality.

Grove Place: Given by Wood, Harmon & Company, developers of Narberth, who favored arboreal names.

Gulph Road: Led to "the gulph," old-time description of a pass through a ravine.

Hardie Way: Named by John R.K. Scott for his son.

Harriton: Plantation of Richard Harrison, house built in 1704.

Haverford: Derived from Haverfordwest in Pembrokeshire, Wales, meaning "the goat's ford."

Holland Avenue: James A. Holland, a Lower Merion Supervisor of Roads, owned the land which was developed here.

Hood Road: Named after Walter W. Hood, one of the organizers of the Merion Title & Trust Company.

Ingeborg Road: German name given by William Simpson to his mansion built here in 1884.

Iona Avenue: Narberth developers named north and south streets alphabetically– Berkley, Conway, Dudley, Essex, Forrest, Grayling, Hamden. Iona was chosen arbitrarily to carry out the sequence.

Kennedy Lane: After John M. Kennedy, important Pennsylvania Railroad stockholder, who had his estate in Bryn Mawr.

Lakeside Road: Road ran past Bailey's Lake, now filled in.

Lapsley Lane: Captain Joseph Lapsley Wilson owned the property on which the Barnes Museum and Arboretum are now located.

Latchs Lane: Corruption of Latch's Lane. Jacob Latch, Revolutionary soldier, had his farm and homestead here.

Levering Street: Was cut through Illinova, the 17 acre estate of Abraham Levering.

Levering Mill Road: Led to ford of Schuylkill on Levering property, also to Anthony Levering's mill.

Llanberris Road: Town in Gwynedd, Wales. Named for the church of Peris.

Llandrillo Road: Town in Gwynedd, Wales. Named for Church of St.Trillo. There are many places in Wales dedicated to this saint.

Llanfair Road: Town in Gwynedd, Wales. Named for the Church of St. Mary.
The full name is:
Llanfairpwllgwyngyllgoegrychwyr ndrobwll-llantysiliogogogoch.

Llanllew Road: After manor of Llanelyw in Wye Valley, Wales. Name given by Benjamin Humphrey to his plantation.

Lodges Lane: Led to mansion of Thomas G. Lodge, wealthy Cynwyd land owner.

Manayunk: From the Lenape "Manaiunk" meaning the lands along the Schuylkill River "where we go to drink."

Matson Ford Road: Led to ford on the Schuylkill River, on the property of Peter Matson, an early Swedish settler.

McClenaghan Mill Road: Led to mills on Mill Creek confiscated as property of John Roberts and bought in 1797 by George McClenaghan.

Meeting House Lane: Leads to the Merion Meeting, a 1695 Quaker house of worship.

Merion: Grandson of a 5th century Welsh prince, from Merionethshire in Wales.

Montgomery: Named for the county Mont-gomeryshire in Wales, which is between Merionethshire and Radnorshire. Name of the 11th century Roger of Montgomery, Earl of Shrewsbury.

Monument Road: Continuation of Monument Road in Philadelphia. Ran past rough obelisk which, tradition says, was erected by Judge Peters in memory of horses killed during the Revolution.

Morris Avenue: Laid out in 1876 through 594 acre property of Levi and Naomi Morris, owners of Harriton.

Mt. Moro Road: After Moro Phillips, of Phillips Land Company, extensive landowners and developers of a century ago.

Narberth: Town in Dyfed, Wales. Name means sacred or consecrated place.

Old Railroad Avenue: Originally part of the roadbed for the Philadelphia & Columbia Railway.

Owen Road: Robert Owen was the first landowner here and his home, built in 1695, is still standing.

Panorama Road: Laid out by Phillips Land Company in such a manner as to take advantage of the view.

Paoli: Named for General Pasquale Paoli, a Corsican patriot.

Parsons Avenue: Father of Luther Parsons had his carriage and wheelwright shops here.

Pembroke Road: Town in Dyfed, Wales. Originally a small village called Pater or Paterchurch.

Penarth Road: A seaside suburb of Cardiff, South Wales. Name means headland, or head of the promontory.

Pencoyd: From Pennychlawd in Denbigh-shire, Wales, birthplace of J. Roberts who built his house in 1685.

Powder Mill Lane: Led to mills on Cobbs Creek, where gunpowder was made during the Revolution and later.

Price Avenue: Price family (corruption of ap Rees) owned nearly all of Narberth since the time of William Penn.

Radnor: Means "red earth," Named for the county Radnorshire, located in central Wales.

Redleaf Road: Redleaf was the home of Thomas Pym Remington, lover of trees, who owned considerable land on both sides of Lancaster Pike in Wynnewood.

Rees Avenue: After Rees Thomas, early Welsh settler.

Righters Ferry Road: Led to ford on the Schuylkill River, operated by Peter Righter.

Roberts Road: Road in Bryn Mawr laid out in 1735 as "John Roberts, miller, road."

Rock Hill Road: Passes by Rock Hill, rocky eminence south of Ashland Hill.

Rosemont: Name given by Pennsylvania Railroad to its station as a compliment to Joshua Ashbridge, whose farm was called Rosemont and who deeded land in 1863 for a station.

St. Asaphs Road: Asai or Asaph, a native of North Wales, was abbot of the Monastery Llan Elwy in 545. There is a church named in his honor in Bala, Wales.

St. Davids: Patron saint of Wales. Grandson of Caredig, who gave his name to a large area of Wales– Ceredigion.

St. Pauls Road: Named by Walter Bassett Smith for St. Paul's Evangelical Lutheran Church.

Schuylkill River: The Lenape name was Ganoshowanna meaning "falling water," "where to drink." The early Dutch named it Skokihl or "hidden river."

Shortridge Drive: After Nathan Parker Short-ridge, banker and Pennsylvania Railroad ex-ecutive, where his 200 acre estate was located.

Sibley Avenue: Squire William Sibley, who died in 1896, developed the property through which the road runs.

Simpson Road: Named by Walter Bassett Smith for the Ardmore Methodist Church (originally named Matthew Simpson M.E. Church).

Soapstone Road: From the steatite quarry found on former 90 acre farm called Soapstone and formerly owned by Clement Griscom, steamship magnate.

Sprague Road: After George S. Sprague, whose property lay on both sides of the road.

Spring Avenue: Part of James Thomas' 100 acre tract. He built his house near by a spring whose overflow coursed along this road.

Spring Mill Road: Leads to a great spring across the Schuylkill River. Remarkable in colonial days for its flow, used today by the paper mill at Miquon.

Strafford: Named for the Earl of Strafford, it was the name of the Wentworth family estate.

Summit Road: Runs along the highest elevation in Penn Valley.

Summit Grove Avenue: Was lane leading to Summit Grove House, a large frame house used in the days when Bryn Mawr was a popular summer resort.

Villanova: From the Augustinian College of St. Thomas of Villa Nova. St. Thomas was a 16th century Spanish bishop.

Warner Avenue: Named for Isaac Warner Arthur, Bryn Mawr businessman and later postmaster.

Waverly Road: From Waverly Farm, name given on the spur of the moment by a farmer, according to a story, while watching waving field of grain.

Wayne: Named for Anthony Wayne, a Revolutionary War general.

Wister Road: Louis Wister was owner of a large tract of land in the area.

Woodmont Road: Alan Wood named his estate Woodmont because it occupied the high ground above the Schuylkill opposite Conshohocken.

Wyndon Avenue: Wyndon, or Wyndham, was name of 18th century residence of Theodore N. Ely. Now owned by Bryn Mawr College.

Wynnewood: Wynne Wood was name of plantation named for Dr. Thomas Wynne.

Youngs Ford Road: Led from John Roberts' mill to the ford on the Schuylkill River which was located on property of the Young family.

THE EDITOR

Dick Jones, Editor-in-Chief and Designer
of *The First 300,* is a 1951 graduate of
Rhode Island School of Design. His career
in New York City included positions at
Esquire magazine and CBS Television.
Dick worked at the Sudler & Hennessey
advertising agency for 12 years, becoming
a Senior VP and Creative Director.
In 1973, he formed Dick Jones Design in
Connecticut. Five years later, he merged the
studio with an advertising agency to form
Dorland Sweeney Jones in Philadelphia.
In over 40 years, Dick has won numerous
professional awards for his art direction;
his work has been published in many
graphic arts journals. Dick has served on
the boards of Connecticut Audubon Society,
Housatonic Girl Scout Council, Art Directors
Club of Philadelphia and American Institute
of Graphic Arts, Philadelphia Chapter.
He is a participant in the Retired & Senior
Volunteer Program of Montgomery County.
He and his wife, Chris, serve on the Board
of The Lower Merion Historical Society
and have been active members of the RISD
Alumni Council since the early 1980s.

THANKS

to **Ted Goldsborough**
for initiating this project and
for his enthusiasm and
commitment to the book

to **Stella Gabuzda** and
Ross Mitchell
whose grant writing expertise
have helped to make
this publication possible

to **Jerry Francis**
for his business know-how
and overall management
of *The First 300*

to **Christine Jones**
and **Liz & Phil Eidelson**
for their editorial
and proofreading skills

to **Sigrid Berkner**
for her computer wizardry
in scanning
these many pages

to **Phil Bagley**
and **Gil Smith**
for managing the finances

to **Thomas H. Wood**
for his endpaper design

FINANCIAL SUPPORT

The Lower Merion Historical Society acknowledges its gratitude for the generous financial backing from these community associations, businesses and individuals.

PATRONS

Smith Hamill Horne

Philip & Ann Bagley

John & Jo Anne Debes

Founders' Bank Quality of Life Award to Ted Goldsborough

Berwind Group

Ken Brier at The Mountbatten Surety Company, Inc.

Jerry & Denise Francis

Chris & Dick Jones

Neighborhood Club of Bala Cynwyd

SPONSORS

John M. Templeton, Jr., M.D.

Mr. & Mrs. Stanton Friedman

Susan & Ted Goldsborough

Mary G. Kane

Manko, Gold & Katcher, llp

Gil & Lynn Smith

Sunoco, Inc.

CONTRIBUTORS

Stella & Tom Gabuzda

Main Street Bank

Jeptha Abbott Chapter NSDAR

Drs. Edward & Carol Huth

Bryn Mawr Civic Association

Frederick Weitzman
300 Rock Hill Road Associates

Eleanor Davis

Meribah Delaplaine

John Fish & Son Jewelers

Founders' Bank

Gladwyne Civic Association

Helen P. Horn

Aram K. Jerrehian, Jr.

Dr. & Mrs. Robin Marinchak

Katherine Muckle

Luise Cook Raymond

Republican Women
of the Main Line

Rose Salios

Ione & Hilary Strauss

Mr. & Mrs. James D. Winsor 3rd

Wynnewood Civic Association

G. Guyer Young III

SUBSCRIBERS

Gladwyne Library League
Jim & Judy Strazella
Catherine Bigoney
James Ackerman, DDS, PC
Amerishop Suburban, lp
James & Jeanette Anders
General Julius Becton
Mapes, Mr. & Mrs. J.R. Benner
Jessie Ellen Burr
Dr. Elias & Rena Burstein
Chadwick & McKinney
Funeral Home
Daniel & Peggy Clark
Firstrust Bank
Dettore Associates
John B. & Mary Ellen Hagner
Edward B. Ilgren
Jewish Federation
of Greater Philadelphia
Amy Karp
Jonathan & Mary Keim
S.K. Kelso & Sons, Inc.
Main Line Chamber of Commerce
Meyer Associates, George Wilson
John W. Powell 2nd
Bruce D. & Wendy C. Reed
Margaret Reid
Delories L. Richardi
Margaretta Richardi
Phelps Riley
Buck Scott
Lloyd & Lamonte Tepper
Charles F. Ward Associates
Felice G. Weiner
Morris & Mildred L. Weisberg
Thomas & Mary Wood

...and...

Main Line Art Center
Main Line Clothing Care
Merion Monthly Meeting of Friends
Jessamine Brandt
Sandra Drayer
William & Mary Goetz
Patricia Goldman
Isabell R. Hardy
Ross Lance Mitchell
Joan C. Roberts
Sidney Rubin
Margaret & Jeffrey Shaver
Fred & Elke Shihadeh
J. Orrin Spellman
Andrew & Helen Talone
Sally Wistar Winsor
Bi-State Construction Co., Inc.
David & Nancy Charkes
Elliot & Carol G. Cole
Florence B. McElroy
Richard & Margaret Schneider
Dana T. Lerch
Mary Ann Curley
Edward & Margaret Semanko
Stephen A. Tolbert, Jr.
A. Talone Cleaning Services
Bryn Mawr Conservancy of Music
Hendricks & Sidebottom Opticians
Rittenhouse Electrical & Supply Co., LLC
Ann Ashmead
Zelda Greenspun
Mary Wood Groves
Ann Hartzell
Lorna Hoopes-Hardt
Dr. & Mrs. James Hykes
Farilyn P. Leopold
Earl & Catherine Moore
Philip & Annette Nowlan
Marion Rodyhouse
David Sonenshein
Jean K. Wolf
Ruth T. Chavez
Victoria Donohoe
F. Homer Hagaman
Mr. & Mrs. Harry Haley
Muriel Noble-Skinner
Ray Woodall
Catherine Bigoney
Francis H. Green
Marion Shumway
David Pearson

AUTHOR CREDITS

THANKS to this talented team who contributed their knowledge and writing skills to *The First 300*. They are historians, architects, educators, journalists, archivists, preservationists and over a dozen enthusiastic "history huggers" from the Lower Merion Historical Society who volunteered their time and expertise to this project.

PICTURE CREDITS

THANKS to those who shared their pictures for *The First 300*. They supplement the many photographs in the Society's collection, thereby expanding our views of the township's people and places.

KEY:

LMHSA (Lower Merion Historical Society Archives)

Hotchkin (*Rural Pennsylvania,* Rev. S.F. Hotchkin, 1879)

King (*Philadelphia and Notable Philadelphians,* Moses King, 1902)

MFMA (Merion Friends Meeting Archives)

All other sources and photographers are identified.

INDEX

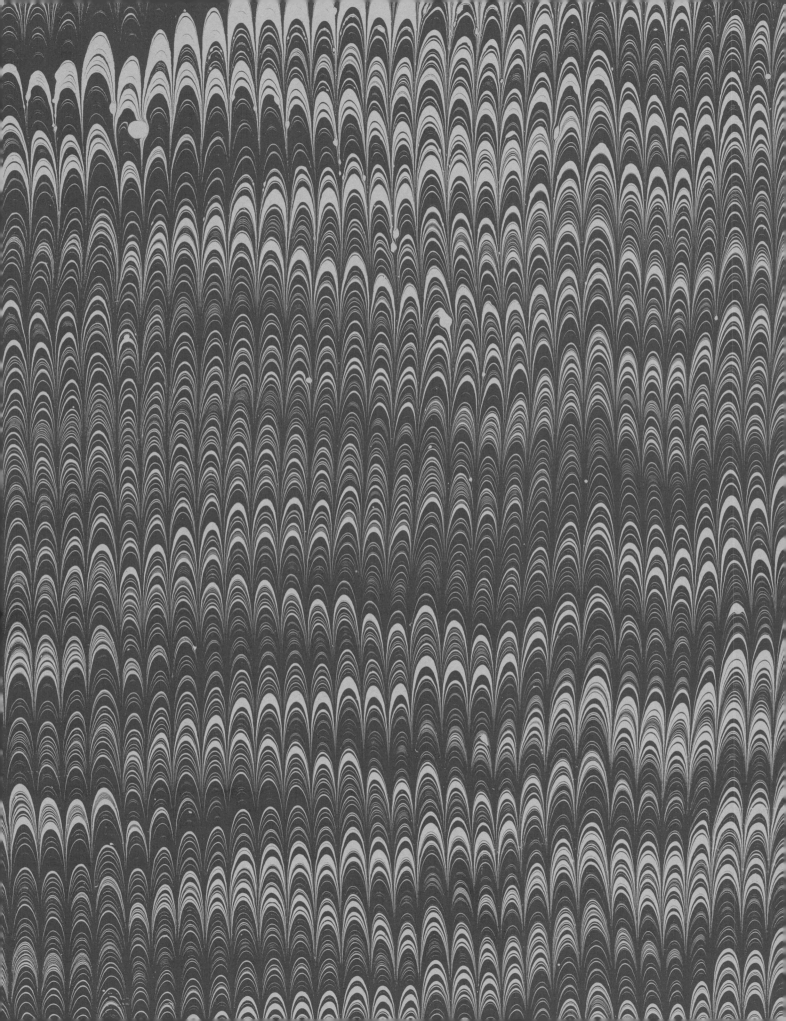